CASSIRER, PANOFSKY, AND WARBURG

Cassirer, Panofsky, and Warburg

SYMBOL, ART, AND HISTORY

SILVIA FERRETTI

TRANSLATED BY

RICHARD PIERCE

YALE UNIVERSITY PRESS
NEW HAVEN AND LONDON

Originally published as *Il demone della memoria. Simbolo e tempo storico in Warburg, Cassirer, Panofsky,* copyright © 1984 Casa Editrice Marietti.

Copyright © 1989 by Yale University. All rights reserved. This book may not be reproduced, in whole or in part, including illustrations, in any form (beyond that copying permitted by Sections 107 and 108 of the U.S. Copyright Law and except by reviewers for the public press), without written permission from the publishers.

Designed by Jo Aerne and set in Sabon type by Brevis Press, Bethany, Connecticut. Printed in the United States of America by BookCrafters, Inc., Chelsea, Michigan.

Library of Congress Cataloging-in-Publication Data
Ferretti, Silvia.
[Demone della memoria. English]
Cassirer, Panofsky, and Warburg : symbol, art, and history / Silvia Ferretti : translated by Richard Pierce.
   p. cm.
Translation of: Il demone della memoria.
Bibliography: p.
Includes index.
ISBN 0-300-04516-6 (alk. paper)
1. Aesthetics, German. 2. Aesthetics, Modern—19th century. 3. Aesthetics, Modern—20th century. 4. Warburg, Aby, 1866–1929. 5. Cassirer, Ernst, 1874–1945. 6. Panofsky, Erwin, 1892–1968. I. Title.
BH221.G34W37413 1989
111'.85—dc19   89-30836
                CIP

The paper in this book meets the guidelines for permanence and durability of the Committee on Production Guidelines for Book Longevity of the Council on Library Resources.

10 9 8 7 6 5 4 3 2 1

To Flavia and Gino

... io vedo il mondo da benigne stelle
adorno tutto in sua novella etade
monstrar di fuor le sue cose più belle.

—MATTEO MARIA BOIARDO

CONTENTS

INTRODUCTION	xi
CHAPTER 1. ABY WARBURG	1
Prologue	1
The Images of Antiquity	6
The Aesthetics of Empathy	14
Genius and History	23
Francesco Sassetti and Renaissance Polarities	35
The Pagan Demon-God and the Apollonian-Dionysian Polarity	49
The Magical World and History	62
CHAPTER 2. ERNST CASSIRER	81
The Renaissance as Conciliation	81
Symbolic Form and Time	100
The History of Symbol Formation as a Broadening of Kant's "Copernican Revolution"	109
The Symbol's Becoming and Consciousness	122
CHAPTER 3. ERWIN PANOFSKY	142
"Eidos und Eidolon" and *Idea*	142

The Theoretical Writings and
Art History   177
The Ideality of the Artistic Problem
and Historical Time   207
Historicism and the Violence of
Interpretation   221

NOTES   237

INDEX   271

INTRODUCTION

Fritz Saxl, in a letter to Hans Meier dated July 15, 1928, concerning the difficulties presented by his astrological manuscript and his daily reports on the activities of the Warburg Institute, wrote that he spent his Sundays reading Kantorowicz's work on Frederick II with great pleasure.[1] Though he noted how the author insinuated personal, arbitrary elements into the portrait of his character, Saxl still appreciated Kantorowicz's attempt to offer a "universal representation," that is, a representation (as he immediately explained) of all material from a single point of view.

There are diverse reasons why one so admires and respects the capacity to trace out a unitary picture, a coherent overall view of a person or an epoch. One might say, along with Arthur Lovejoy, that this is a question of metaphysical pathos or "monistic pathos," an aestheticizing veneration of the number one.[2] Or one could agree with Ernst Gombrich and identify the vice in this taste for unity with the persistence of a Hegelian view of history whereby single facts are considered moments in the evolution of a universal spirit, which Gombrich interprets as a residue of theological tradition.[3]

In any case, whether this is a question of psychological motivation or of philosophical heritage, there is no doubt that what leads us to admire a work of historiography for its intrinsic unity is both the difficulty this task entails and the necessity of doing it.

The difficulty is twofold: it consists in the fact that the past, even the most recent past, presents itself in a fragmentary state, and it also lies in the changes we ourselves constantly undergo, so that without a rule of life—whether it be conventional or existential—our very physical survival would be jeopardized. The necessary nature of the task of historical synthesis stems from the ambition every historian has to interpret the material known to him. This ambition was no less alien to Jacob Burckhardt, for example, than it is to Gombrich in tackling Renaissance documents, even though their two inquiries and systems result in clearly opposite conclusions. And since even the driest chronicle cannot help being animated by an interpretative design (if the compiler has any interest at all in his work), we should seek out the monistic basis for that design, because in order to interpret one has to connect and disconnect, two operations that must be formulated from a single, underlying viewpoint.

Hence, the interpreter must not only establish for the historical past those relations useful to his task of clarification and understanding, but he must also recognize in himself, in his own present and past experience, the regulative principles that lie behind the choices he makes, the direction his research takes—whether it aims at establishing unity for the historiographic model he is proposing, or at destroying all possible models in the name of the absolute indeterminateness of historical knowledge. And all directions, be they univocal or the result of various courses, are such only insofar as they have a stable reference point that at every step indicates their origin. Yet it is precisely the stable reference point (or better, the origin that accompanies movement and change as its own possibility) that is the most difficult to find because we are surrounded by the manifold and changeable, which we can interpret only on the basis of a unifying criterion but which continuously does violence to the limits we have set, until an extraordinary virtue resolutely opposes that manifold and changeable. And it is that virtue to which we render homage when reading the great historiographic works that, despite their interpretative arbitrariness, become models even for their detractors.

The tendency to cultivate the sense of unity does not have an aestheticizing nature; it is not the satisfaction of a taste or a pleasure of the soul but, on the contrary, is determined by the necessary effort to give meaning to what surrounds us. Plato did not shut himself up in his arduous speculation on the number one because it seemed more beautiful to him than the other numbers,[4] but because he sought in it the criterion for the manifold so as to make it comprehensible.

With the profound self-directed irony and humor typical of the Hamburg scholar, Aby Warburg's famous and oft-repeated saying "The Good Lord hides in details" implies a serious awareness of the situation in which the historian finds himself. He faces a world of details, of minutiae, in all of which something is concealed that is most certainly not the "Good Lord" but is the most obscure and obstinate of "evil spirits", the broadest meaning, the unitary sense without which what Panofsky calls the "sense of the document" is precluded and which the historian knows he can attain only by means of two faculties that are difficult to hold together and reconcile, temerity and prudence.

Warburg's oeuvre demonstrates this determination to find the unitary criterion for the knowledge and consciousness of an epoch, a determination that partly stemmed from the historians he had become acquainted with in his youth—above all Burckhardt, Justi, and Usener—and partly rested upon his idea of history as a tradition of images and words that imply and communicate vitality and energy. And Warburg's life itself was marked by a constant determination to pursue his goals and to put to use as intensely and profitably as possible the economic and cultural means destiny had bestowed upon him. He not only utilized his huge patrimony to found the splendid and unique library that bears his name and around which some of the greatest twentieth-century historians have gathered, but he also used the important position his family had occupied in Hamburg for centuries to help found there the university that attracted the talented persons on whom he counted to build his school.

It is, however, inexact to speak of a school without clarifying the meaning this word had for Warburg—or rather, the meaning it took on in light of his intentions and the nature of his personality. Usually "school" means a center where disciples gather around a scholar whose teachings set them on a certain path of study and research. In Warburg's case, though, the school was made up of already established scholars, each of whom came from a different area and had his own well-defined and singular intellectual force. Warburg himself always refused academic posts. In his scholarly solitude, he availed himself only of the collaboration and comfort of friends who, quite different from him and sometimes much younger and with other interests, shared his passion for iron discipline in scholarship and his acute sense of individuality and freedom of historical research, as well as the responsibility of imposing his own historiographic model.

It was this broader, higher concept of school that allowed great scholars in Warburg's milieu to come to the fore. In his teaching, these scholars found not so much an example to be followed or criteria to be imitated as a nucleus of possible historiographic research to be carried out according to each historian's talent and inspiration and to be extended in many different theoretical or art-historical directions. In a certain sense then, we must imagine Warburg's character as being intolerant of the traditional concept of "school" and "disciples." He aimed only at sharing his own work with culturally independent persons who, like himself, had intellectual tenacity, so that their collective energy would multiply rather than be split up and thus dispersed.

Perhaps Warburg's concept of history and the individual is now too distant from us to be thoroughly understood. But his school and those who were part of it, or for whom it was a center of interest and study for a certain period, are indicative of a spirit based above all on the coexistence, in the mind of each scholar, of different disciplines that together take on the form of an organic whole. Since this was Warburg's idea of the totality of learning, every scholar who came into contact with the Warburg Library and Institute attempted to relate and react to these stimuli by delving into the various areas of research with his own resources and insight. Thus the unique personalities of these erudite philosophers and historians contributed to that wealth of production which is marked precisely by variety and distinctness.

This may help us to understand why the presence of a thinker like Ernst Cassirer was so dear to Warburg despite the fact that his philosophical experience was so different from Warburg's and that his conception of history developed, in that period, to a certain extent in opposition to Warburg's. What they had in common was the aptitude to investigate the most recondite testimonies of humanity's tendency to represent itself through culture. Another point in common was the need, at that crucial moment in history, to make every effort to inculcate younger generations with the values of civilization so as to thwart the nightmare that was in the making—a catastrophe which these scholars' restrained and reasonable example, of course, did not manage to avert. In 1928, when Warburg did his utmost to persuade Cassirer (who had had an enticing offer from the University of Frankfurt) to stay in Hamburg, it was no longer possible to conceal the urgency of this pedagogical mission; and it was this that convinced Cassirer to refuse the brilliant post he had been offered.[5]

INTRODUCTION   xv

The gloomy, weary letters that Cassirer, Saxl, and Panofsky wrote from abroad in the autumn of 1933 to resign officially from their posts at the University of Hamburg, and to take their leave of the outstanding burgomaster Von Melle,[6] betray their shattered hopes in their studies of that period and a tragic feeling of futility. But these scholars continued to work in other countries, because each of them had maintained and developed his own intellectual solidity as well as what Thomas Mann would call his own moral-psychic world. They themselves were the center of the Warburg Institute experience.

The reason for limiting this book to an inquiry into only three personalities, among the many belonging to that school and to the period when they worked at the University of Hamburg and the Warburg Institute, then, lies in the nature of Warburg's teaching and personality. The analysis of his work, and of Cassirer's and Panofsky's writings in the 1920s and in the sphere of their common experience, does not aim at finding proof of an affinity or intrinsic unity on a theoretical or historiographic level (which for that matter does not exist), but sets out to demonstrate the differences and in part the obvious contradictions between them. The choice of these three scholars corresponds to the aim of finding out what premises lay behind Warburg's teachings, how they are to be grasped by following the course of his writings and historical thought, and what consequences this method of inquiry had for those colleagues who were on most intimate terms with one another and were the most gifted from a philosophical and theoretical point of view. One might say that the method Warburg employed in his research took on particular importance in the different philosophical approach given to it by Cassirer (who was immediately and instinctively won over by it), and that the method was expanded theoretically by the research with which Panofsky demonstrated his great intellectual gifts and which laid the foundation for his iconological method of dealing with art-historical problems.

The connection between symbol, image, and creative imagination, on the one hand, and historical time and the unfolding of meanings, on the other, has been viewed as the motif that draws these three scholars together, for each constructed his view of history and historiographic approach on this fundamental theme.

The writings of Cassirer and Panofsky, who belonged to the two succeeding generations, have been limited to the production of the 1920s and early 1930s, not to contradict the principle of individuality that emerged from the institute, but because that period of collaboration and common aims had a meaning for those scholars without which one would not be able to understand Warburg's unique heritage.

Given the differences among these three intellectuals, it is natural that their approach to the question of the symbol and historical time should differ. Warburg's art-historical writings do not allow for a direct theoretical scrutiny. Despite the many cultural implications in them, those essays are almost exclusively concerned with the matter of the work of art. In order to track down their historiographic and philosophical meaning, it is necessary to analyze the persons and subjects interwoven in Warburg's experience. The figure of Warburg thus does not emerge prominently and immediately, but rather through the stage setting, so to speak, that partly describes the late nineteenth-century German scene through which he passed and which impressed certain lifelong models upon him.

In general, the thesis implicit in Warburg's oeuvre—precisely because it is never expressed in a wholly explicit manner and yet is fundamental for the purposes of this book—can be fully brought to light only through a complex account of its motivations.

Another kind of limit is necessary for the treatment of the same subject in Cassirer. Except for isolated cases, all references to his important philosophical works written before the 1920s, as well as the works written after the early 1930s, have been deliberately omitted. In Cassirer the theory of the symbol and its historical development presupposes the broader treatment of these concepts that he effected in his entire oeuvre as well as his relationship with the Neo-Kantian schools and with his own epistemological conception. Though bearing all this in mind, I have limited the critique of Cassirer here to his studies on symbolic forms in which, more than elsewhere, one notes the nearness of Warburg's teachings and that of his colleagues at the institute in that period.

I have attached particular importance to Cassirer's *Individual and Cosmos in Renaissance Philosophy*—really only one episode in his vast production—because it allows for a comparison with Warburg's view of that historical period and, above all, because through a critique of Cassirer's method of inquiry one can also shed light on his conception of history and thus of the symbol as the expression of the relationship between knowledge and reality in time.

This book aims at verifying how different conceptions of that relationship could still converge and influence one another, giving rise to a common, conscious evolution of these ideas. Such differences and such approximation to the historiographic solution to the problem emerge with greater clarity from an analysis of Panofsky's writings, which are also limited to the same period. Panofsky explicitly brought to light the theoretical consequences of his teachers' oeuvre and tried to account for the difficult equilibrium between historicism and autonomy of interpretation in historiography.

In fact, every writing on history is an ideal course through a reality that is bequeathed fragmentarily, with oversights and omissions whose meaning in each case has its raison d'être. Human memory is powerful but unstable. In order to grasp it in its permanence and not in its precariousness, the historian must be as faithful as possible to the objective data and at the same time must comply with his own concepts and vast cultural experience.

Panofsky takes in the heritage of the philosophy of symbolic forms by interpreting it as a consequence of Kantian critical idealism, and hence within more rigorous limits than those used by Cassirer in his formulation. On the other hand, he endeavors to use it to account for those oversights and gaps, that mysterious instability that allowed tradition to settle in, and impress itself upon, collective memory, just as Warburg had done with such perceptive intuition.

The image of Warburg that emerges both from the premises of his historiographic reflection and from the results they produced in those who—each in his own way—understood him, is one of power and unity rarely granted to a person in this century. Thus the vague figure whom Ernst Gombrich depicts in his highly documented "intellectual biography"[7] as irresolute and fragile, who emerges from the fragmentariness of his notes rather than from the completeness of his published works, is quite improbable. In his reconstruction of Warburg's thought, Gombrich cannot conceal his aversion for the foundations of that historical inquiry. Already in 1969 his *In Search of Cultural History* had questioned Warburg's cultural world by criticizing Burckhardt's oeuvre, which according to Gombrich is of Hegelian derivation. In this work, Gombrich confuses the history of culture constructed along the lines of a unitary scheme with the history of the spirit conceived on the basis of the idea of progress—or at least, as he would have it, through the teleological evolution of the spirit that grows upon itself. This is not the place, however, for a point-by-point criticism of Gombrich's thesis of the Hegelian philosophy of history, a thesis which seems to ignore the meaning of Hegel's philosophical categories; nor is it the place for a discussion of Burckhardt's relationship with Hegel.

Rather, in this volume I attempt to clarify Warburg's relationship with Burckhardt. More generally, I focus on the difference between a concept of history understood as progress (which appears in Cassirer's view of the evolution of the spirit within the framework of its symbolic expression) and a concept of history understood as a totality of documents whose meaning is to be found only by tracking their basic unity, which in itself is of a nontemporal nature. Warburg's complex idea of an "age of transition"—that is, an epoch abstracted from the course of time—is taken up again by Panofsky on theoretical grounds. In these writings, Panofsky makes a subtle and profound assessment of the suppositions that underlie the enigmatic balance between historical relativism and the absoluteness of category with which the phenomenon is judged.

The world of history is a utopian domain from which nevertheless come documents that have the most intense vehemence and vitality. And with patience and courage the historian must attend to the task of giving a plausible reality to that world by means of the facts and what they conceal. What is concealed therein is also something that goes beyond the temporal limit, which we strive to establish in the very moment when, in interpreting it, we transcend it.

The writing of this book and the formulation of its basic thesis were made possible by attending the lessons and seminars of Professor Gennaro Sasso and also by the original idea for a research project that he gave me years ago, for which I am very grateful.

Special thanks are due to Professor Raymond Klibansky for the interest shown in my study and for the special advice he so generously gave me. I am also grateful to Professor Valerio Verra for his active help in having this book published.

I think back with gratitude to the conversations I had with Professor Filippo Mignini on the subject of this work, his friendly and steadfast

INTRODUCTION   xix

encouragement in my many moments of doubt, and his patience in reading over the manuscript.

I also want to thank Fabrizio Desideri and Emilia Desideri Passaponti for their cheerful and trusting support.

Thanks to the aid of the Deutsches Akademisches Austauschdienst in Bonn I was able to carry out fruitful research at the Deutsches Literaturarchiv in Marbach am Neckar, at the Philosophy Seminar Library of the University of Hamburg, and at the Staatsbibliothek in Hamburg, where I also had interesting conversations on the topics of my research with Professor Heinz Paetzold. I also did research for quite some time at the Warburg Institute Library in London, where I was able to consult the Warburg Archive thanks to the kind help of Professor J. B. Trapp and Mrs. Anne Marie Meyer. Thanks are also due to the Vatican Library; the Gregorian Library in Rome; the library at the Institute of Philosophy of the University of Rome, whose kind personnel were always a great help to me; and last, the Hertziana Library and Goethe Institute Library, both in Rome, which allowed me to obtain texts not available elsewhere in Italy.

I would like to express a grateful thought in memory of Miss Frances Amelia Yates, with whom I had many an occasion to talk during my visits to the Warburg Institute.

CASSIRER, PANOFSKY, AND WARBURG

1

ABY WARBURG

Prologue

In October 1929 at Hamburg, Ernst Cassirer read the memorial address at Aby Warburg's burial service. It was the most inspiring speech given on that occasion by the late scholar's colleagues and students. The impression Warburg had made on the philosopher when they had met five years earlier, and from the time Cassirer began frequenting the Warburg Library, was so great, the understanding between the two so intense and immediate, that Cassirer's brief speech had a much stronger, more ardently sincere ring of affection and esteem than is usual in a commemoration.

In this particular moment of grief, with the straightforwardness of feeling that distinguished him, Cassirer fashioned an extraordinary parallel between his own suffering over the death of a dear friend and colleague and the suffering of Warburg's own life. Warburg had struggled against life's onslaughts, yet had used them as a way to investigate the meaning of the entire history of humanity. In this identification Cassirer abandoned his usual serenity of mind and optimism to put himself entirely in the person of his friend, who was so different from him in temperament, and he thereby evoked a truthful picture of him with great precision and heartfelt sympathy.

Warburg's presence in the culture of Hamburg had asserted itself with such force and determination that it would surely have left a lasting mark had not subsequent historical events obliterated even that manifestation of exceptional vigor. The University of Hamburg was founded in 1919, and Warburg was one of its most impassioned supporters. He also lent his support to research into the fields of the so-called sciences of the spirit, or cultural sciences, that were cultivated up to the end by the scholars and students there. Together with his historical-cultural research, the Warburg Library was the scholar's life-long commitment, reflecting his personality and with it the aim he pursued in study. Cassirer says that an enchanted air emanates from all those books—which even in the most remote corner reveal the focal point round which they have multiplied—and a welter of images and primal impulses of history is transmitted to visitors, until behind this world there looms the figure of its founder and master.[1] Warburg made no distinction between great and insignificant works, because he was certain he would grasp the whole, the organic meaning of a totality, in every historical moment. The focal point out of which radiate those "energy tensions" that animate history is the distant past, where the "pathos formulas" (*Pathosformel*)—those gestures of terror or passion in which people sought a bulwark against the mysterious power of the irrational—were created as a permanent patrimony of humanity.

Cassirer stresses exclusively and insistently the motif of suffering, of painful experience that was reflected in the observation of the historical world and in the search for those demoniac symbols that bind our earthly existence. Singularly, from among the facets of the figure of Warburg, Cassirer chooses only the Dionysian side, ignoring the Apollonian one, the pure contemplation of beauty, because in the art of observation and in the capacity to penetrate cultural phenomena through his own inner struggles, Warburg resolved and liberated that tension which otherwise would have destroyed him.

In projecting Warburg's nature onto the objects of his study, Cassirer recognizes the power of Warburg's intuition, which has revealed the function of certain mythical forms and pivotal figures of religion, the function of the symbol and of the concept of Fortune in Renaissance art, and above all the meaning of astrological imagination. We are familiar with Warburg's aversion to every form of superstition—such as the one that makes men slaves of the power of the stars and planets—and we know that, with nostalgic intensity, he looked back to the Renaissance as the epoch that waged the most passionate and determined battle against the images of the astral cult in order to emancipate intellectual energy. This constant battle, which yielded only rare, short-lived victories, was the *geheimer Punkt*, the secret nucleus or reference point of all his exploration into the epochs and customs of humanity. His devotion to the history of art was not a cult of beauty per se; he tried with the "courage of truth" to demonstrate that the search for a beautiful form was nothing but the idealization of the fears and conflicts that disrupted an epoch and led it, by means of ancient paths, toward new self-awareness.

But Cassirer does not go this far in his evocation of Warburg's oeuvre. And it is truly singular how, in this pain-filled representation of his friend, he does not make use of any of the themes he himself dealt with in his philosophy. He does not speak of historical progress or of the evolution of the symbol, nor of the ideal as the final redemption from the sensory; he does not dwell on the symbolic form attaining its final and positive purpose. Instead he is wholly absorbed in tracing as faithfully as possible the portrait of a scholar who—as Schopenhauer said—led a heroic and unhappy life. And even the quotation from Schopenhauer is not fortuitous. It is not a culture used to achieve a rhetorical effect but rather a clue Cassirer gives to set us on an interpretative track, because the nineteenth-century thinkers and historians who were Warburg's masters continuously referred to the author of *The World as Will and Representation*.

In the last page of his address, Cassirer delicately touches upon Warburg's final hour, a conversation he had with the philosopher in which he expounded his plans for a study that had been suggested to him by Cassirer himself: research on Giordano Bruno. Cassirer does not hesitate to express his surprise at noting how Warburg's acumen had passed well beyond a traditional understanding of that episode in the history of philosophy and how a theoretical problem had once again become for him an experience of life. The art historian had been struck by the theme of the infinite as an object of reason, but reason that is embraced with the same heroic feeling that induced that late-Renaissance figure to become absorbed in magic in order to emancipate himself from it in the end through speculation. Employing a myth far removed from his own philosophical faith and personality, and referring to an early quotation of Warburg's, Cassirer speaks of Icarus's flight, doomed to a tragic end but exemplary in its unconditioned and desperate ascent to a superior sphere, free—at least in intention—from the painful constrictions of the finite world. In this poem of death, actually extraneous to Cassirer's taste but consistent with the dual figure of "pain and greatness" that recurs in German culture from the time Schiller set "heroism" against "happiness," we have a rare synthesis of Aby Warburg's life experience. It renders his inner tensions, exasperated by the vengeful demons of paganism that he wanted to see defeated, and his obstinate search for a coherent principle of historical analysis that would afford a primal and necessary meaning to every manifestation of civilization.

The pathos formulas are permanent reproductions of life which, due to their origin in the passions and sensations men have always endured, tend to be regenerated continuously by their primal energy. In fact this primal energy has only one impulse, which sometimes raises it almost to the absolute, only to make it fall once again when it has worn itself out: the impetus to give shape to, determine, and circumscribe an otherwise incomprehensible destiny, in order to make it accessible to the imagination or to thought. The image, be it a mimic gesture, a propitiatory dance or a work of art, grows out of the overwhelming need the senses have to assert themselves in a lasting, tangible, and visual manner. The image also grows out of the equally essential capability on the part of reflection to abstract the sensory in forms in order to make it typical and permanent. This dual nature of the image occurs in all phases of its history. Not even the most primitive graffito or the sound uttered in a moment of terror to call upon a god—either as a form of exorcism or as a supplication—can do without these two aspects of the formation of the image. Philosophical abstraction in its highest stage, the Platonic one, makes exemplary use of myths or mathematical symbols to indicate its farthest limit in the sphere of expression.

Warburg firmly believed in this twofold nature of the image, but instead of giving it an epistemological basis, he searched for its incessant reproduction in diverse historical periods and circumstances. Tradition is not always and solely the conscious search for a link with the past, but it is above all the obscure connection history has with its essence, the subterranean course of forms which, albeit changing, remain identical, since there is only one motive that determines them and it is rooted in the very nature of the civilization that expresses itself through them. From a distant past these forms make their mark according to how various epochs understand them and are disposed to accept them; then the forms reemerge in the illusory and often splendid guise of new products of the forces of time. For Warburg, the historian is he who seeks the motives peculiar to an epoch, but who spares no effort to discover the infinite ties this epoch has with the permanent substratum of history, and thus is able to reconstruct its authentic vital tissue with overall harmony and coherence.

Cassirer pursues the same goal of offering an all-embracing and well-grounded picture of the formation of symbols; but though he starts off from postulates similar to Warburg's, his speculation leads to a different conclusion. He does not follow the symbolic form in its mysterious wandering over the centuries. It is not the butterfly bursting free from its chrysalis, in Warburg's popular and recurring metaphor, the delicate Nymph which, in a fortunate but intensely agitated moment of its long existence, with a deft movement sheds the cumbersome conditioning of tradition. For Cassirer the symbol is rather the very source of change and temporal becoming, because in it there occurs the continuous and necessary ascent from the bonds of the sensory to reach the purely intelligible and dwell in the utmost abstraction, where its true freedom manifests itself as its ideal essence.

The in-depth study of that unity of knowledge and of the multifarious links that help to give the most exact picture possible of the history of culture, which had attracted Cassirer when he first came to the Warburg Library, united the philosopher and the collector of images in their common erudition and precision of research. But it did not affect Cassirer's faith in the ideal progress of humanity that he believed could be fully established by means of his theory of the symbol. His championing of the thesis that history took place by opposition and contrasts was not sufficient to allow him to see the contradiction between a temporal course conceived as necessary and the positive reality of opposites. From that linear movement toward a goal—the definitive overcoming of the sensory in the symbolic expression typical of the exact sciences—opposites prove to be weakened and nullified from their very foundations.

Cassirer's Hegelian vision of the world, ambiguously contaminated by Kant's apriority and by scientific positivism, did not affect the mutual understanding between the philosopher and Warburg's milieu that led to intense collaboration at Hamburg in the 1920s. The conviction that perfect agreement could be achieved occurred above all because Warburg himself and his most direct disciples would never have dreamed of denying the idea of progress or of not recognizing it as a working part of history. Warburg's formulation of historical becoming as evolution from one civilization to another, from one way of thought to another, toward greater spiritualization is reflected in the following theses: of a struggle for liberation from suffocating medieval traditions; of having recourse to the pagan deity in its primal purity as a sign of the already accomplished formative process of the modern individual conscious of his own strength and projected toward future conquests; and, finally, the thesis in which the accent is placed on Luther's contempt for superstition and prognostications. The clarity of this formulation varies in Warburg's work. It was less conspicuous in his early writings and became increasingly marked as he deepened his interpretation of artistic history as the history of battles never totally won. The more he tried to react against his growing pessimism and the increasing intricacy of the subterranean connections he had discovered, the more he strove to lead everything onto a totally linear plane, thus to observe the accomplished scientific sublimation of magic.

There is a moment in Warburg's work when he and Cassirer seem to be in perfect consonance,[2] but it is followed almost immediately by a somber, disconsolate reflection on the angst in present-day consciousness, which demonstrates how arbitrarily that image of progress had been superimposed on his basic temperament. All the more reason why Cassirer's funeral commemoration of Warburg's character is praiseworthy. This time it is no longer the searcher after, and persecutor of, demons who is seeking comfort in the fecund working optimism of his philosophical counselor. Now it is the latter who—in the dismay and grief of the final, unheard farewell to the person who no longer exists, and almost overwhelmed by the reality of time which no longer seems to lead to a fullness of sense[3] but rather manifests itself in the irrevocable theft of existence—identifies personal *Erlebnis* (inner experience) with historical interpretation and, in creating an authentic image of Warburg's character and teachings, makes his own admiration and painful sense of loss stand out amid the motif of unhappiness and heroism.

The Images of Antiquity

Among the points of common interest that consolidated the harmony between Warburg and Cassirer during the short period they worked together, the most congenial one was undoubtedly their passion for ancient Greece. Both Warburg—the diligent investigator of crises and flaws in history, of the dramatic suspension of the ages of transition— and Cassirer—the trusting theoretician of conciliation in historical continuity in relation to its evolution toward the spiritual realm of freedom—sought in classical antiquity the origin of civilization, its true and most deep-seated nature, during its development as well as in its darker moments. The creation in Greek art of images rich in meaning was viewed by Warburg as the most fully realized attempt to give permanent form to the expressions of fear and veneration that had been impressed upon human memory since its primitive existence. Usener's pupil was in fact convinced that the sensory manifestation of the obscure and irrational terror of the soul when faced with the unknown was a means for developing a defense against the recurrence of the annihilating experience of chaos.[4]

Usener saw in the origin of words, of simply calling or indicating with the same gesture, a spiritual excitement,[5] a sensory impression that sprang from a conflict with the nonself. The word is the result of the attempt to fix in a possible identity equal impressions, the recurrence of which demonstrates they are permanent and nameable. The word refers to a sensory experience that in repeating itself is known and constant.[6]

The focal point of Warburg's entire interpretation of the Renaissance is the reemergence of images consolidated by habit and tradition which the vigorous genius and intense feeling of the Greeks established in archetypes that remained firmly anchored to human sensitivity. The continuation or repetition of an immediate emotive response in a symbolic language and the will to supreme refinement and universal comprehension in the works of Greek genius are the two forms of energy that gave birth to Western culture. In order to exalt, or even to free themselves from these forms, succeeding civilizations had to return to them constantly and master them so as to exploit their unique fecundity in the outward expression of a world view.

The unity of Warburg's research into the modes of the rebirth of ancient paganism is based on his possession of the tools of erudition and on his interpretative method, whose comparative points of reference were the nineteenth-century schools of history and philology. But above all, it is based upon the conviction that there was one, single impulse that produced images and that translated the mysterious perception of the infinite and supernatural into symbolic idealization as an alternative to the suffering over one's finiteness and the sensation of hostile nature. This unity, therefore, lies at the base of a common psychological tension. In this regard, reading Darwin's *Expression of Emotions in Man and Animals* was of fundamental importance for Warburg. The analysis of the wealth of information collected on this subject by the English scientist had revealed that "the same state of mind is expressed throughout the world with remarkable uniformity; and this fact is in itself interesting, as evidence of the close similarity in bodily structure and mental disposition of all the races of mankind."[7] The tendency to make the origin uniform was also common to Usener in his research on religious fragmentation into personal gods and "momentary gods." He quoted the theory of his teacher Welcker, who held that all the individual gods sprang from the primal concept of Zeus,[8] and cited as one of his sources Schelling's thesis that at the beginning of every religion lay a relative monotheism, the presence in the world of an indeterminate concept of divinity with absolute power.[9]

In his study, Darwin says that "all the chief expressions exhibited by man are the same throughout the world. This fact is interesting, as it affords a new argument in favour of the several races being descended from a single parent-stock."[10] Darwin's three principles of the developmental phases of expression gave Warburg the idea of an energy of the image during its historical course. The starting point is the principle of serviceable associated habits, that synthesis which meets an immediate need. Then there is the principle of antithesis, the reaction to habitual states of mind under the pressure of the new image that concerns a still unknown danger. Last, there are actions caused by the constitution of the nervous system that are totally independent of will and to a certain extent even of habit (the principle of the direct action of the nervous system).[11] These three principles explain the hereditary nature of a predisposition to certain acquired movements to which an analysis of expressions must refer in each of its historical-evolutionary stages. In addition, Warburg enunciates a thesis of the modification of reflex actions, that is, those actions that depend upon the nervous system because of a particular circumstantial need.

It should come as no surprise that the search for a psychological explanation of the stylistic motif of movement—as a part of a broader category, *Völkerpsychologie* (folk psychology), that attracted the attention of the nineteenth century—led Warburg to become interested in a book like Darwin's. In fact we must consider that he did not make a clear-cut distinction between the origin of myth and the origin of that symbolic act that goes under the name of the artistic phenomenon. Both represent that self-knowledge produced between the primordial chaos of the psyche and logical order. In his first studies on early Renaissance art, Warburg turned his attention to another evolutionist, Tito Vignoli, author of *Myth and Science*. The German translation of this study (1880) can still be found in the psychology section of the Warburg Library with Warburg's annotations, almost all of which, significantly enough, concern the passages on movement in a state of tension.[12]

In this work Vignoli studied the origins and anthropological conditions of various myths in order to gain knowledge of psychic phenomena and the "hidden laws of the exercise of thought."[13] Myth is "man's psycho-physical reification in all those phenomena he can apprehend and perceive,"[14] and in this does not distinguish itself from science; the spontaneous and necessary, "intrinsic and inevitable" function of intelligence lies at the base of both.[15] What is of most interest regarding Warburg's conception of the symbol is Vignoli's search for an apriority of evolutionism, which he finds in the establishment and perpetuation of certain factors of the species, and his distinction between the origin and the necessary sources of myth (which take on form in that apriority) and the manifold forms of its successive evolution.[16] At the base lies one *sole generating act,* a principle of animation, a "psychic force in general," which Vignoli determines as a reflective action over and above intelligence with which man intuits intuition itself, thus inwardly doubling the use of his entire psychic life.[17] Man's cognitive reduplication is due to the fact that, besides his perception of external things, he also possesses the intimate perception and emotion of that perception,[18] so that not only the object before him but also the "psychic type" of that object as it was impressed upon him intellectually come to life.[19] The very personifications that man used from the outset to give shape to nature's phenomena help to personify the phenomena of his interior actions, ideas, and concepts.[20] The process from phenomenon to type belongs in equal measure to myth and to science: in both cases one proceeds from observation to identification and classification, step-by-step toward a "most universal unity."[21] The myth is a primordial and spontaneous activity, and the imagination, "creator and animator of phantasms in man," later intervenes to elaborate upon and perfect its form. Vignoli says, in the style of Vico (whose authority he often invokes): "It is thus that poets mold symbols from reality."

Vignoli's bizarre thesis is that myth and science develop in parallel and have the same sole origin—from an apprehension, or perception—even though they represent a duality of effect; science in fact is the gradual exhaustion of the myth in the objects it has consciously investigated. One apriority of the intelligence that dominates in myth as well as in science is abstraction. Its diverse development is of a psychic nature: at first unconscious, then explicit, and finally causally determining objective processes. The production of the psychic type begins from the inner image we create for ourselves in the state of abstraction from reality. This type, called the "phantasm," has an ideal nature, is fixed in the memory, and becomes explicit both in myth and in artistic manifestations.

The progress Vignoli specifies in this sort of psychological history of apprehension consists of a development of all human activities that are primal and permanent and whose forms evolve together. Warburg had significantly underlined a passage which we can easily imagine he agreed with: "The various branches of science are only subjective necessities for the successive and gradual order of our comprehension of things: they are classifications of method and in themselves do not specifically correspond to any individual personality of nature. They are all parts of the whole."[22] Thus the young Hamburg scholar, in his search for a psychological motive for the unitary act of consciousness and intelligence, had encountered an evolutionary scientist and, at the same time, an idealist theoretician of the universality of knowledge, a concept that he himself would later establish as a condition for the arrangement of the different disciplines that were to converge in his art-historical studies. The observation of a repetition of the motif of "accessories in motion" as a constant in Renaissance art made it necessary to give a more thorough explanation than mere aesthetic commentary could ever offer. The animated hair and flowing clothing, which become a primary stylistic component in the representation of myths and legends both in ancient Greece and in the Christian tradition, constitute a pathos formula that reveals a secret anxiety sublimated in art, a need for the sensory and external manifestations of an inner conflict. In Darwin, Warburg found confirmation of his thesis according to which the free expression of a sentiment by means of external signs renders it more intense.[23] And the art historian often emphasizes the intensification of external movement as the dominating artistic intention theorized in Leon Battista Alberti's treatises, pursued poetically by Poliziano and Lorenzo the Magnificent, and utilized by early Renaissance painters and sculptors—all of whom considered it a principle of distinction from medieval aesthetic patterns, a lively attribute of elegance and grace as well as a means of showing off their antiquarian erudition.

Just as the conquest of a criterion to grasp the deity and give form to the unfathomable was, for primitive man, salvation from the danger of being physically and psychically overwhelmed, and just as the cult of the dead tended to keep the dreaded impending nothingness in check,[24] so the profound need that animates the artist's hand lies in the impulse to make external that form inside him which urgently presses upon him as the perception of, and meditation upon, life. In their festivals, poetic celebrations, and preparations for their funeral monuments, the citizens of fifteenth-century Florence sought those expressive motifs of antiquity that would free them from superstition and give form to the powerful impulse stemming from the renewal of life—motifs in which the daily battle waged against the uncertainties of Fortune would take on a definite aspect.

Darwin says: "We have also seen that expression in itself, or the language of the emotions, as it has sometimes been called, is certainly of importance for the welfare of mankind. To understand, as far as possible, the source or origin of the various expressions which may be hourly seen on the faces of the men around us, not to mention our domesticated animals, ought to possess much interest for us."[25] Even though the images of antiquity seem to change and evolve, though they sometimes assume disguises that hide their true likeness, or in their incessant migration disappear from certain historical periods only to reappear in others, their permanence in human memory is marked by the universal nature of the psychic energy that engendered them and by the formal expression that gave them the power to resist the passing of time.

In speaking of the plenitude those symbols achieved in ancient Greece, Warburg demonstrates an awareness of the idealizing power of Greek art and reveals his connection—albeit from a standpoint of openly avowed opposition—with the interpretation eighteenth-century Germany had given of the classical ideal of beauty. Despite the fact that nineteenth-century criticism, culminating in Burckhardt and Nietzsche, directly influenced Warburg's interpretation,[26] the classicist aesthetic conception was equally influential in his works. This conception was grafted onto his historiographic analysis like a subterranean leitmotiv, but it was endowed with such vigor and suggestiveness that it was still part of the European aesthetic consciousness at the beginning of this century. For that matter, the certainty that led most of German culture in the past few centuries to regard Grecism as the highest expression of the human essence in artistic and philosophical terms is quite alive even in Nietzsche, who speaks of the Greeks being endowed with "self-sufficient grandeur.... The Greeks, as charioteers, hold the reins of our own and every other culture."[27]

Cassirer also constantly refers to Greek philosophy as the transcending, in Platonic dialectics, of that impossibility to justify the movement and the manifold to which the thought of Parmenides and his followers had led. Many times in his historical-philosophical works as well as in the more specifically theoretical ones, he affirms that philosophy's first conquest was Parmenides's definition of an abstract being and that Plato in turn took that concept forward by transforming the monolithic image still clothed in the mythical heritage of Parmenides's being into a dialectics of relationships, a conception of nonbeing as a positive reflection of the manifold and of movement. This Platonic position was fundamental for philosophy's successive development toward the conquest of what Cassirer held were pure relations or "functions" that were to pave the way for the establishment of the philosophical bases of modern science.

In a work published in 1932 on antiquity and the rise of exact science, Cassirer distinguishes between the contradictory concept of natural science in Platonic philosophy—in which the knowledge of *physis* once again falls into the category of myth and is based on likeness—and the completely new concept that research in the natural sciences had assumed with Kepler and Galileo.[28] Yet he tries to demonstrate that the fathers of modern science moved in the same direction as Plato (though remaining within the framework of nature and hence of the sensory and perceptible) precisely because they no longer believed that the means to grasp the sensory should in turn be hampered by the limitations of the empirical world, but wanted to base their research on universal rules.[29]

"As a pure Pythagorean and Platonian, Kepler pursues and finds a connection for the fullness of the sensory in the number and in measurement." With the dexterity of an exegete, Cassirer develops the passages of Kepler's writings that hark back to Plato and sees in the scientist's works a continuation of the rebirth of the authentic Platonic concepts and texts in the immediately preceding age. And he has no doubts concerning the actual use of the Renaissance heritage on the part of modern science. The sensible-intelligible dichotomy which, as far as natural phenomena are concerned, Plato resolved in myths, obtains in the new science of physics the principle of its transcendence in universal laws that are not engendered by the empirical world but are regulative of sensory experience. Over and above all the evident references and unquestionable opposition, in principle the methodical bonds between antiquity and modern times can be noted and have never been dissolved.[30]

As can be seen in this picture of thought relationships—of which this is only an example, but which can often be found in his writings—Cassirer tended to trace ideal lines which, because of their inner energy, reduce the differences and opposition to pure circumstances that are important for historical analysis but quite unable to break the ideal bond. This is nothing but faith in the relationship with antiquity that does not rest only on an analysis of the historical phenomenon, but also upon an "eternal providential" design, as it were, of the human spirit that grows upon itself. Cassirer replaces the ideal of Greek beauty, which is reproduced in those epochs that are similar in feeling and that simply lend themselves to imitation, with the ideal of history that automatically regenerates itself upon its own bases, since its aim is implied in them. Therefore the reference to antiquity in Cassirer takes on the lines of an ideality different from the recondite ideality in Warburg's erudite thought, which serves rather as an authority on whose base ingenious epochs find the strength for renewal and autonomous "rebirth." In this case it is a rebirth of the universality of life in all its forms, whereas with Cassirer it is the claim to universality on the part of a particular science that makes itself autonomous.

Cassirer's choice of the symbolic form as the nucleus round which his thought develops is determined by the symbol's consisting of a mediation between the sensible and the intelligible, between the external world of the perception of the datum and the epistemological faculty to elaborate upon it and lend it form. This middle position of the symbol—suggested to Cassirer by the three evolutionary phases of expression in the aesthetics of Friedrich Theodor Vischer, the roots of which lie in Hegelian philosophy[31]—becomes the focal point for the progressive emancipation from the sensory by means of which the mind fully asserts itself in the purity of the intellectual act, which establishes authentic and definitive relations in the temporary certainty of the world of experience. Since the Greeks first saw this need to transcend the sensory and formulated its theoretical bases, any intellectual attempt to produce that progress must turn to them.

As can be seen, the formulation of Cassirer's speculation on this subject is contradictory, but here it is only necessary to observe how from a similar philosophical formulation there should stem a method of analysis of the value to be attributed to the rebirth of antiquity substantially different from the one followed by Warburg in his research on the Renaissance. Both in the consideration of the typical properties of that age when the study of classical texts was at its height and in the historiographic verification of the transformation of the symbolic form in time, the unifying principle that informs Cassirer's research and assures that it will always lead to its predestined goal consists in submitting the plan of history to the deduction of a logical apriority that legitimates both the unitariness of the subjects of research and the reality of the progressive becoming of history itself.

The Aesthetics of Empathy

Although his research was limited to the observation of artistic phenomena, Warburg broadened the scope of his investigation to encompass everything that contributed to an understanding of the spirit of the times. The work of art is conceived as a reflection of the life of the period and its needs. It is therefore necessary to track down the customs, circumstances, and ideas that engendered it in order to make an interpretation that is both faithful to the work of art and consonant with the spirit of the civilization that produced it. At the same time, the work of art reveals intentions that go beyond its scope and belong to a need that is deeply hidden in the psyche, and the historian must penetrate the course of this intentionality, or at least try to imagine what it is, by utilizing the elements that the past and the present—in other words, his own cultural heritage—offer him.

At the beginning of his 1893 dissertation on Botticelli (his first completed piece of research), Warburg remarks on his endeavor to clarify which forms of antiquity stirred the interest of Renaissance artists and spurred them to imitation: "We will also observe in brief that this attempt is meaningful for psychological aesthetics, since here, in the milieu of artists intent upon their creations, one can note in its becoming the sensitivity to the aesthetic act of 'empathy' as a powerful creator of style."[32] This passage is accompanied by a note that cites two works Warburg referred to with regard to psychological aesthetics: *Das Symbol* (The Symbol) by Friedrich Theodor Vischer and *Über das optische Formgefühl* (On the Optical Perception of Form) by Friedrich Vischer's son, Robert. Besides the precise indication of the aesthetic principle that was the basis of his reflections on the feeling antiquity stirred in the Renaissance artist, this mention of the theory of empathy bespeaks Warburg's particular bent in tackling this investigation. In fact, this task meant he had to identify himself as far as possible with the atmosphere and mentality of the period in question. As Cassirer had rightly noted in his speech at Warburg's burial service and just as many commentators were to point out later, the gift for transferring his own life experience to the personages and events of the past he had decided to investigate was an intrinsic part of Warburg's character. But often in his oeuvre there is a warning addressed to those who want to understand a distant epoch, a warning to withhold judgment until such time as erudition and intuition have attained the difficult process of historical mutation from the present to the past under investigation. In order to find out which school he referred to in following his historiographic instinct, it is worth quoting a passage from Usener's *Götternamen* (Names of the Gods), in which a similar program is enunciated: "Since at the outset we find no fact in our consciousness that can clarify the impulses and gestures of prehistoric man, a speculative method such as that used in the so-called philosophy of religion is thus excluded. Only by devout delving into these spiritual traces of a vanished period—hence through philology—can we learn to make past experiences our own. Only then can analogous schemes flash and resound within us little by little and can we discover in our consciousness the threads that connect the old with the new."[33] And in analyzing the conceptual becoming of the primordial names of the gods, Usener reaffirms: "Only profound philological research into the language of these ancient representations will allow us to overcome the prejudices of our consciousness, [which is] separated from the ages, and lead us to intimate understanding."[34]

Warburg approaches the description of Florentine festivals with the same attitude: "An excessively modern judgment would obstruct our appreciation of the true psychological value of the artistic process to which this symbolism of costumes owes its origin and raison d'être."[35] Feeling in conformity with the object, which was part of Usener's as well as Warburg's character, is not an artistic or magical faculty, but the fruit of philological research bent on ascertaining every datum, on putting every concept to the test, and on gauging every connection before stating that it is certain. If intuition at times plays an overriding role in this historiographic method and induces one to draw the occasional forced conclusion, it nonetheless belongs to that inspiration typical of the great historians of the past which, side by side with possible errors of interpretation, paved the way for important discoveries in the often obscure realm of history.[36]

So it was with particular feeling that Renaissance artists turned to antiquity as an inspiration for their creations. The choice of the stylistic patterns to be revived and imitated responded to an inner need and a pathos both ancient and new, and it led these artists to contemplate and reproduce antiquity with highly charged involvement.

The art theory of empathy that Warburg mentions is not to be identified generically with the psychological schools of the second half of the nineteenth century that sought a metaphysical basis for the sentiment of sympathetic involvement because, as Benedetto Croce rightly observed in a brief work written in 1934, a distinction must be made between these schools of thought.[37] The thesis Warburg was close to and which had more of a speculative character than a psychological one, was formulated in 1873 by Robert Vischer, who continued his father's aesthetic research and was a competent and seasoned art historian. His book on Luca Signorelli served as an example to Warburg for the abundance of documentary material used to reconstruct the various aspects of the life of the times. Vischer seriously grappled with the problem, which his father had left unsolved, of a mixture of the sensible and intelligible, of nature and mind, in that intermediary phase of human consciousness that is the symbol. Vischer concluded that this symbol is a unity, but the problem to be solved is how to arrive at this unity on the premise of a dualism. Empathy—that "feeling inside the other person," the contemplating subject and contemplated nature becoming identified and one, whereby the former becomes nature and the latter is animated—rests upon an expressive capacity of human sensitivity that is transferred and observed in nature.

Friedrich Vischer had already noted how the meaning of every formal symbology was an intimate identification of image and content which, in a still unconscious stage in the natural religions and myths, had been an exchange between the observed object, the phenomenon, and the transcendent sense that was immediately attributed to it. In the aesthetic symbol, in the artistic form, this exchange takes place on the basis of a conscious identification of the inner ideal with the external object, thus giving rise to a symbolic image, a moment of mediation of this movement of the soul in order to take possession of the phenomenon. More than relating to a cognitive arrangement of the real in the phenomenon, the symbol conceived in this way seems to be the fruit of a metamorphosis. But it is change in a reciprocal direction—both toward the imaginative power of the subject and back to the material that is observed. Robert Vischer takes up this theme and tries to go deeper than the original dualism between subject and external world in order to explain how it is resolved in the symbolic unity of the gesture, of the word and, last, of the artistic phenomenon.

He begins with an analysis of the nervous centers which act in unity with the psyche upon the vision of the external object, determining reactions of sympathy with, or antipathy to, the form. The representations spring from the original perceptions and impression they make on the nervous groups and on the soul. In aesthetics this is solely a matter of mixed representations that are both subjective and objective, hence representations of a conscious relationship between the self and nonself.[38]

Robert Vischer's conception of both representation and object is unclear. The pure Kantian intuition and the apriority of space and time, elaborated in Schopenhauer's speculation on intellectual intuition, generate in Vischer's analysis continuous confusion and terminological imprecision that in certain passages borders on theoretical shoddiness. He explains the attainment of inner will, of the self's intimate need for harmony, in terms of evolution, as his father had done, and according to the scheme—later inherited by Cassirer—of a historical process from sensory expression to concept. While intuition, with respect to the character of the image, is dominated by a direct clash with objective reality, representation has greater inner freedom, an unlimited capacity for contemplation. "It does not have the clarity of reality, but neither does it have its blinding power, since form is both transfigured and spiritualized by means of its interiorization. On the other hand, this independence from the petty conditioning of reality may also cause a doubly intensified intervention of the material stimulus."[39] In fact, reality exerts an exact and constrictive discipline upon inner representation, lacking which the material stimulus is exaggerated. Vischer considers this, which he calls the "talent of exaggeration," the authentic power of representation, its "power of imagination." This engenders a self-sufficient image that is totally new, though still bound by a sort of "immature sympathy for subjective, private play and for anomaly." "Only inner fantasy truly abstracts from the confusion and irrationality of nature and, accompanied by the unconscious norm of bodily perfection, takes the liberty of creating harmonious single forms, microcosms."[40]

Only art or external fantasy, which has the acquired capacity to have an "objective intuition" of reality, can lead these inner images to total clarity and purity. Fantasy is thus a specific common action of the three principal forces of the soul: feeling, representation, and will.

Vischer's idea of nature is confused. It is the binding discipline from whose narrow confines inner representation, cultivated in fantasy, escapes; yet it is also a blind, irrational force in which fantasy establishes the order of lovely, harmonious form. However there is not only the form attained in the inner creative process; there are also external forms, which he obscurely calls objective forms, toward which the representation of the corporeal self shifts to become identified with them because of a feeling of pleasure.[41] Vischer does not clarify what kind of forms these are. Initially, though, they appear to be not simple images of exteriority but images confused with the external world until they seem to belong to nature itself, like the nonself, the absolutely other than the soul.

Nature thus can appear as the irrational, which however is not indeterminate but rather seems to possess an extraordinary power of constriction and limitation. At another time nature is the rule of a well-ordered cosmos, entirely regulated by mathematical laws. "Everything in the world is subject to the rules of mathematics," the number dominates all things.[42] Although he intends to demonstrate that the symbolic image (the "symbology of forms" he inherited from his father) is truly a whole, a mediation achieved between internal and external, Vischer goes on to identify two types of forms, the subjective ideal ones and the objective real ones: "What else is this form [the objective one with which the subjective form has identified itself], if not the form of a content identical with it?"[43] "It seems that I belong to myself despite the fact that the object remains other than myself, since I am transferred and magically transformed into this nonself."[44]

It is evident that for Vischer there exists an innate sense of the whole, and the efforts made by the symbolizing will are directed at its conservation as well as at the increase in the harmony of our inner feeling. We originally perceive the universe as unity in sensation: the process leading from the feeling of one's opposition to the objective world to the conscious identification with an external form in artistic creation is a process in which reality is idealized in the harmony of taste, in pure aesthetic pleasure.

Feeling of oneself is an abstraction from the primal unity with the world in pure sensation; it is an individualization which in turn evolves in acquiring feeling from the other and thus extends to a generalization of the self-in-humanity (*Menschen-Ich*). "Progress properly speaking is nothing else but a renunciation and scattering of the feeling of oneself, which is got only in relation to the whole."[45] The ideality of fantasy is the recovery of a harmonic totality; it is the idea of a universe that receives its measure from fantasy itself.

What perhaps impressed Warburg in this problematic attempt at

establishing the aesthetic sense as the self's empathy with the object—
and what must have been useful for his interpretation of the early
Renaissance style of expressive movement—was the thesis according
to which representation is a mixture of moldable, pliant elements penetrated by the universal contraries (quiet and motion, self and nonself)
in a mysterious whole.[46] If one observes an immobile, stable object,
one can put oneself entirely in place of its intimate structure, its vital
center, Vischer affirms. This is the empathizing (*Einfühlen*) of the form
of the still phenomenon, which corresponds to the study of physiog-
nomy and is dominated by the atmosphere (*Stimmung*). In opposition
to this is mimic or active empathy, which is dominated by affection
and produced in relation to an object really or only apparently in
motion. In any case, the perception of movement or of an object's
tendency toward movement is fundamental to the manifestation of
empathy.[47] Empathy is the support for the nature of religious personification, mythical formation, and the free fantasy of aesthetics as they
move along an indirect path toward a spiritual energy that can attain
a greater objectivization of itself. In fact, the vital power of the phenomenon and the spiritual value attributed to it are connected in a
psychic feeling of empathy whose perfection is reached only after passing through the realm of experience and education.

The aesthetic act is based upon the will of fantasy, which is imposed
by an inner participation in the relationship between the various symbolic forms. This participation also generates empathy, since will consists of an impulse to action and movement, and hence tends to satisfy
a need for pleasure. And imitation is the way in which this impulse
moves the sentiment of empathy outward to the forms of reality found
in an image. Indeed, perceptive movements are already imitations, or
better, mediations between subject and object. "Artistic imitation . . .
is originally the adequate result of an inner dynamic event consonant
with it. The activity of the eye has stimulated a process in the inner
nervous system, in the entire psyche and in the entire person. Representing this being consonant is the recondite aim of every ingenuous
formation of images, and the opinion whereby this is rather a paradigm
existing in nature, is a form of self-deception."[48]

Form now appears not only in fully realized artistic expression, but
even in primitive symbol formation, a being consonant with the self
and nonself through the power of the imagination. After Schopen-

hauer's scornful rejection of the "thing-in-itself" that Kant "let slip through his fingers," Vischer hastens to deny reality to formal models as essences existing in nature, which he could not explain in any way whatsoever and which would have posed serious problems in his attempt to account for the way that subject and object harmonized in empathy. In making forms into psycho-physical as well as spiritual entities, however, he is wholly unable to verify their purely ideal nature: they are at once what gives rise to complex symbolic movement, to the tension between opposite poles of feeling, and the result of this movement. In order to justify this contradiction he is forced to give, to what should be a structure of aesthetic knowledge, a historical-evolutionary framework that at least once—as we have already seen—he explicitly calls progress.

The artist who possesses a healthy spiritual individuality that is equally conscious of the sensory nature of his general vital impulse, is never content with vulgar imitation. "Insofar as he transfers to the object the instinctive and reflective [sic] unit of measure of human conformity to a norm, he represents in a whole the perfect human being and in a whole his own semblance as it is transfigured by the illusory magnificence of the world. He makes the phenomenon harmonious, so that—thanks to him—it achieves the utmost expression of human harmony in feeling and of the divinity of everything."[49]

Fantasy consists in the senses and the soul feeling in harmony, and in this consonance each confirms itself in a sort of identity; they are fused together, as it were, without any residue of an abstract or sensory nature. Art is therefore a strengthening of sensibility, like a superior physics of nature.[50] It is both purely subjective and purely objective, since subject and object are one thing alone in the artistic act. From this mixture of elements belonging to Neoplatonic aesthetics and to Kant's theory of taste, to post-Hegelian idealism and to nineteenth-century psychology, there emerges above all a notion of art that undoubtedly fascinated Warburg and influenced his interpretative inquiries. For Robert Vischer the highest aim of art is to represent a conflict of forces in movement: the physiological one of sight and the nervous system, and the other one of vital corporeal and psychic feeling, the spiritual energy of the imagination and the regulative and harmonizing will of fantasy. In fact, he defines movement as "the form of the relationship between the forms of single corporeal elements."[51] Warburg certainly agreed with a theory of imitation that considered this instrument of artistic reproduction a creation inspired by the agreement that is generated through empathy between the individual feeling of life and the external movement of forms, rather than a passive repetition of nature or of the stylistic models of the past.

By referring to empathy at the beginning of his studies on Renaissance art, Warburg stresses the fact that Florentine works of art were not limited to being mere imitations of classical models (the very imitation Winckelmann had urged the artists of his time to practice). He suggests that the new spirit of novelty and also the limit of Renaissance artistic expression lay in a "sentiment," that is to say, in an identification that was not natural but filtered through the imagination with what Renaissance men saw—or wanted to see—of themselves in the great works of antiquity. From these statements emerges the 'setting' of Warburg's wide-ranging interpretative approach whose working principles are noted here.

Like Burckhardt, Warburg is willing to acknowledge that the term *Renaissance* is not appropriate to define the nature of the epoch.[52] In his eager approach to classical culture, the Italian of the quattrocento fought an arduous battle against the medieval figurative tradition and against the boundless world of transcendence the preceding age had cultivated with great intellectual vigor. He saw in antiquity the possibilities offered by a vast patrimony of beauty, and the new conditions of political autonomy and individual freedom spurred him on to seize upon those possibilities, to raise his existence to those extremes of harmony and pleasure, and to cultivate himself in external images of refinement and elegance as well as of the ideality of his passions and intuition of his own time. Given the new approach to the antique, every interpretation of texts or imitation of forms was considered different and surprisingly fecund; but the contrast with a custom that was in the process of changing and with a mentality that was about to be eclipsed by the modern one, was also strongly felt. This awareness of living in a period of transition—an awareness more or less defined intellectually by the Renaissance artist, as well as by his patrons and counselors—gave rise to the melancholy of the transitory, the anxiety of the present, the intention of turning to those forms which he himself might never attain, the haste to fathom and consume his own existence in this battle against time. At the end of the chapter on

Renaissance festivals, Burckhardt mentions the "beautiful song that accompanied the scene of Bacchus and Ariadne" ascribed to Lorenzo the Magnificent, "whose refrain still echoes to us from the fifteenth century like a regretful presentiment of the brief splendor of the Renaissance itself."[53]

Warburg's writings on Botticelli embrace all these motifs. Later on he would expand and deepen them, but always within the bounds of the interpretative unity he had achieved.

Genius and History

The influence of Warburg's great teachers is already apparent in his 1893 essay. In his portrait of a Botticelli who painted upon the advice of Poliziano, who in turn was inspired by Homer's hymn to Venus and by the Latin poets, and in the long comparison made between these poetic texts and the stylistic details of Botticelli's paintings, we feel the influence of Lessing's *Laocoön*, which had led Warburg to decide to devote himself to the study of art history.[54] The structures of his study and Lessing's are almost symmetrical: Warburg showed that the painter was inspired by the poet, just as Lessing had affirmed that the sculptors of the Laocoön group had been by Virgil. Additionally, since the Renaissance poet and painter were on quite familiar terms, in his poetry Poliziano provided the details that Botticelli could use in his painting.[55] This construct is also an homage to Lessing, who said that there is a great difference between the aesthetic formulation of poetry and that of painting or sculpture and then offered a long and truly prodigious analysis of the tools appropriate for each artistic medium. In this analysis Lessing made a significant juxtaposition between the arts: painting and sculpture flourish in spatial extension; poetry operates in time and is thus necessarily inclined to express perception as a succession of elements and to lend its descriptive power to becoming, in which the reader's interest either wanes or is protracted.[56] Yet in his verses, Poliziano was careful to anticipate the pictorial sense that was to be depicted by Botticelli. The painter was fascinated by the classicizing material his illustrious friend offered him but nonetheless remained faithful to his own experience as a goldsmith and chiseler of precious details.

The reference to Lessing cannot but evoke the other great scholar of antiquity, his contemporary Johann Winckelmann. These eighteenth-century German masters had opposing views, and Warburg's preference for Lessing is already foreshadowed in his early works. Even the allusion to the relationship between poetry and painting is a clear reference to Lessing, since Winckelmann did not believe that a work of art as important as the Laocoön group could have had a precise literary model or that it could have been adapted to that model. And in fact he dated the group—erroneously—to a much earlier period. Winckelmann believed that the sculpture of the golden age of Greek art was its own raison d'être and that a description of it could not go beyond the limits the work itself established; every cultural or historical element was suspended in the very act of offering itself to us for contemplation. Winckelmann's thesis was greatly subverted by nineteenth-century philological criticism and then definitively lost its influence in the chaos wrought by twentieth-century aesthetics. And yet the subtle connection, or contrast, that Lessing formulates in his *Laocoön* appears to be the result of a merely pedantic reconstruction compared to the inimitable coherence of vision and sentiment with which Winckelmann contemplates the Apollo Belvedere or the Bust of Hercules.

To understand how difficult it is to divorce oneself from the view of antiquity so memorably established by Winckelmann in his writings on Greek art, one need only recall how his most violent adversary in the nineteenth century, Nietzsche, was still so influenced by his thought. And naturally his reading and interpretation of Winckelmann—which were presumably fervid and diligent—were filtered through Schopenhauer's philosophy of art. The Apollo Belvedere that Schopenhauer describes with the same passionate participation—"The head of the god of the Muses, with eyes looking far afield, stands so freely on the shoulders that it seems to be wholly delivered from the body, and no longer subject to its cares"[57]—still lies before Nietzsche's gaze when he points out the "measured restraint, freedom from the wilder emotions, and philosophical calm of the sculptor-god" in the Apollonian dream world. "His eye must be 'sunlike', as befits his origin; even when his glance is angry and distempered the sacredness of his beautiful appearance must still be there."[58] There is another detail that could not have failed to make an impression upon

Nietzsche's restless spirit: he touches upon the philosophy of the sylvan god "which caused the downfall of the melancholy Etruscans." Here the reference to Winckelmann's thesis concerning Etruscan art is evident; he affirms that it is inferior to classical Greek art and stresses the melancholic nature of these less evolved people. In fact, a melancholy nature, though a sign of genius and of profundity of reflection, is prone to overviolent feelings that cannot be led to "that gentle agitation, which renders the soul perfectly susceptible to beauty."[59]

The detailed precision with which Warburg tracks down and reveals the presence of those "accessories in motion" that had so struck him in early Renaissance art tends to point out a stylistic motif central to that art. It might at first glance seem that the pathos of animated, intensified movement is without doubt set against the "quiet grandeur" that Winckelmann viewed as the fundamental characteristic of Greek genius. If drapery flowing in the wind and the mobile tension of muscles were really present in antiquity, this means that the Greek artists expressed themselves in terms of external agitation and pathos of movement. But Warburg is not yet disputing Winckelmann; on the contrary, in concluding his three-part study of Botticelli's production, he expressly states that the fault for that insistent fluttering and billowing of veils and drapery lies in the lack of artistic independence on the part of the Florentines of the time. This art is unfavorably compared to the poetic models that it attempts to reproduce because it has not yet found a self-sufficient and unitary means of expression.[60] With a final quotation from *Winckelmann* by Karl Justi (another of Warburg's teachers), according to whom "initiative is characteristic of genius," Warburg utters his final reproof of Botticelli, whose character was too "pliant," too easily impressionable and passive either to make a faithful rendering of antiquity or to create a new form.

Justi distinguished the artist's primary substance, which is the individual element that determines the artist's capacity to make autonomous aesthetic choices, from the secondary substance, which is his contact with his environment (what Panofsky calls the "historical inner experience"). In his early work Warburg keeps these two different aspects of the artist's personality in perfect equilibrium; later on he tends to focus on the analysis of the secondary substance, dwelling only rarely on the primary one—for example when he encounters it in Dürer, Leonardo, and Piero della Francesca.

Making a parallel between visual art and poetry may be useful for a historical reconstruction of the period and, in the case of Lessing, for offering arguments in favor of a later date for the Laocoön group. However, since Lessing defined the different and even contrasting stylistic criteria of the two media, the evocative power and autonomous capacity for invention of the sculpture group with respect to the description of the tragic episode in the *Aeneid* remain the same. Lessing and Winckelmann were thus in basic agreement concerning the strong sense of restraint and measure applied to expressive pathos that makes Greek sculpture a unique example of harmony and intensity in the history of art.

Fascinated as he was by the Florentine world that was rising before him in such a vivid, concrete form, Warburg viewed Botticelli's works more as the result of literary imitation than as an autonomous creation of the artist's primary substance. It was perhaps this harsh criticism, which somewhat attenuated the significance of Botticelli's genius, that led Justi to react rather coolly to his young pupil's paper, as Warburg seemed to be animated more by an eagerness to show his worth, and by a critical approach already too free and singular, than by prudent historiographic rigor.

In his early research on Botticelli Warburg hints at the precise aesthetic and historiographic method of inquiry that he will develop. His intention was to underscore the recurrence of a stylistic pattern that corresponds to a particular type of sympathetic identification with ancient models. Early Renaissance art in Florence imitated—while augmenting its movement—what it considered the lovely and graceful expression of intense emotion. The creation of a stylistic pattern corresponded to Renaissance painters' new sensitivity to antiquity that manifested itself as the transferral of their own sense of life into those examples of the past. At first Warburg felt this procedure acted as a brake on inventiveness, but during the course of his studies he comes to think of it as the symbol of Renaissance emancipation from the paradigms of previous art. But what interests him above all in the analysis of style is precisely the supposition of a certain choice: it is that sense of life he often mentions to indicate the features of an age of transition during which Renaissance consciousness, split by the rapid changes in civilization, brings to the surface its anxiety as well as its enthusiasm, with both emotions immediately revealed in every facet of existence.

Warburg often returned to the motif of life as energy and the anxious will to movement and becoming in his writings, demonstrating that he had fully taken in Burckhardt's lesson in this regard. In fact, Burckhardt also frequently takes up this idea in his consideration of art and history. Life is what determines and guides the choice of a certain intensity or of a certain pathos for any artistic reproduction. The inn scenes of the great Flemish painters, which the Basel historian (unlike Hegel) praised, possess that capacity for involving the viewer offered by the awakening of an interest in life which is reproduced with such agreeable realism.[61]

Warburg feels that life is the totality of aspirations, thoughts, and defeats that an age has passed through and that the artist reproduces, by dwelling on either contemporary aspects, Christian legends, or pagan myths. In each subject the accent (or its lack) on certain stylistic details and the effort made at imitating certain models reveal an overview of the world and a way of life in which the artist perceives a unitary conception of existence, or the ideality of the aims pursued by that age. In Warburg's later writings, in particular the lecture on the Palazzo Schifanoia frescoes in Ferrara, his research is based upon artists of less genius because, having less creative power, they made more effort to adapt to tradition, thus offering us what Usener would call "conceptual transparency"[62] and giving more certain references to their sources. For—to repeat Justi's observation—initiative is characteristic of genius.

Given that the theory of genius stems from the common ground of aesthetics and from the emergence of modern individuality,[63] the genius-artist's milieu and the culture that educated and nourished him make up the secondary substance, the contribution of circumstances extraneous to his birth and development. But the primary substance is initiative, the power to dominate the surrounding world in a unitary view that can only be obtained in him and through him. His initiative is the capacity to produce independently of any rule or discipline. "The environment does not make men significant, it merely acts together with talent, destiny and will. Of all these factors will is the most tenacious force. Without will the other three are almost nil, but will can counterbalance their adversity."[64] The determination of will is an innate gift that the artist intuits in himself and which he is driven to cultivate at all costs. To use an image of Schopenhauer, who for once made this concept comprehensible, the "method of genius" is like a force that vertically cuts through the horizontal stream of rationality and is capable of invention, of rendering visible and comprehensible the idea, the "thing-in-itself" of the will which in that linear process of causes and effects has no other way of making itself perceptible.[65]

The problem of the genius's rationality, his conformity or nonconformity to rules, is central to eighteenth-century art theory and appears in its most complete form in Lessing's thought, according to which the genius is free from formal discipline, for he himself is the creator of artistic rules. He is not subject to the rules that tradition has taught him but rather establishes them, thus founding a new and different expression of the same ideal. Kant affirms the same thing in his *Critique of Judgement*: "Genius is the talent (or natural gift) which gives the rule to art."[66] Its first property is originality, which consists of creative imagination that, strengthened to an exceptional degree by nature, utilizes the concepts of the intellect to express the inexpressible rather than experience. Kant, however, limits the genius's activity to the sphere of art; his is an essentially aesthetic trait inherent to the beautiful and thus to a subjective dimension. He has no relationship with science, his creations cannot be imitated, he cannot communicate how he came by the ideas he has expressed. Kant considers genius as such inferior to scientific talent, since scientific talent works for the greater perfection of knowledge and education, while art is not subject to progress but rather has a finite limit beyond which it cannot go and "which presumably has been reached long ago."[67] The genius is conscious of his talent and puts it to use "after the example" of the genius that preceded him, but in an independent manner. Art is the conception of a purpose and as such must be subject to rules. So Kant also continues the German Enlightenment polemic against the *Sturm und Drang*'s parading of extravagance and disorder. "Genius can only furnish rich *material* for products of beautiful art; its execution and its *form* require talent cultivated in the schools, in order to make use of this material as will stand examination by the judgement."[68]

The genius makes free use of his cognitive faculties and yet is subject to a standard—the rule of taste, by which he must eliminate that dangerous tendency not to dominate ideas and thus lose himself in senseless unrestraint. Having denied genius a place in scientific progress and in the causal chain that regulates the discovery of the laws of nature, Kant nonetheless recognizes that even genius has a binding limitation and grants it a role in human progress. The rule of taste, "while it brings clearness and order into the multitude of the thoughts [of genius], makes the ideas susceptible of being permanently and, at the same time, universally assented to, and capable of being followed by others, and of an ever progressive culture."[69] Kant strives to reduce to a minimum the margin of irrationality of genius, admitting and even desiring constraint upon the genius's freedom rather than on the rule of judgment, and on the abundance of the imagination rather than on the intellect.[70]

Schopenhauer also holds that the work of the genius is of an exclusively artistic nature, but for him genius appears as the ability to free oneself from the limits of the will and consider things independently of the principle of sufficient reason in order to grasp the ideas that lie beyond every relation, in pure contemplation. Art "plucks the object of its contemplation from the stream of the world's course and holds it isolated before it. This particular thing, which in that stream was an infinitesimal part, becomes for art a representative of the whole, an equivalent of the infinitely many in space and time. It therefore pauses at this particular thing; it stops the wheel of time; for it the relations vanish; its object is only the essential, the Idea."[71] Genius is the aptitude of wresting oneself from the conditioning that the will works by means of individual aims and personal interests, and in this sense represents the total objectivization of the will, knowledge removed from relations and the chain of causes; it is losing oneself in intuition.

In Schopenhauer the exposition of the properties of genius is filled with contradictions, but one above all is central to the argument that concerns Justi's conception, and in part Burckhardt's and Warburg's as well. The genius is "unusual energy of that whole phenomenon of will" which manifests itself through the "vehemence of all his acts of will." In him intuition prevails upon intellect, and action, which has been abandoned by "colorless concepts," proves to be irrational. But if art is the forgoing of particular aims of will and of the system of relations that will dominates through the principle of sufficient reason, how can genius be a strengthening of will itself? In the concluding pages of his main work, Schopenhauer points out how at the basis of every annihilation of will, in sanctity or aesthetic contemplation, one catches sight of the obscure limit of nothingness, since everything in the world is a phenomenon, that is to say, a manifestation of will, and the end of will is also the end of the representation of the world. Art conceived as the work of genius will thus be suspended over a vague borderline between that maximum of will that is will itself becoming absolute with respect to relations, and nothingness which is the lack of the concrete products of will—phenomena. This will be an art of the contemplation of the idea, but also incapable of effecting any representation: its products, abstracted from space and time, cannot be seen or heard, nor even painted, carved, or written. Schopenhauer seeks to obviate this drawback by describing the creations of the individual arts as caused by the conflict between subjectivity, into which will has insinuated itself, and objectivity that immediately contemplates nature itself, an ideal world emancipated from the illusory phenomenal world governed by particular aims.

The extreme consequences of his thought are treated with great clarity by Nietzsche, who states that knowledge of art itself is illusory, "because as knowing beings we are not one and identical with that being who, as sole author and spectator of this comedy of art, prepares a perpetual entertainment for himself."[72] The genius coalesces with the primordial artist of the world and only then does he intuit the essence of art. He turns his eye on himself and contemplates himself. This passage of Nietzsche's demonstrates even more clearly the impossibility of creation on the part of the genius: what need would he have to create, in fact, if he already contemplates himself, and above all what would distinguish the "act of artistic creation" from the artist's coinciding with the eternal identity of subject and object in "creation"?

By defining will as the most important attribute of genius, Justi implicitly keeps his distance, at least on this essential point, from Schopenhauer and restores to the individual genius—together with his independence from history and from any idea whatsoever of progress and evolution—a rationality all his own, since willing presupposes consciousness and intellectual exercise. Robert Vischer then explicitly insists upon the opposition to Schopenhauer's position on the part of art theory based on the will of fantasy.[73]

This theory of genius as will was strongly impressed upon Warburg and his school. Saxl considered the wingless angel in Rembrandt's painting of Hagar in the desert a tremendous effort on his part to free himself from a tradition deeply rooted in figurative art and make his choice through an initiative that was violent in its historical context.[74] Panofsky presents Dürer's figure of Melancholy as a highly personal interpretation of the ancient iconography of Saturn and his temperaments: in that engraving the age-old existence of a symbolic form takes on totally new and personal importance and meaning, and Dürer's genius, the power of his sentiment, created a synthesis of the data at his disposal and interpreted them according to his artistic intention.[75] Warburg notes in the same engraving the fully realized process of the spiritualization of a symbol for the most part related to the fearful superstition of preceding ages.[76]

The genius thus makes a mark on the course of history and determines the decisive transformation—that in which the results of so many partial endeavors are summarized and transfigured. But what influence or coherence the episode of the genius-artist has in the course of history is not easy to determine from this thesis. If, as Schopenhauer affirms, it reveals the light of ideas to contemplation, it cannot be taken in by the world of rationality and of the principle of sufficient reason. Once the rupture between these two spheres (contemplation and rationality) has been effected, it will be impossible to take in any reciprocal influence. In fact Burckhardt observes that Renaissance culture concerns only a limited circle of intellectuals interested in cultivating the ideas of antiquity, but it does not act upon the general public. And he (so hostile to the masses and yet so scrupulously aware of their presence and the problem they pose) adds that this is a universal datum pertaining to all civilizations, since culture can develop only as the heritage of the few.

Progress on the other hand involves all of mankind; therefore it cannot be entrusted to culture and the artistic genius has no power to make proselytes and make a mark on the course of evolution. His oeuvre lives outside of time, in eternity or—in relationship with historic time—in the instant, before which and after which it is not really anything.⁷⁷ The creations of artists "look like youth rescued and perpetuated."⁷⁸ In his view, the term *Renaissance* is partial and restricted because the genius and novelty of this age do not end with the rediscovery of antiquity, they do not live in a real historical process ranging from antiquity to modern times; rather the talent developed in life in all its forms has an autochthonous and autonomous sense. "It was not the revival of antiquity alone, but the union with the genius of the Italian people, which achieved the conquest of the Western world."⁷⁹ However Burckhardt himself, who only rarely experienced the weakness of doubt, hesitates when faced with this image of a heroic Renaissance. Immediately afterwards he says that "the amount of independence this spirit maintained in this union varied," and, further on, he even speaks of an alliance of the greatest independence between the two distant epochs. Though through the analysis of the social conditions Burckhardt attempts to redeem the political and civic maturity, the desire to live intensely, and the meaning of the 'great event' that the Renaissance represented, as one proceeds in the chapter on the revival of antiquity, he increases the value of classical culture's contribution to the new epoch, above all with regard to its function as a guide with its wealth of objective truths in all spiritual fields.

What distinguishes the Renaissance from the preceding "barbarism" is the particular spirit of self-consciousness it brought to bear in its possession of ancient culture.⁸⁰ This is the motif Warburg sets out to deal with in his art-historical research. The choice of accessories in motion tended to "grasp from what is living the instant of an external motion";⁸¹ the Nympha recurring in the imagination of the time was the ancient mythical girl that emerged from centuries of oblivion, as fresh as a creation of the moment, the symbol of a hitherto unknown energy of renewal. "The nymph was one of those attractive creations in which the Italian quattrocento, in its wholly peculiar and masterly fashion, fused the genius of art with the feeling of antiquity."⁸² "Florentine genius worked with that typical and peculiar harmonic fusion of original artistic power and imitative skill."⁸³ The homage to Burckhardt is evident in these passages, as is the importance attached to the festivals as occasions in which one seized the opportunity to see the living figures celebrated by antiquity.

The theory of genius as the harmony in an individual of all the elements of the external world and tradition is extended to the entire

Florentine Renaissance, conceived as an epoch of genius in human history. But Warburg does not pose the general problem of the participation of the masses in culture and of the popularity of the Renaissance, as Burckhardt had done. With melancholy and profound mistrust in the future, Burckhardt witnessed the emergence and consolidation of the popularization of culture in the Western world without ever for a moment believing that culture would emerge from it reborn, or at any rate solidly established. Though he saw that the world of classical values that had accompanied him in his studies and convictions was collapsing, he did not think of abandoning it. Instead in his historical meditations he constructed for that world the only sphere in which genius, inventiveness, and the sublimity of the creative act made any sense for him—the sphere of art. During the Renaissance this sphere produced the magnificence of the various city-states and the absolute dedication to the ideas made "evident" by the ancients, the wealth of trade and commerce and the freedom of the individual genius.[84] Burckhardt's view of history becomes in Warburg a view directed at the inner realm of the psyche and a meditation on the possibility that art may clarify in history what is buried in the penumbra of the human soul.

The dominion of art lies in the sphere of the symbol, which helps the imagination to free itself from the depths and express itself. It is necessary to find those symbols that, with the utmost power of expressive synthesis, represent the externalization of an inner world thus entrusted to feeling, which contemplates it, and to intellect, which judges it. Once this is done, symbols continue to live in humanity's consciousness. They lie in its more or less hidden and latent zones; they migrate through civilization among those persons who can most openly take them in; they seek in some persons that self-knowledge that will allow them to reemerge in their original guise or in simple nudity, as was the case with the Olympian gods.

What relationship do these symbols have with the potential progress of humanity? Wherever they are found in their original meaning, the initiative of that epoch is most intense; since they are creative, they transmit energy and offer themselves to speculation through the spiritual tension they emit. When a people has exhausted its inventive and creative capacities, these symbols withdraw or disguise themselves until they are unrecognizable and then migrate, because they, along with energy, are bearers of the same restlessness that produced them. At this stage oblivion replaces memory, because the symbols come from the depths and conserve for humanity authentic memory which, as Bergson says, emerges only from the depths and is not a mechanical connection of data in recollection. Since memory is lacking, self-consciousness wanes, as does the impulse to produce an external world of perfection in one's image.

Progress and genius, when the latter is understood as a fortunate mixture of historical memory and striving after a certain intensity of life, do not seem to influence each other. If genius is produced by the will to emerge from a conflict, as Warburg seems to mean, it cannot survive the fulfillment of its task; for even while it is celebrating its triumph its moment has passed, its energy is drained and the course of time continues indifferently.

Warburg's concept of the symbol therefore does not seem to have any trait susceptible to evolution, but only characteristics related to the expression of the spirituality, self-consciousness, and vital instincts of a certain epoch. But this line of thought does not remain unchanged in Warburg's research into the survival of the ancient world. In any case, in order to give meaning to history, it would be important to know whether the regeneration of tradition, the conservation of memory, is conceivable as a spontaneous fact, an intrinsic nature, of the symbol.

Gertrud Bing, Cassirer's pupil and Warburg's secretary until his death, states: "Tradition for Warburg was not a stream on which events and people are borne along. Influences are no matter of passive acceptance, but demand an effort of adjustment, an *Auseinandersetzung* [discussion] as Warburg says, which includes that of the present with the past."[85] But what is it that provokes the fatigue of this encounter, the interest in the discussion? It is not enough simply to say that it is the ancient works of art that spur one to revival, because their reappearance cannot be casual, and because the desire to intensify and imitate them requires all those circumstances that in reality are difficult to establish concretely. Warburg is so convinced of this that in an essay central to this problem of the relationship with antiquity he states that, as far as the Laocoön group is concerned, if the Renaissance had not discovered it, it would have had to invent it, precisely by virtue of its disturbingly passionate eloquence.[86] On the other hand, if ancient tradition consists of already consolidated symbols that celebrate, once and for all, the achievement of great expressive intensity, what is it that kindles or consumes their evocative power? In reality they are always present in history and are bound to it as if to a second nature; they disguise themselves in other forms that often contradict them and often decrease their evocative power and make them appear to be what they are not; and yet they preserve themselves, ready to reemerge totally intact when the time and place are favorable and well disposed to them. They do not struggle at all against time, but rather survive in time. Warburg says that the history of human expression is in the last analysis their history, not determined progressively, but by changes wrought on a framework of permanence and identity. Only the encounter that every history must have with time, which generates change, produces that restlessness, that pathos which coincides with the symbol's capacity for metamorphosis. Changing in appearance but not in structure, and thus having a history, the symbols of the past remain intact until such time as the somewhat extra-historical and extra-temporal appearance of genius brings about a more intense qualitative change, which is at the same time a reconquest of their primal power.

Francesco Sassetti and Renaissance Polarities

The inappropriateness of the term *Renaissance,* which Burckhardt had found too restrictive and Warburg also criticizes, is in the final analysis based on the twofold character of the historical process: first, the essential influence of antiquity on a cycle of renewal; second, the autonomous impulse to take in and cultivate such an influence (which is itself caused by the convergence of favorable circumstances, determined by a sort of fortune, above and beyond any historiographic attempt at reconstructing a linear design).

The feeling of the brevity of life and of the immortality of an illustrious past engendered the genius of the Renaissance. This engendering occurred in history, that is to say, in that course of events made up of lights and shadows that the scholar tries to lead to the uniformly visible surface of rational consciousness. Rationality means a verification of causality, and it is the motif of the causes that determined the choice of certain stylistic models of the Florentine Renaissance which links Warburg explicitly with Burckhardt.

Warburg's 1902 paper, "Portraiture and the Florentine Bourgeoisie," was intended as an appendix to the Swiss historian's *Notes on the History of Art in Italy*. He appreciatively underscores the "empirical" paths in that masterly art-historical research in which, rather than making a unitary judgment of the epoch, Burckhardt breaks down the historical problem of that civilization into parts that stand by themselves—figurative art, society and politics. In this posthumous work, to whose destiny Warburg wants to link his study, "[Burckhardt] paved the way for a third empirical course: he did not disdain the labor of investigating the direct connection the individual work had with the background of the epoch in order to interpret the ideal or practical needs of real life as 'causality.' "[87] Warburg is also striving for the same causality of existence in its totality of feeling and experience, because he sees in it the sources of that admirable artistic production and its ideal, which constitutes one of the most tangible documents in the Renaissance. The empirical course is the only one that dwells not only on the personality of the artist or on the purely aesthetic judgment of the work of art, but also witnesses and scrutinizes the sphere of concrete relationships between the artist and his patrons and, in general, his environment, a sphere that has no immediate link with the philosophy of art but rather with "life."

When Burckhardt describes the portraits by Flemish painters, with their realism and devotion to detail, he says that "their criterion was anything but that of beauty, and not even that of energy, but rather that of a certain measure of honesty"[88]—as though one had life itself before one's eyes. And then again: "In all of them there is a new world made up of an intransigent spiritual and material adherence to life."[89] These concepts are less evident references to Flemish art if we think of them in the context of the portrait as it became part of the legendizing idealization of the Italian artists. Warburg thus had to abstract and isolate in the sacred representation of a Christian legend those motifs he was seeking in the Florentine archives that represented the relationships between patrons and artists, and between the patrons and the political and economic world in which they operated so successfully.

In order to explain the unusual iconology that Francesco Sassetti wanted Ghirlandaio to use in the frescoes of his burial chapel, Warburg tries to "understand the universal of the mentality of eminent personages of the past on the basis of single facts in their actual existence."[90] The empirical course thus moves through the thousands of documents that have survived in archives, and it has the intellectual awareness of a "natural union between word and image."[91] It is the right granted to the art historian to make use of written testimonials in order to reveal the personality depicted in a portrait or the symbol requested by the patron of the work. Beyond this, and with specific reference to the Renaissance, it is the art historian's task to join intention and information with the artist's capacity to be in accord with that model and let himself be carried away by a common expressive aim. This union is natural because that age felt it could express its will in works of art that were the symptom and result of life. Life was in fact taken in and circumscribed in its worldly value, in the promise implicit in political power, in the activity of commercial enterprises, and in the desire to take on shape by means of pictorial images in which the acts of existence would assume a permanent and universal meaning.

At the base of that civilization Warburg grasps quite well the fertile contrasts in the Renaissance conception of life, that polarity between idealization and real life the quattrocento Florentine felt he could conciliate. Just as 160 years earlier Giotto had depicted with fervid devotion the solemn scene in which St. Francis receives approval of the Order from the Pope, so between 1480 and 1486 Ghirlandaio painted a fresco of the very same scene in the Sassetti Chapel in Santa Trinita church, this time setting it in Piazza della Signoria in Florence, with Sassetti himself, in an attitude of elegant and discreet self-satisfaction, together with his family and in company with a benevolent Lorenzo de' Medici.

With realism and evocative power, Warburg identifies the personages in this fresco, including Poliziano and the Magnificent's young son. They participate in the religious ceremony in the pagan form of the image—the portrait—which captures them in their worldly power and prestige. Thus the aesthetic idealization of the image corresponds to a realism that the Tuscan painter derived from the Flemish masters.

The Florentine Renaissance certainly did not disdain Northern artists; on the contrary, it was the custom to enhance one's collection of paintings with Flemish works, and the rich merchants who traded with northern Europe often had themselves painted by the best artists from that area. With great sensitivity Warburg describes the existential vicissitudes of Angelo Tani and his wife, linking them with the various portraits they had commissioned during their lifetime; the realism of these works faithfully reproduces the different phases of their life, the changes and passages of the events and personalities of the Florentine lord and his wife, whom he brought with him at a tender age on his business trips. That sure and balanced realism conformed to the ruling class of the time, and in Florence as well artists sought to learn its technique and to apply it.

In addition to the immediate inspiration afforded by Burckhardt,[92] the description Warburg gives of the Sassetti Chapel has much in common with Winckelmann's description of ancient statues. There is the same delving into the realism given to the image—based on an erudite awareness of the world to which the image belongs—in order to describe both the concrete features of that civilization and its degree of idealization in artistic form. Winckelmann pursued the aim of delineating the nature of the Greek ideal of beauty and furnished us with the documents of a life which tended in every way toward aesthetic harmony and the calm, balanced reproduction of solemn gestures. Warburg does not perceive therein a universal tension toward beauty but a quest for conciliation of live and active contrasts in the Renaissance consciousness. The majestic yet realistic form given to the faces of the Florentine political personages bears a sense of self-consciousness that seeks a moderate but vigorous dominion, halfway between Heaven and Earth, between the Christian religion, the classicizing ideal, and worldly concreteness.

Warburg uses the term *idealization* to mean what is found in Ghirlandaio's portraits (even though they were influenced by a natural realism alien to the Tuscan milieu): an aspiration to transcend the individualizing detail typical of the portrait in the artistic universal. The mirroring of Greco-Roman antiquity in this stylistic process corresponds to the use of the classical myths as a way of reflecting events of the Florentine quattrocento, even while evoking scenes of Christian history. In *Birth of Tragedy,* Nietzsche deplores the decline of myth in Euripides, where psychological refinement and character representation prevail. In Sophocles, these characteristics still do not obstruct the power of the myth; later on, though, they become typified in masks that slightly evoke Dionysian music but are already basically estranged from it. The myth in fact, "as a unique type of universality and truth towering into the infinite," "cries to be conspicuously recognized."[93] In it the "universal will" is totally expressed and made visible, expanding in our consciousness "to the copy of an external truth."[94] At the root of Warburg's conception of the symbol, and of Florentine art as a restoration of its universal character by means of a style that tends toward the ideal, is also an echo of this metaphysics of art as the transfiguration of individual will in the idealizing tension toward cosmic unity.

In the works discussed up to now we have seen the development of the motif of a polarity between "paganizing" idealization and the actuality of Christian faith. To this is added another polarity, this time of a geographic nature—that between Northern realism and Florentine classicism. Warburg speaks of a "superior Roman plastic language"[95] as opposed to Flemish art, thus displaying an obvious predilection for the revival of antiquity in fifteenth-century Florence. The motif of a north-south polarity is a constant in the entire school that grew up around Warburg; it extends the Renaissance milieu over all of Europe through the imprint of conflict and an effort at conciliation. More than his followers, Warburg believed that Italian Renaissance painting was superior to the Flemish, which he felt was still too bound to medieval tradition. "The realistic costume style '*alla franzese*,' which seems so naive and innocent, was the main enemy of that new pathetic style *all'antica* that only with Pollaiuolo's heroic manner animated the weighty, luxurious clothing."[96] The revival of antiquity is above all the rebirth of an ideal. Here the classicist influence of the ideal of beauty makes itself felt in all its effectiveness—that ideal which, according to Winckelmann's famous dictum, the Mediterranean peoples, because of their nature and education, are inclined to cultivate. The interpretation of the artistic phenomenon as an aspiration after the ideal and as the representation of that ideal has followed a long and complex course in the history of art theory, which can be summed up as a history of the interpretation that grew up around the Platonic doctrine of ideas.

Panofsky deals with this subject in *Idea,* a book that came into being in Warburg's circle and that will be discussed at length in the third chapter. Panofsky's investigation ends with seventeenth-century aesthetics and with the accomplished transformation of a concept of idea still more or less openly derived from Plato's doctrine into the ideal, as well as with the loss of the transcendental notion of idea and the delineation of the subject-object relationship in its modern meaning. In Winckelmann one notes a determination of the sphere of the ideal that is partly new and partly tied to a more ancient sense of transcendence and a determination of the contemplation, implicit in transcendence, of the work of art as a visual manifestation of the idea. In fact he held that beauty is immanent to the nature of things, since its cause is to be found in all creatures. On the other hand, since philosophers had given to universal beauty the property of perfection, "of which humanity is not a fit recipient," we can only have a concept of human beauty through the "collected and united" "single acquisitions of knowledge," and this concept is exalted the more we are able to rise above matter. "This idea of beauty is like an essence extracted from matter by fire; it seeks to beget unto itself a creature formed after the likeness of the first rational being designed in the mind of the Divinity."[97] Such an image can only be the simplest one possible (that is to say, the most unitary), and what is manifold in it—since it is mediated—is yet full of harmony and uniformity. The unitary character of supreme beauty that is contemplated is devoid of feelings of pleasure and passion, as they would introduce something extraneous into it. But since human life in its course of development cannot distinguish beauty, the object of contemplation, from the passions that guide it, there must also exist for us an active and passionate character for beauty, and this is expression.[98]

The transformation of the notion of the ideal at the dawn of Romanticism is expressed in the most definitive manner in Schiller's essay *On the Naive and Sentimental in Literature*, which Thomas Mann, though criticizing its central thesis, rightly points out is so important for all German culture: "This [is the] classical essay of the German people, which at bottom makes all the others superfluous because it contains them all, but in whose antithetical world reality and life are never entirely resolved."[99] Schiller distinguishes the state of man as still identical with nature—one and the same with nature and thus filled with necessary and real sentiments and thoughts—from man in the state of culture who has lost the harmony of his senses and is only striving for unity. "The correspondence between his [cultured man's] feeling and his thinking which existed in *reality* now only exists as *an ideal*; it is no longer in him but outside him, as an idea which must first be realized, no longer as a fact of his life."[100] In the state of natural simplicity the poet is thus defined by an *imitation of the real* as faithful as possible; while in the state of culture, since harmony with nature is merely an idea he strives after, the poet aims at transforming reality into the ideal or, more precisely, into a *representation of the ideal*. But the ideal is infinite, Schiller says, and therefore cultivated man can never attain the completeness which natural man, who moves in a finite reality, is allowed to reach. Cultivated man, however, has the advantage over natural man because the result he is striving for, even if he does not achieve it, is the infinite, and his course is marked by *degrees* of unceasing *progress*. "In so far, however, as the ultimate goal of humanity cannot be reached except by means of that progression and the natural man cannot progress except by cultivating himself and as a result merges with the former, then there is no question as to which of the two deserves greater merit with regard to that ultimate goal."[101] If natural man prevails in the plastic arts, which are forced to act within a delimited space and hence with full materiality, in poetry or art expressed through concepts, matters are different; the power of Homer's poetry over the *physical* world of forms is greatly surpassed by what in the work of art cannot be depicted and expressed—that which is commonly called the *spiritual*.[102] The sentimental poet's works are the fruit of reflection, since he is not one and the same with his material but is set in a relation of the object with the idea, and the force of his composition may derive from the uncertainty and tension of this relationship.

This is not the place to discuss Schiller's thought in its historical complexity and characteristic contradictions; suffice it to say that it appears as a discriminating line drawn between two ways of conceiving the ideal, one still partly operating in Winckelmann's reflections on beauty and Greek art, the other taking on its full modern meaning in Hegel's philosophy. In *Science of Logic* Hegel deduces—or feels he has deduced—affirmative infinity and gives a complete definition of the ideal, in the same way that Schiller attempted to capture it in art: "Ideal being [das Ideelle] is the finite as it is in the true infinite—as a determination, a content, which is distinct but is not an *independent,* self-subsistent being, but only a *moment*."[103] In a footnote Hegel even distinguishes the term *ideal*, which refers to the beautiful, from the term *ideell*, which is used in this philosophical definition in affirmative infinity.[104] The meaning of ideal that now emerges in all its clarity proves to be immediately connected to an idea of progress. In fact, ideality for Hegel is "essentially the process of *becoming*, hence a transition."[105]

With Warburg the problem of Renaissance idealization takes on both connotations of the concept of the ideal. On the one hand, there is the classicist one of Neoplatonic derivation according to which the work of art represents an ideal of beauty whose model lies in the golden age of ancient art; in imitating the Greek style the Italian Renaissance artist strives to attain the universal and the typical as was expressed once and for all in ancient times. On the other hand, the meaning of this idealization changes into its more modern definition precisely when Warburg puts his interpretation of Renaissance works into a concept of culture in which operate all those elements that Burckhardt considered essential for understanding the artistic phenomenon (beyond mere aesthetic appraisal). Their nature then takes on a broader scope and is dominated by opposites, by polarities.

The striving after an ideal of life, or of a representation of life, is recognized in the contrasts and polarities between which the character and will of Renaissance artists were torn. In the High Renaissance, already at the threshold of the modern age, these polarities gave rise to the "spiritualization" of the ancient symbols, the sublimation of their ambiguous essence—both positive and negative—into an autonomous notion both of the object represented and of the artist's duty. And this is the period of Dürer, Raphael, Leonardo, and Michelangelo—what Werner Kaegi in his work on Warburg calls the Apollonian phase of the Renaissance.[106] For the Hamburg art historian this second, more modern and "dynamic" meaning of the ideal emerges along with an ever uncertain and obstructed delineation of the ideal of human progress and of the linear course toward a solution of the conflicts that generate fear as well as superstition in the soul.

With regard to Ghirlandaio's portraiture, Warburg certainly extolled its increased tendency toward idealization in the classical sense and toward formal perfection compared to the realism of the portraits painted in Northern Europe. Yet he did not fail to be influenced somewhat by Burckhardt's work in this field of research, which in fact made the perception of the origin of that conflict clearer to him. For Sassetti's aim of making the figures of his family and of his powerful friend Lorenzo the Magnificent stand out in a special way, and the tone of classical worldly celebration in that painting, could not be extraneous to the will to participation that drove Northern artists to paint realistic scenes even in the most banal details, with a fondness and an intimacy between eye and vision that made the painting—over and above the value of the subject—so interesting to the viewer. Burckhardt describes seventeenth-century Flemish genre painting, whose roots lie in fifteenth-century Northern realism, in terms of the magic of participation. Was it not perhaps this magic and an analogous desire for perpetual involvement that inspired the learned and refined Tuscan painter in the service of his enlightened patron?

In 1907 Warburg also examined the scenes of country life on Burgundian tapestries. Once again, in comparing Northern and Southern stylistic choices, he admitted that there was a reciprocal influence at work even though the preference for a certain style was autonomous. Medieval tradition, with its realistic continuity in the North, was opposed—with partial victories and partial compromises—in Italy, only to be revived in the North when the South had exhausted its idealizing force. The Greek satyr was most fitting for the Italian Renaissance mentality, but this too became the stale reproduction of a form once its particular burst of evocative energy was spent. Then Brueghel's Northern jester of medieval court origin came back to life.[107]

The comparison with Northern popular comicality reminds Warburg of Botticelli, whom he had so severely criticized in earlier writings; now he states that this artist felt the rebirth of antiquity as a liberation from the courtly materialism and splendor still linked with medieval tradition. Here the art historian finally seems to recognize Botticelli's artistic independence in the free movement he rendered so sublimely,[108] lending the figures that plastic simplicity now made possible by its being emancipated from the heavy and complicated Flemish dress. Nevertheless, this is still a "hesitant" imitation of antiquity, for Botticelli had also learned the art of minute ornamentation which, though a part of the new style, played a role of decorative overabundance.

The personality of Francesco Sassetti inspired some of Warburg's best writing. The rich Florentine merchant—who merged his economic fortune with that of the Medicis, had his burial chapel built and decorated with such sure artistic taste, yet drew up a will pervaded by medieval values—illuminated Warburg's conception of the Renaissance as an age of transition that oscillated between the old and the new. In the worldly experiences and striving after harmony that so characterize both Sassetti and the age, Warburg seeks the motive underlying a rebirth which, far from being the culmination of new ideas and forces, is rather a difficult period in which vital energies struggle to defend their value and spirit of initiative partly by taking refuge in the tradition of their forefathers, but also partly by taking in aspects and concepts of the modern classicizing style.

Sassetti's intelligence was directed at worldly matters; it questioned the nature of his capacity to dominate events and lead him and his family to a safe refuge where they would be sheltered from the whims of Fortune, which at a certain point in Sassetti's life seemed to be intent upon striking out at that very capacity. His will (which Warburg reproduced in its entirety), drawn up in 1488, is totally within the bounds of old-fashioned traditionalism; the father wisely saw to the destiny of his heredity, playing on the sense of loyalty to the family name and of its members' reciprocal honesty, rather than drawing up secure legal dispositions. The prevailing tone is one of severe exhortation to prudence and virtue. And the first mention made of Fortune—whose ends are unknown to mortals—is a bitter and dignified admission of the presence of an enemy whose unfathomable power must be gauged at every moment, an enemy against which the family had to be united and in accord, an enemy that could not be faced in open combat but rather had to be carefully spied upon and kept in sight, so that it would not overwhelm the family.[109]

The acquired sense of an individuality through which one can act with total free will is contaminated by the awareness of the precariousness of worldly matters, of the impossibility of knowing what fate has in store for riches entrusted to ships that cross stormy seas and are menaced by ferocious pirates. It was exactly the nature of their trade—carried out or impeded by the winds of Fortune—that led Sassetti and his contemporary Giovanni Rucellai anxiously to ponder the meaning of that pagan deity and avidly to seek an answer in ancient texts and philosophy.

In the metaphorical use of ancient figures—Fortune depicted on standards, coats of arms, and in the art of devices, a symbol of a bizarre power that could turn out to be either favorable or adverse—both Sassetti and Rucellai reveal how, in that period of transition marked by subjective behavior and action, they aspired to a new equilibrium between diverse energies.[110] Can the audacity of the will resist the snares and dangers of Fortune? There was no unilateral answer to this question, so that a conciliatory meeting ground was sought after, something that might seem contradictory in a rigorous system of rational deductions.[111] By effecting an in-depth iconological investigation into the meaning and reason underlying the images that accompanied that age-old question, Warburg judiciously reconstructs the design that lay behind that attempt at conciliation, which had to reckon with no little resistance to the new artistic ideal of the Renaissance. The symbolism employed in the minor artistic genre of devices shows us the classicizing representation of Fortune, who holds up the sail of a ship, as Rucellai's crest.[112] The etymological sense of Fortune as tempest is represented in the pagan style in those accessories of motion that Renaissance man likes so much because they were bearers of the energy and will to worldly power that was identical with his individualism. "We find united here popular pagan sentiments, classicizing artistic fantasy and theological humanism—bent on elaborating, as a threefold conceptual tangle, the still living divinity of *Fortuna Audax,* openly pagan in both idea and aspect."[113] Fortune holding a sail, set on the facade of Santa Maria Novella church as its founder's emblem, was no cause for conflict in Rucellai's mind, since his Christian piety suggested to him that he accept adverse fortune as a divine punishment for his shortcomings, which he was as aware of as he was of his worth. At the same time, as an ornament to the facade of his palace, it was the expression of a classical joie de vivre for having been so farsighted as to bind his fate with that of the Medicis through a felicitous marriage. The symbol of the goddess Fortuna, who had been invoked in the difficult times of doubt both as a spur and restraining force to audacity, becomes in the happy period of success an encouragement of intrepid and valorous action.[114]

Thus *Fortuna Occasio,* her forehead covered with a tuft of hair offered up to the skilled helmsman's grip, expresses the astuteness of taking advantage of a good wind and of the positive risk in seizing the propitious occasion, which presents itself only once to the intellectual virtue and courage of the condottiere.[115] "It works in both Rucellai and Sassetti in the same sense, as a figurative formulation of the compromise between the 'medieval' faith in God and the self-reliance of Renaissance man."[116] Sassetti in turn chose the centaur as the emblem on his family coat of arms, and the frieze that decorates the burial niche in Santa Trinita church had many of them. This ancient, elementary deity that participates in the frenzy of a pagan dance symbolizes liberating energy in compliance with an already consolidated early Renaissance style. This motif is accompanied in the burial chapel by the one of David with his sling which depicts the biblical shepherd and his destiny as king. But in the coat of arms on Sassetti's bookplate, the sling borne by two centaurs abandons its Old Testament character and emerges as the pure expression of dynamic energy, and the motto that accompanies it is indicative of the merchant's frame of mind: "*A mon pouvoir.*"[117] With the same contradictory attitude that in Sassetti's personality and life betrays his anxious longing for conciliation, there was another motto which appears more often in his manuscripts: *Mitis fata mihi,* or *Sors placida mihi.* Thus the audacious outburst of the first motto is tempered by the exorcism formula: "He thus counterposed the passivity of the Latin ejaculation with the French motto, whose longing for action is intensified in a classicizing manner by means of the centaur's temperament."[118] Otherworldly Christian piety and pagan admiration of the earthly once again conflict in the burial chapel, where, after a detailed description, Warburg notes how the symbols of that equilibrium between contrasting forces that mark Sassetti's character still submit to the patron saint (St. Francis) and to the incumbency of solid Christian elements with which he tried to exorcise the pagan demon whose unrestrained energy one wanted to imitate but at the same time still feared. In observing the "placid realism" that Ghirlandaio manifests here—which a few years later will be transformed into an animated and surer ability in classical representation—Warburg considers the "Sassettian civilization" the producer of a "retarding effect" in the change in style from the Middle Ages to the High Renaissance.[119]

Therefore every attempt to revive antiquity is accompanied by a corresponding opposition to the solidity of tradition. The dichotomy confirms the age-old persistence in human expressiveness of a symbolic energy tending to create types which insure the essential sense of its own unbridled longing for renewal. This tendency to typify lends an idealizing value to the attempt to revive antiquity—that is, it is a quest for a symbol sensitive to the expression and reinforcing of the idea.

Warburg does not fail to mention the speculative premises of this symbolization of Fortune. When Rucellai asked Marsilio Ficino to explain the arcane relationship between audacity and fate, the philosopher's reply was marked by a theological humanism of Neoplatonic origin, while Sassetti's more earthly and cautious conception betrayed that exhortation to ethical virtue which was to be found in one of the books in his library, Giovanni Argiropulo's translation of Aristotle's *Nicomachean Ethics*. Although his soul was "in diverse senses divided," Ficino tried to offer a unitary explanation of the motif of prudence with respect to Fortune that did not contradict either the Christian faith in God's omnipotence or the Neoplatonic thesis of an intellect that disposes worldly matters in conformity with its superior order. In his long and meditative written reply, the Florentine philosopher clarifies the relationship between nature, virtue, and Fortune. Nature per se is inanimate, and intellectual rule, like the essence of goodness, is far removed from it. It is therefore necessary to take nature back to an intellectual basis so that its order can acquire meaning also from the viewpoint of the flux and becoming of things that so disturbed Rucellai in his commercial undertakings. Ficino explains the base of that intellectual process that produces order as a striving after an end. The natural substance thus has a beginning and an end and moves between these in a circular fashion in the intellect, in goodness, and in life. Hence prudence is not only a gift of nature, which in itself does not bestow gifts, but is a gift of the intellectual basis, which is the source and origin of nature itself. Prudence depends upon our natural corporeal constitution and upon its beginning in the intellect, in goodness, and in life. It is thus conferred by a nature determined in superior spheres and lies beyond man's actual capabilities. Fortune has no rules that conform to our desires and intentions, but it is also determined from on high and, contrary to appearances, has a precise order of its own. Therefore one behaves well with respect to Fortune if the base of nature ordered by the intellect—which in turn gives order to nature—likewise orders us to conform to it. It is therefore necessary to adapt oneself to the path indicated by Fortune; here lies the greatest wisdom, as it stems from the consciousness of not being able to oppose that superior order. Ficino, however, also indicates certain valid means for dealing with Fortune: prudence, patience, and magnanimity, which are gifts of the natural and intellectual basis of everything.[120]

Ficino also says that in the war with Fortune very few emerge victorious, "and those few only after intellectual hardship and great labor"; he thus offers a gleam of hope—albeit very slight in what is basically a pessimistic and contradictory letter. And in the end he urges Rucellai to make peace or come to terms with Fortune and to go wherever she beckons so as to humor her and not be overwhelmed by her. (Let us not forget the dry and heavy-hearted confession in Sassetti's last will: "I do not know where Fortune will take us ... nor howsoever she will behave whenever I chance to meet her.") And in the case of concord with the wind of Fortune the philosopher prescribes the most appropriate virtues with which to follow it: "All this we will achieve, if within us power, wisdom and will are in accordance." These are the gifts most likely to humor propitious fate, and their character is much more active and strong than that of the three gifts of prudence, patience, and magnanimity, almost as if personal vigor could in turn work a positive effect upon Fortune herself. Thus in naming that virtue most appropriate for facing the terrible deity without undue fear, the Neoplatonic philosopher confirms the divided state of his soul.

Warburg perfectly grasps the ambivalence of feeling that characterizes his attempt to define Fortune within his iconological explanation of the symbol that accompanies it. According to this interpretation, Fortune—before which the sagacious man acts with intelligence that is first and foremost prudence and, in the most difficult moments, even philosophical patience—in her classicizing symbol and in the style in which she is expressed, in reality reflects a will to vigor, energy, and active feeling and consciousness of oneself and one's power. This latter meaning however does not contradict the former one, because prudence is also understood as the ability to foresee. Warburg, in compliance with Ficino's teachings (inspired by the "divine Plato"), repeats the rule whereby one defends oneself from Fortune with the very gifts that Fortune herself—or the superior order to which she belongs—bestows. Since it is necessary to have a cautious but varied relationship with fickle Fortune, Renaissance man interprets his role in the world that surrounds him as an exercise in courage and farsighted intelligence.

In dealing with the theme of Fortune—which is much broader and more complex than it appears in this brief discussion—Warburg finds an exact correspondence with his thesis of an ambivalent Renaissance torn by forces that in one light seem positive but in another become hostile and menacing; a divided epoch suspended in that transition that signifies precisely continuous flux, the impossibility to find satisfaction in the tranquil certainty of one's recent past, or in the peaceful expectance of a foreseeable or desirable future.

And the burial chapel on which Sassetti employed all his worldly intelligence and artistic taste in order to make it magnificent, also reveals, in its prudent coupling of symbols, the basic anxiety that animates his last will and testament: that allusion to his advanced age that makes him "mortal every day," that pessimistic attitude concerning any real certainty of success for his descendants, and that tone of habitual domestic intimacy rather than exaltation of a power which was already seriously threatened by Fortune.

The Pagan Demon-God and the Apollonian-Dionysian Polarity

The hypothesis of an organic evolution of style was rejected by Warburg, who upheld the view of Renaissance man's continuous oscillation between conflicts actively at work in history and his consequent attempt at conciliation. In his 1912 lecture on the frescoes in Palazzo Schifanoia in Ferrara, he once again repeated his criticism of the term *Renaissance*, this time considering it too "mystical."[121] The mysticism in the word consists in its taking on a meaning of historical palingenesis through the ideal vehicle of antiquity, and one fails to note that renewal is really a slow, painful tumult of conflicting motifs and different types of polarity, in the uncertainty as to which of the two will in the end prevail. Pagan demonism survives as a second nature in the Olympian deity, where it is idealized but never totally defeated, and it again appears up to the end of that intense epoch that dominated Western civilization for two centuries and was characterized by a migration of images and motifs of classical antiquity as well as by Hellenistic astrological superstition.

Warburg sets about explaining this sphere—which was disagreeable to him—where the "beautiful things" that had fascinated him in his preceding studies no longer existed (and here again one perceives his personal bias for the classical style, a bias that however did not affect his rigorously objective research) in order to find an iconographical basis for his thesis of the substantial persistence of ancient images. Northern realism was not lacking in experiences in the field of ancient pagan motifs; on the contrary, they flourished there, and were cultivated along the lines of astral demonology, in which the figures of Greek mythology found the means to survive and then became an essential contribution to the rebirth of antiquity in Italy.[122] Here the Middle Ages, and in particular their prolongation in Northern civilization, are a sort of mediator of Greek civilization, though in a manner that later—in a dramatic period for Warburg both on a personal and professional level—takes on the detestable forms of superstition and reaction against renewal.

The key to the cycle of months in the Palazzo Schifanoia frescoes was explained by Warburg, who discovered in those composite and mysterious representations the iconographic motifs of the ancient deities who had passed through Eastern and medieval symbology in the form of Indian Decans and, only because of the authentically classicizing spirit of the Italian Renaissance, once again took on their classical characteristics. These latter had wandered for centuries from East to West, North to South, shedding their external aspect but preserving their original substance. The figures painted at Ferrara are symbols of the fixed stars and of what their ancient name concealed and signified in becoming the matter of astrological speculation and divination. And astrology, says Warburg, is nothing but a fetishism of names projected into the future.[123]

Critical iconology—the science founded by Warburg from the time of his conception of the symbol and the conflict it bears in historical time, a science whose worth for historical investigation he made explicit in his 1912 paper—carries out its task of burrowing into images that would otherwise be incomprehensible and discovers in the principal texts of ancient-medieval astrology that the figures that dominate the middle zone of the Ferrara frescoes are the Indian Decans of ninth-century astrologer Abū Mā'sār under whose travesty there "beats a Greek heart."[124] Evidently at the Ferrara court in 1470, the use of medieval astrology still persisted, since only the earliest symptoms of the artistic restoration of the Olympian gods can be found there. Warburg feels he can discern these symptoms in the planetary gods' being replaced by the series of twelve gods from Manilius's *Astronomica*. And the *restoration* (the word used in this context by Warburg) of the classical gods rejects their demoniacal form and resuscitates that more elevated ideal style that marks the passage from the early Renaissance to its more mature phase. "With this will to restore antiquity, the 'good European' began his struggle for enlightenment in that age of the international migration of images that we ... call the Renaissance age."[125]

In a moment of particular scientific enthusiasm, Warburg lays down the bases of critical iconology as opposed both to a general evolutionary theory that does not take into account the important contribution made to art history by a "historical psychology of human expression" and to an overhasty schematization of aesthetic formulas and the theories of genius.[126] This new science must overcome the rigid confines of successive ages and consider "antiquity, the Middle Ages and the modern age one connected epoch" so as to illuminate the stages of its general development. It is necessary to note how at this point, having realized a thorough formulation of the new discipline, which he indicated as an essential contribution to the history of art and civilization, Warburg maintains a coherent balance between the thesis of the steadfastness and persistence of the image as an expressive substratum, in spite of its many transformations, and the idea of historical development that conforms to the connection between the various ages. And it is precisely the term *connection* which, during the course of development, refers to a continuity that is basically stability and permanence. But at this point the humorous figure of the "good European" and the "struggle for enlightenment" make their appearance, revealing in turn a twofold basis in Warburg's conception of history: the subtle irony directed at an ideology of the "naive" and "good" Renaissance man (a prefiguration of modern civilized man); and a calm trust in that idea of progress as an emancipation of the most ideal and intellectual aspect of humanity, which is counterbalanced by the concept of the restoration of ancient virtue that was able to make the

Greek deity of the universal, of the equilibrium between individual and cosmos, emerge from the demons.

The twofold polarity that Warburg observed in Renaissance art becomes a motif of contrast and overcoming in the genius of Dürer. In his essay "Dürer and Italian Antiquity" (1905), Warburg fully brings to light the meaning of the motif of movement as the expression of pathos that he had been seeking as a common denominator for the entire epoch—a motif which he had hitherto only partially explained, and this only in connection with the spirit of the time. Here Warburg openly opposes Winckelmann's "unilaterally classicist doctrine," which conceals a basic aspect of antiquity itself, the pathetic-Dionysian one. Intensified movement and idealizing serenity constitute a polarity which Warburg now explicitly reveals in the works of antiquity. In studying the iconography representing the death of Orpheus, Warburg notes that "the typical pathetic pantomimic language of ancient art, such as Greece had elaborated for this tragic scene, here makes its weight felt, directly determining a style."[127]

This unbridled movement, which the Middle Ages had checked by confining the characters of the scene in an incomprehensibly static position, is reproduced by Dürer with untempered intensity, just as he had learned from his contact with, and study of, the Italian art of his time. At the beginning of the sixteenth century, Italians felt that Dürer's work lacked decorative pathos as they noted how his original Northern imperturbability got the better of his imitation of Southern vivacity. In the stylistic formula he uses to render the tragic myth, for example, the German artist succeeds in breaking down the restraints imposed by the Middle Ages on expression, just as he acutely penetrates the classical duplicity of style between the Apollonian perfection of proportions and the Dionysian pathos of intensified movement. But he also becomes the mediator between the classicizing style in its achieved formal perfection and the Northern European realism given to faces, gestures, and pictorial details in everyday objects. In Dürer's hands, however, these objects become symbols. Their realistic cover is nothing more than the overpowering meaning they take on thanks to his exuberant imagination. "Antiquity aided him in his Italian mediation not only as a Dionysian stimulus, but also as an Apollonian appeasement."[128] Here the character of Warburg's opposition to Winckelmann is made explicit; it remains operative in his later writings and gives him that key to the interpretation of the Renaissance that makes his historical research so unique. Moreover, the influence wrought on the Hamburg scholar by that conception of classical antiquity that had arisen from the terrain of classicism and German romanticism, and which had found its most passionate expression in Nietzsche's *Birth of Tragedy,* now takes on a precise and amplified form.

Nietzsche's work was basically a philological investigation of the origins of Greek culture—through its religious customs and its creation of the pagan cosmos of Hellenic deities—onto which was grafted the pessimism of Schopenhauer's philosophy. The result was a book filled with obscure tension, written with the desperate anxiety to be free from Christian moralism and from the separation of man from the transcendent in order to regain a oneness with nature that was the tragic will to express passions so as to transcend them in the Apollonian representation of the dream of life. In his violent conflict with the contemporary world, with the philosophy of Hegel and the philistine religion from which it had issued, Nietzsche proclaims the eternal essence of Greek religiosity, whose restoration he aspires to with all the fury of an intimate belief in the impossibility of such a task.

The polarity expressed in this tormented work must have had a profound and lasting impact on Warburg's approach to the Renaissance. Nietzsche's formulation of the birth of Greek tragedy as a question of an essentially psychological nature touched the very basis of Warburg's search for those psychic tensions through which the Renaissance, with great effort and pain, must have freed itself from the conditioning factors of the preceding age. According to the classicist conception and also to a feeling common throughout the modern age, what set the Greeks apart from all other peoples was their aspiration to beauty. In Nietzsche's opinion this aspiration originated in the pain of privation, in the pessimism of existence. But, expert philologist that he was, he could not but inquire into the origin of that violent and dramatic civilization of suffering and horror of the world that reveals itself in a preceding epoch—in the age of the great tragic myths. In conformity with the law by which every manifestation of civilization grows out of its opposite and in opposition to it, one would be led to think of a more ancient stage in the Greek evolution toward beauty, one in which life was satisfaction and happiness. This consideration leads Nietzsche to the bitter confirmation of a much grimmer and more pessimistic reality: the fullness of life in all its forms conceals within itself the germ of the most disturbing laceration, which at a certain point finds the strength to come to light in the powerful and dynamic expression of the tragic myth.[129] For the philosopher there ensues a conception of art as the appearance of reality,[130] as a redemption from that opposition that manifests itself in the being and becoming of life and that imposes either a plunge into suffering in order to determine its forms in full and reveal the authentic force of the drama of the soul, or a transcending of this unbearable contradiction in the dream of beauty, in the formal order that distinguishes and reconciles, pacifying the tumult of instinct. There is, however, no trace of evolution in all this. Each of the aspects—the Dionysian and the Apollonian—struggles to assert itself, but conceals within itself the tendency to its opposite. But in the *Birth of Tragedy* there is one aspect that dominates the other: the Apollonian solar contemplation of phenomenal rules, which establishes a truce over the subterranean unleashing of the passions, is subject to a random and unmotivated violation that gives rise to horror and hence to the Dionysian.[131] The Dionysian is always latent, even in the dream of life. And the Apollonian is a veil temporarily set over the Dionysian, ready to be rent at any moment for those whose piercing glance penetrates the reality of what appears to be.[132]

The Dionysian is thus the overwhelming element, the one most authentic in revealing the nature of things. It consists of the eternal essence of a primordial unity with nature, whereas the Apollonian is the eternity of appearance, the pure illusion of nature.[133] For Nietzsche, the Dionysian corresponds to music and the Apollonian to the figurative arts, among which he places epic poetry. At the base of this distinction—which is not to be found in Warburg since it would exclude his field of inquiry—is the aesthetics of Lessing of a formal conditioning of intense emotions in Homer and in the representation of classical visual art. Warburg transfers Nietzsche's dichotomy totally into the sphere of the figurative arts, which, as in the case of Greek tragedy, are a continuous alternation between elements of pathos that manifest ardent vitality worthy of the "Dionysian merrymakers" and stylistic elements composed in a superior harmony that is achieved by means of an effort at symbolizing through the study of exact formal proportions. The essence of the Greek soul has been defined as at once Apollonian and Dionysian in tragedy, in which the universality of art is expressed. According to Warburg, this essence is also reproduced in Greek figurative art; and that very universality, that expression of an absolute will which becomes representation, is awakened in the psyche of Renaissance man because of his particular emotional instability and therefore lends itself to new solutions of the same conflict.

When the power of intensified movement outdoes even the ancient models, as in the case of Pollaiuolo or Donatello, Warburg realizes that the Greek dichotomy has become even more strident: "Pollaiuolo's Hercules, who chokes Anteus and defeats the Hydra, got from ancient sculpture itself the tumultuous pathos of the virile athletic ideal; he is really almost more ancient than antiquity itself."[134] Because of his modern expressive attitude in a milieu nurtured on the classical tradition, Pollaiuolo knew how to render the vigor of combat, tragic weeping, and the dance that echoes antiquity.[135] The same thing occurs in Donatello: "Donatello and his pupils are carried away by a tragic, hypernervous pathos which in the case of some pupils actually leads to an orgy of movement that attempts to surpass in pathetic, expressive impulse the very ancient reliefs that serve as their model."[136]

In his imitation of a pagan sarcophagus depicting the funeral of Meleager, Donatello understood the need to communicate what he found to be essential therein—the struggle of ancient grief over the death of a man driven to the point of finding its expression—and saw "that this expression, in this moving formulation, means an inestimable increase in humanity's pantomimic language."[137] The attack against classicist aesthetics becomes insistent and exclusive: "The essential matter is that here the primitive quattrocento which we contemplate with such pleasure for its 'naive' placidness, precipitates into the extreme baroque style of movement, and the responsibility for this lies precisely with the pagan art of their ancestors."[138] This time the polemic is against Schiller, who in his famous essay on literature had defined man's oneness with nature as a naive state. Nietzsche also shows that this ingenuousness, for which modern man is so nostalgic, is by no means a simple or serene stage, but is rather the highest effect of Apollonian culture, which "has always to overthrow some Titanic empire and slay monsters, and which, through its powerful and dazzling representations and pleasurable illusions, must triumph over the terrible abyss of world contemplation and the keenest sensitivity to suffering."[139]

The similarity between Warburg's and Nietzsche's texts is striking. Nietzsche had given an example of naïveté in the "immortal naive" Raphael, who, in the allegorical painting of the Transfiguration, had succeeded in representing that "appearance of appearance" which is the essence of the Apollonian dream atmosphere. We feel our profound relationship with the Primal Unity, with the nature of its cosmic meaning, and we thus learn to consider the world of experience, of becoming, of causality, as the world of appearance. The abstraction of this empirical reality is then conceived as a representation of that fundamental unity and offers itself to our perception as a phenomenon of the phenomenon, an appearance of appearance. It redeems us—through the *principium individuationis* sublimated in the figure of the god Apollo—from that world of suffering and torment which in turn is necessary so that "the individual may be impelled to realize the redeeming vision."[140] Naturally, for Nietzsche this is a task that belongs to the sphere of art, which celebrates the achieved union of human expression with the authentic sense of the original reality, that which lies beyond the phenomenon, which neither science nor philosophical speculation manage to reach since they are limited by the phenomenon and cannot, in that state of pure knowledge, go beyond it. Art is therefore the true metaphysical activity of mankind.[141]

A surprising parallel with Nietzsche's inspired example is found in Warburg's essay on the idealizing classical Renaissance style. The path he follows through the intensely animated style of the Florentine quattrocento leads him in turn to Raphael. Warburg traces the depiction of Trajan's victory over the barbarians on the Arch of Constantine through its rise as a powerful molder of style to its climax in the Battle of Constantine in the Vatican fresco.[142] "The time of uncertainties between the realistic painting of the present and the idealizing classical style are over." Unbridled dynamism and quiescence, the oppressive presence of the masses and the individualization of the dramatic center, are placated here in the "consoling" impression provoked by a judicious unitary design. In the same fashion, the figures of the gods painted by Raphael and his helpers at the Villa Farnesina in Rome restore consummate formal beauty to pagan divinity.[143] But this was not the origin of the entry of the classical world into the early Renaissance. "One is not so well disposed to recognize antiquity as a strong artistic influence in the Quattrocento exactly because its rationalistic nature is felt to be an essential element."[144] This interpretative error, which stems from the theory of the ancients' "quiet grandeur," tends to make Renaissance man the primitive individual of the modern age, alien to the imitation of rigid formal rules of Greco-Roman culture and totally immersed in his individual power of renewal.[145] Beyond observing that Warburg explicitly sets his interpretation against Winckelmann's, one notes once again his implicit criticism of the idea of a heroic, self-reliant Renaissance that already possesses within itself the motives of its expressive power—a notion forged by Burckhardt in his historiographic method of making an independent analysis of each of the various cultural spheres.

Warburg now feels he is in a position diametrically opposed to Winckelmann's; the Laocoön is not at all a terrible myth placated by the dominion of formal equilibrium and by the stoic self-control of the priest, but is on the contrary an example of that disturbing passionate eloquence that had penetrated the Florentine Renaissance with such evocative intensity. "Now we resolve little by little to consider this classical restlessness an essential quality of ancient art and civilization; the studies made of Greco-Roman religions teach us more and more to regard antiquity as almost symbolized in a Janus-faced herm with the faces of Apollo and Dionysus. The Appollonian ethos sprouts up together with the Dionysian pathos almost like a double branch from the same trunk rooted in the mysterious depths of the Greek motherland."[146] The double root of the formal poise achieved by Raphael, who left the contrasts behind him, offers the most profound sense of the relationship Renaissance art had with antiquity. And since the two elements are at once inherent to the same artistic expression, it is not possible to conceive of its history as an evolution. The one conceals the other and prepares the predominance of the other, as can be seen in tragedy, where the dominion the Apollonian has apparently conquered at the expense of the Dionysian proves to be illusory in the most crucial moment of the drama, when the Dionysian effect, which "transcends all Apollonian artistic effects,"[147] explodes. The two deities that mythically sustain this "aesthetic game" end up speaking each other's language and this results in the harmony of primordial musicality. This song unleashes a liberating power among the spectators, as if the passions that make existence unhappy and unresolved had found an outlet in the common action of the two components of the Greek spirit.

There seems to be no place for progress in this eternal struggle for liberation; once the origin is conceived as polar and dynamic, the definitive calm of the victor no longer exists; on the contrary, the primitive obsession will rise again continuously side by side with the powers of order. And yet in Raphael's art, as in Dürer's, Warburg perceives the subsiding of pathos into a superior formal poise. The ancient form in its fullness followed its complex course through the centuries thanks to the enthusiasm and confidence with which it was received and reshaped in the quattrocento.

It is legitimate to doubt whether the theoretical parallelism noted in the quotations from Nietzsche and Warburg corresponds to an authentic reversal of the classicist thesis. All Nietzsche's striving for an expression of the primal demoniac nature of the Greek soul is really addressed to an exaltation of the formal dominion over the chaos of change without rules. The very prevalence of the demoniac in tragedy can manifest itself precisely because its language at the same time rests upon the order of Apollonian form, which has been conquered once and for all and has imposed its own rigid stylistic limits upon unbridled emotion. As much as one may founder in the contradictory strife between the dream of beauty and the will to evoke the wild conflicts of the psyche, that strife is placated in an accomplished compromise thanks to which the catharsis of the spectators in tragic art is possible. Nietzsche's restlessness and anxiety are expressed much more in his vivacious language than they are elaborated on a theoretical plane, and he cannot help conceiving of the Greek world, with all its lacerations, as a world that achieved the highest level of expressive power because of its deeply rooted sense of measure. In fact, what is the interpenetration of opposites, the moderating and revealing action of one on the other, if not a reciprocal measuring?

Erwin Rohde, who set out from the same bases as his tormented friend, observes already in Homer that simplification, reduction, and uniformity of the confused and exuberant cult of souls, dispersed into so many regional particularisms, which gave rise to Homer's Olympian Panhellenic deities. This is "the special poetic task ... that Greek idealism in art continually set before itself."[148] "Out of their own natural feelings and reflection this most intellectually gifted nation evolved the great ideas that nourished succeeding centuries."[149] And the greatness of those people above all was that, in the many-sidedness of the different forms, the "individual factors restrained or balanced each other" in a "general condition of equipoise." No sudden change characterized that culture, precisely because it did not fanatically pursue and embrace one idea at a time but cultivated itself in the measured enterprise of realizing a synthesis of different influences.[150] The discipline of philology—which in effect Rohde did not violently criticize as did Nietzsche—tempered the tone of this scholar in his later years and undoubtedly made the results of his analysis of the Hellenic soul more farsighted.[151]

Nietzsche did not succeed in abandoning the concept of ideality and, though transfiguring it into the appearance of a dream, he pursued it constantly in *Birth of Tragedy,* so much so that he later criticized himself exactly on this point.[152] The same thing occurs with Warburg, who admits the attainment of a perfect form at the end of the Renaissance's effort to make an ideal synthesis emerge from different polarities. Briefly turning back to his interpretation of Dürer's engraving of the motif of Melancholy, we can note that he even goes so far as to give an almost optimistic interpretation of the symbolic image realized by the German artist. "The most creative act properly speaking that makes *Melencolia I* the folio *par excellence* of humanistic comfort against the fear of Saturn, can be understood only by recognizing that it is precisely magic mythology that is spiritualized in artistic transformation. That menacing astral demon who eats children ... gives rise in Dürer, thanks to a humanizing metamorphosis, to the plastic incarnation of the man in active meditation."[153]

Thus by means of art, astrological matter is spiritualized. Moreover Dürer, owing to his humanism infused with genius, is able to transform the demon into a fecund thinker. There is a substantial difference in interpretation in Panofsky and Saxl's 1924 essay, where the meditative "worker" is typified in his melancholic nature and in his suffering. For Panofsky the metamorphosis lies in the personalization of temperament, in the fact that the ancient demon with his characteristics becomes a sort of heroic lament of the genius, a personification of pessimism vis-à-vis the actual possibilities of attaining the beautiful form by means of the magical-scientific tools at his disposal. In Warburg's view, on the other hand, we are faced with the accomplished sixteenth-century exorcism of the demon. The Apollonian has triumphed over the Dionysian, bipolarity has found a solution in formal humanism and in "spiritualization."

In addition to the demon-god polarity, therefore, there is another constant factor that accompanies the Renaissance from its beginning: the tendency to idealize, in accordance with the teachings of the Greeks, to give an expression of oneself capable of conciliating contradictions in the upper sphere of artistic reproduction through severe formal measure and stylistic commitment that was also and above all the study of the tools fit for painting and architecture. Winckelmann certainly did not believe that "quiet grandeur" and "noble simplicity" had risen up as if by magic among the Greeks. In his *History of Ancient Art* he undertakes a long inquiry into the causes and circumstances that led the Greeks to that perfection which—whether we like it or not—has remained paradigmatic in the history of Western civilization. When he compares Egyptian art to Greek art, he turns to science: "But, in art, knowledge precedes Beauty; being based on exact, severe rules, its teachings at the beginning have necessarily vigorous definiteness."[154] It was science, or better, the possession of a perfected technique of reproduction, that freed Greek art from the straight lines and stylization of form in archaic Greek art or in evolved Egyptian art, which had remained faithful to that style. In the same manner, during the Renaissance, perspective developed side by side with the evolution of mathematical science and of the infinite, until it became at once a criterion of expression in works of art and an independent geometric science.[155]

A thorough analysis of Winckelmann's theory of the causes and nature of the beauty of Greek art reveals nothing that is in actual contrast with the definitive meaning of the delirium of polarization in Nietzsche. One may merely note how the eighteenth-century historian's hand was guided by the influence of aesthetics based on Platonic philosophy,[156] while Nietzsche, though still an heir of that school of aesthetics, tries to break up its theoretical force with the thesis of the root of bipolarity lying at the base of the stylistic unity of tragedy. Instead of inquiring into the nature of that idea of Platonic origin which was still central to Winckelmann's aesthetics and which fought against the tension expressed in the ideal as the aim of artistic achievement, Nietzsche takes his cue from Winckelmann's analysis in order to move toward the attainment of the ideal constructed upon the opposition and merging of the Dionysian and Apollonian. The schema of a Primal Unity which the breaking down into opposing psychic forces tries to regain through artistic illusion—as if the duality that has thus taken its place in the world could have as its foundation a Primal Unity and lead back to it—is a schema superimposed in Hegelian fashion upon the motifs of classicist theory. But this schema, in seeking to oppose Hegelianism, weakens that theory without really disputing its basic nucleus.

In accepting Nietzsche's formulation of the Apollo-Dionysus polarity, however, Warburg seems rather to be borrowing a conceptual configuration that allows him to give a more specifically theoretical sense to that motif of polarities on which he based his art-historical deductions. In reality the theme of oppositions in which the Renaissance struggled is more closely connected to the motif of an age of transition than to an expanded conception and total acceptance of Nietzsche's philosophy. Warburg's study of the frescoes in Palazzo Schifanoia may have allowed him to confirm his theory of the pertinacity of the symbol against the generic idea of historical evolution, but it also put him in contact with the demoniac essence of ancient pagan deities. Now while the metamorphosis of the Olympian god of form into an astrological demon, confirmed by nineteenth-century studies of ancient religions, weakened the vision of a heroic Renaissance striving for the transcendence of contrasts in the ideal, it also began to torment Warburg's mind with the premonition of a world perennially threatened, and often overwhelmed, by superstition, a world in which the triumphs of humanism were only episodic occurrences that cost such tremendous efforts to achieve that more often than not they were considered unbearable by civilization.

Warburg thought he had found in Nietzsche a philosophical basis for his ever more determined opposition to Winckelmann, for his concept of striving after the ideal, and above all for an interpretation of antiquity as suffering and pathos. Actually he understood Winckelmann much more thoroughly than he himself realized. In fact, in the 1912 work he asserted that Botticelli could fashion his classicizing world "because ancient plastic art itself showed him how the world of Greek deities dances its round in superior spheres to the sound of Platonic melody."[157]

And yet it is exactly the entry of Nietzschean terminology that marks the abandonment of the scheme of permanent bipolarity and of the basic identity of symbolic form. Onto this theoretical formula is superimposed the observation of the Renaissance's course toward a more conscious humanism and toward a transcending of the demons. This humanism no longer means a quest for a rationalistic transformation of the irrational forces that battle for possession of human nature; here it consists of hope in concrete progress.

The Magical World and History

The long, bitter pause caused by the First World War brought about those tormented premonitions concerning the future of humanity that so seriously undermined Warburg's psychic health,[158] forcing him to leave the natural sphere of his studies and his precious library, which contained all the documents and witnesses of the migration of images in the Renaissance, an age that was so decisive for the fate of modern man. After the war during which the tragic, ill-fated nature of this century began to take on shape, Warburg collected and published the notes from his laborious research into pagan divination and the meaning it took on in Luther's time. As a preface, he remarked on the fragmentary nature of that work and on his regret at not having been able to dwell more at length on many of the details to which his diligent intuition continuously led him. He did not hesitate, however, to make public the temporary results of his study, which had been carried out in a mood of great enthusiasm but also in a state of anxiety, as he sensed his impending illness.

The astral deities, already examined in his study of the Ferrara fresco cycles, had migrated from Hellenism via the Near East, Spain, and Italy toward Germany, and had preserved their character as calendar gods that marked out the divisions of the days, months, and years with mathematical precision but also with the overriding influence of very ancient mythical evocativeness.[159] In rejecting the solar image of the Olympian gods taken as mere artistic phenomena, Warburg found it necessary to probe their nature as religious beings, which as such are more difficult to oppose. These premises already reveal how, with the increasing pessimism that permeated Warburg's earlier works, the entire beauty of the Olympian world was negated by a much more desolate reality which that world (and the erudite culture that sustained it) conceals only for a moment but must uncover upon more careful scrutiny. The religious essence that had found felicitous aesthetic expression now has quite different roots in humanity—in its suffering and perversions rather than in the ephemeral rule of taste. With the breakup of the unitary idea that those deities had represented, Hellenism handed them down in the form of demoniac beings with sinister antithetical power, a form that, according to Warburg, they had possessed from their origin. These deities were amenable to rational calculation and as a mode of orientation in space and time. At the same time, they became idols with which man in his regressive, infantile fear tried to come into union in order to save himself from their evil influence.

Even though one perceives the echo of Nietzsche's Primal Unity in the definition that Warburg gives of the cult of these demoniac beings as the recovery of a "primordial, unitary mood with a great capacity for vibration," it is evident that he has no Dionysian reverence for that primitive sensation. In the passages given over to the different relationship Luther and Melanchthon had with the magical practices of astrology, there is rather the vibration of the same tone of dry reproval, and at times even of actual disgust, with which Burckhardt tackles the question of the mystery cult and the decadence of the pagan world in the chapter entitled "The Daimonization of Paganism" in his *Age of Constantine the Great*. The historian describes the process of the breaking up of Hellenic polytheism into a myriad of minor and major deities which the educated pagans in the third century A.D. turned to when, in the uncertainty and great spiritual confusion of that time, they embraced popular superstitions in order to find a new means of salvation. Burckhardt underscores the role played by Neoplatonic philosophy in this "lamentable" shattering of the unity of the pagan world by merging the most categorical aspects of superstition with speculation.[160] Within an overall view of decadence in the state and society that favored an increased interest in otherworldliness, Burckhardt admits that the explanation of demonism, which spread to the various manifestations of life in that time, had roots that lie well beyond any analysis of preceding religiosity: "New tendencies such as these draw their essential strength from unplumbed depths; they cannot be merely deduced as consequences of antecedent conditions."[161] Singularly, side by side with a sort of pagan monotheism, there arises a host of particular deities that must be appeased and worshipped with a number of ceremonies that are sometimes openly uncivil and obscurantist. In particular, Burckhardt's analysis of the power astrology had on life in the imperial age and the judgment he brings to bear on those atheistic and amoral practices are somewhat parallel to Warburg's research. The Swiss historian interprets that late and frantic devotion to magical rites as a sign of the intrinsic weakness of pagan will. "The need for superstition was grown the more desperate in the degree that the natural energy with which the individual confronts fate had disappeared."[162]

In Burckhardt's view this is the propitious occasion to emphasize, as he was wont to do, the inconsistency and impotence of philosophy when it came to redeeming this age from its astrological mania: "It is a humbling testimony to the human spirit's want of freedom in the face of great historical forces."[163] Even with great intellectuals and "noble personalities," philosophy remains in "shadowy byways," oscillating between the different forms of superstition. In spite of its conception of the "absolute One" that thinks itself and permeates the entire world pantheistically, Neoplatonism considers demons "demiurgic intermediary beings." "The ancient gods thus became superfluous, unless they were daimonized and included in the ranks of these lesser powers."[164]

But whereas Warburg sees a continuity between the images of astral deities handed down by the Indian East to late Hellenism and then to the Renaissance itself, Burckhardt makes a clear distinction between the essence of ancient Indian and Germanic medieval tradition, which was a source of "grandiose mysticism of a more or less conscious pantheism," and the "mysticism of polytheism" that characterized the age of Constantine and demoted the gods to the state of demons, depriving them of their strong and definite personalty.[165] He is therefore led to consider the new Christian religiosity and its harsh condemnation of paganism not responsible for the latter's decadence. The Christians found themselves in a battle against an "art of conjuration aimed only at initiates and arrogantly oblivious of the great masses, whose belief in their old gods and heroes it only confounded."[166] Christianity was able to triumph because it offered a clear and exhaustive answer to the problems the age was seeking to solve, abandoned as it was by the support of its own former civilization.

I have presented these observations of Burckhardt's because they demonstrate how the influence of this nineteenth-century master acted incessantly upon Warburg's thought, not only in the early period, as Kaegi affirms,[167] but also in his later confrontations with the pagan demons. Naturally, this must not prevent us from recognizing the difference between the two historians' interpretations of the Renaissance.[168] In his *Age of Constantine the Great* Burckhardt goes on to say that "men had learned to separate the beautiful artistic form of the god completely from its daimonic nature."[169] This observation is useful in clarifying Warburg's position in his investigation of astrological demonization: in his 1920 essay he is interested in analyzing in which cognitive values of the age logic and magic coexisted, because he notes how at the end of the fifteenth century, in Italy as well as in Germany, two conceptions of antiquity were counterposed: the very ancient practical-religious one and the new artistic-aesthetic one. He himself thus separates the divination "of art" from that "of omens" and weaves into the verification of the latter the history of the spiritual battle for the prevalence of the former.[170]

Speaking of Melanchthon's belief in astrology, which Luther not only did not share but actually loathed, Warburg presents the spiritual head of Protestant Germany as a pagan soothsayer who attempted to appease the objections raised by his intellectual realism as a scholar against that pure superstition with the consideration that in the astrological method "there survived in a practical manner that harmonizing conception of the world of the ancients that was precisely the essential basis of his humanism with its cosmological tendency."[171]

The complex question of how Gauricus, an avowed enemy of Luther, changed the revolutionary monk's horoscope by falsifying his date of birth so as to "demonize" him and thus give vent to his hatred of this earthly messenger of misfortune for the Catholic Church, and the influence all this had on Melanchthon and on popular iconography regarding Luther, is a clear example of how the propaganda pamphlet literature of the time wrought its hold over visual representation and betrayed a typical aspect of the overall mentality of that age. The story of the different dates of birth for Luther and the polemic it engendered is also proof of the persistence of the pagan totemic belief in historical consciousness, which seeks to emancipate itself intellectually during the Reformation.[172]

In Italy around 1520, when Raphael and his school painted the frescoes of the Villa Farnesina,[173] "antiquity was venerated almost as a Janus-faced herm, with a dark demoniac countenance that called for superstitious worship, and a serene Olympian aspect that called for aesthetic veneration."[174] Although they lie within the elegant conciliation effected by High Renaissance creativity, the two aspects—Apollonian and Dionysian-demoniac—are viewed by Warburg as solidly established in the artistic and cultural conception of the age and its relationship with antiquity. The law of polarity is so intrinsic to historical becoming that it impinges upon every attempt to transcend it in the name of harmony and measure. And this difficult equilibrium almost makes historical development vain, or better, renders the manifestations of possible progress precarious. Thus the splendor of rebirth is obscured by its very brevity, by its aesthetic and formal nature behind which a restless soul is grappling with itself: it contemplates and pursues beauty but at the same time endures the demons and the restraint of the superstition that beauty conceals and bears unresolved within itself.

"In the transition period of the early Renaissance, pagan-cosmological causality found expression in the idealizing classical symbols of the gods; the degree to which these are filled with human likeness determines the varied development which leads from religious demoniac worship to purely artistic and spiritualized transformation."[175] An example of the triumph of spiritualization over superstition lies in Dürer, where the demon Saturn is rendered innocuous by the meditative activity of the creature irradiated by the demon itself. Melancholy's pensiveness is the same pensiveness typical of humanistic meditation which transforms the immediate identification of man with the demon into scientific speculation. The result is self-awareness gained by means of the naturalistic use of the tools of astrological exorcism according to the intellectual principle that the Platonic academy was striving to determine.[176]

Luther, steadfast in his Christian faith against the pagan mythology that was raging around him, is also a worthy representative of that polemic in favor of the interior, intellectual, and religious emancipation of modern man.[177] This is the true rebirth of classical antiquity which, through a rigorous reading and interpretation of the ancient texts in their entirety, rises up against Arab-Hellenistic antiquity and celebrates renewed vitality against the "mummified *acedia*" of the Middle Ages.

Therefore in Warburg's opinion, antiquity, in the Renaissance spirit—that which rediscovers Aristotle's *Nicomachean Ethics* and *Problemata*—opposes the Hellenistic belief in demons that held sway in the Middle Ages. It is difficult to understand how this optimistic conclusion could stand side by side with the pessimistic tone that stems from the vision of a primal bipolarity of the Apollonian and Dionysian in antiquity. From the images of the Olympian gods this vision aroused the demons that govern fear, only to recover—by means of, and yet against, these demons—the solar fascination of beauty and meditative tranquility. The Apollonian-Dionysian duality is verified in the alternation with which these two motifs manifest themselves in the following ages through the principle of historical connection. The two aspects, inherent to the same human symbolizing faculty, like a law of expression that continuously reproduces the bipolar archetypal nature of the psyche, unfold in history separately: the Apollonian belongs to classical Greece and is transformed into Dionysian demonology during the autumn of Hellenism; Hellenistic ambiguity predominates up to the triumph, after the Renaissance struggle for form, of the spiritual emancipation of modern man.

We thus have two historical schemes in Warburg's analysis of the Renaissance. One visualizes the quattrocento as the reawakening of the ancient Greek symbolic typification, as opposed to that stylization of those symbols effected in the Middle Ages that obscured their original idealizing energy. The other fixes the pagan symbol in a basic ambivalence, in a spiritual-psychic antithesis, which in its uninterrupted working on the destinies of civilization is reproduced in the Renaissance as immanent conflict that only exceptional humanistic and religious virtue work out in the original creation of a new era.

The polarity between the Middle Ages and the Renaissance and between Northern realism and Italian idealism are transfigured into that mythical polarity evoked by Nietzsche in his analysis of Greek tragedy which takes root in the very essence of human nature and in its expression in symbols and images. This mythical polarity is the

Janus-faced herm, the power of metamorphosis of the divine into the demoniac and vice versa. The nineteenth century had fully penetrated this domain of humanity's primitive symbolic energies: the demon that is transformed in the evolution of the god's cult; the primordial monotheism that breaks up into a multitude of demons and heroes; the poetic idealization of Homer that takes the heroes back to the personal essence of the Olympian gods; and classical art which reproduces them in perfect formal equilibrium, until the Roman imperial age and late Hellenism once again divide that universality into demonology and the chaos of superstition, as Burckhardt had learned from Creuzer's research.[178]

Both these schemes involve and imply each other in all of Warburg's oeuvre, but in the last works greater emphasis is put on a moralistic-anthropological judgment of history than on the aesthetic-erudite judgment of stylistic details and their relationship to temporal becoming. It might seem that the theorization of that structural ambivalence of the psychic phenomenon, which leads to symbolic expression, should serve to articulate the connection of epochs but not to support the idea of progress in civilization. In fact, this is all the more reason why it should have denied this idea by considering the course of history a tormented oscillation of the image from one pole to the other of its primal constitution.

"Luther and Melanchthon revealed the reason for this participation in the surviving magical practices of pagan belief, which was so paradoxical in a unilinear historical conception, because they both attempted, in quite different ways, to come to terms with this prognosticating superstition."[179] "Unilinear" thought belongs to Christian faith in history conceived as salvation, which contradicts that vision of the cosmos on which astrological belief and the magical conception of the world were based. The viewpoint of a constitutive polarity of civilization that historical time reveals without being able to resolve also contrasts with this unilinear historical conception. And yet, in that very work written in 1920, Luther and Dürer are presented as exponents of that triumph of spirituality over superstition that is considered the true beginning of modernity. Warburg no longer speaks lightly and ironically of the "good European" and the search for "enlightenment"; these concepts are instead verified in humanism's victory over divination and furnish polarity with a resolution that seems to lead to one unequivocable road—the progressive development of the modern age.

The pagan god transformed into a terrible demon and used in anti-Luther propaganda in order to arouse fear of, and contempt for, the head of the Protestant Reformation betrayed an outlook on history that was so pessimistic that it proved unbearable to Warburg in those tormented years of his life and led him to seek concrete proof of human progress. As he himself had once recognized with the resignation typical of a profound and honest historian, the astral demons would drive him away from "beautiful things." The observation of the attainment of that process of stylistic idealization carried out by the Renaissance had been transformed into the will to idealize the course of history as a passage from an age of superstition to one of liberation from that "irresistible and very ancient human instinct" of mythological causality.[180]

What, according to Warburg, are the postulates of what he continuously calls "mythological causality"? At the beginning of his paper on divination in Luther's time, he makes a distinction between logic and magic, the two elements that coexist in the age under observation. "Logic, which through a conceptually distinctive definition creates the space between man and object pervaded by discursive thought; and magic, which in turn destroys that very space by creating ideal or practical links between man and object and brings them together through superstitious practices—these two forces still constitute for the prophesying thought of astrology a primitive unitary tool that the astrologer can use both to effect mathematical measurements and work magic. The epoch in which logic and magic . . . 'flourished as if grafted onto a single tree' . . . is really outside of time. And in the representation of this polarity from a historical-cultural viewpoint there are still undiscovered cognitive values that contribute to a more profound constructive criticism of historiography, whose doctrine of evolution is determined solely by a purely temporal concept."[181]

In this passage Warburg cogently affirms that temporal evolution containing a polarity, a coexistence of opposing conceptual tendencies, can take place solely in that form which the historian must refer to constantly with his data: the form of pure astronomical time which, however, cannot be attributed with the force of substantial evolution. He affirms that the age that manifests an ambivalence of cognitive values lies "outside time." With this expression, which bespeaks a clear-cut historiographic choice, Warburg intends to reiterate that concept of "age of transition" that is a leitmotiv of his oeuvre at least as basic as his pathos formula.

The age of transition is characterized by one or more polarities; it is a period in which historical time is suspended and as such does not take part either in evolution or in progress. But the link the age of transition has with the totality of historical epochs, the "connection" of the historical whole, makes this particular solution of a conflict reproduce in an evident manner—with its accentuated expressivity and ambivalent character—the very nature of the course of history. This solution completely annuls any possibility of evolution and in a certain sense makes the "before" and "after" of history a mere convention. How, in fact, can the course of time, which is conceivable only as something successive and hence linear (both a straight line and a circle) be interrupted? And how can a chronologically identifiable event be "outside time," if not by virtue of the fact that one distinguishes between chronological time and the time of historical becoming, thus negating the latter? If the former is indeed evidence taken as a convention, the latter can admit of an "outside," a suspension, only by questioning its own reality and nature. The historiographic concept based on polarity and conflict cannot therefore be reconciled with the concept of evolution, of becoming in a historical sense and direction.

At least one consideration must be made at this point, however: this concept of history also makes it impossible to speak of an age of transition. What would the transition spring from and where would it lead if no other support were given to the "before" and "after" than the purely temporal one? The very concept of transition implies a becoming, and since an entire epoch is characterized by change, this becoming must have a particular qualitative nature that makes the epoch different from the preceding one and sets it in relation to a future and to its fulfillment in the "after." The age of transition thus has a total relationship with the time of historical evolution in a direction that is certain. Warburg's peculiarity, though, lies in not allowing the epoch to exist in the certainty of a direction, as those historiographic models based on the idea of progress so often do, but in presenting it in that uncertainty of the future that, to use an expression in Ernesto De Martino's anthropological theses, might be called "the risk of one's own presence [being-there] when faced with not being-there."[182]

In 1923 Warburg gave a lecture in the nursing home at Kreuzlingen to an audience of nonexperts and fellow patients, in which he took up the threads of his studies on the Pueblo Indians in New Mexico and Arizona. Here he stated that the Indian lives in a heterogeneous state of *transition*. In the snake-dance ritual, which seeks to control the demoniacal power of lightning, and in the tangible projection of this dangerous natural phenomenon into the serpent that crawls menacingly toward its prey, Warburg sees "an instrument for orientation ... midway between magic and logic," a symbol that man in transition interposes between himself and the world.[183] The question the Hamburg scholar poses in this anthropological investigation is closely connected to the meaning of his studies on the Renaissance: "To what extent can these remnants of pagan cosmology still obtaining among the Pueblo Indians help us to understand the evolution from primitive paganism, through the highly developed pagan culture of classical antiquity, down to modern civilized man?"[184] We see in this research project how the historical vision embraces a gradual process in which transition is the most troubled and restless phase, comprising the painful anxiety of unbridled flux and at the same time the effort to establish a causality that will serve to dominate fear and free man from the oppression of an extraneous world. The purpose is to establish a connection between the subject and natural forces by means of a symbol that magically links the individual to the hostile power. The emotional release through religious magic is not typical only of primitive and savage peoples. "Two thousand years ago in Greece—the very country from which we derive our European culture—there were certain ritual practices in vogue which surpassed in their blatant monstrosity the things we see among the Indians."[185]

The nature of Warburg's vision of demonology expresses itself here quite clearly: ancient Greece gave us Plato's thought, but it also gave us Hellenistic demonology with its cruel rites. The classical age gave rise to an ambiguous age of superstition. The evolutionary thesis is therefore contradicted by this conception which integrates the successive epochs and observes them in a sort of ideal contemporaneousness, which is the coexistence of contrasting tensions.

Here once again we have the motif of the orgiastic cult of Dionysus and the Laocoön, the symbol of an antique passion and of the tragic pessimism of antiquity. But the serpent is also a symbol of benevolence in a deity: it belongs to Asclepius, the god of healing.

In this conceiving of the symbol as a connecting force between the individual and hostile nature, Warburg unconsciously coincides with Cassirer. In the second volume of *Philosophy of Symbolic Forms,* which concerns mythical thought, the philosopher analyzes this same problem of mythical causality, which is completely different from the causality of scientific thought. In myth or in the forms of magical thought there is an identification of the symbol with the object it represents, and the purely conceptual representation of the object in a causal link that coincides with the epistemological function of the subject has not yet been formed. Friedrich Vischer's essay on the symbol suggested to both Warburg and Cassirer the theory of an intermediate phase in the formative process of the symbol, when one no longer believes in the primitive symbol but remains tied to it because of the intrinsic power of the image.[186] This is the degree of development that obtains between magic and logic. The tension between these two poles opens a critical point "where the symbol is understood as a sign and yet remains a living image,"[187] and this is the phase that Warburg calls the age of transition. The bipolarity met with in this intermediate phase is translated by Warburg into a conflict between the spiritualizing Apollonian and the demonizing Dionysian.

If, however, it makes sense to speak of a polarity between logic and magic in the Renaissance, which had inherited both from the preceding ages, what sense does it make for a unilinear view of history to institute this very same polarity in the primitive symbol, when the "passage" to the abstract concept of natural causality was yet to be achieved? In this sense Ernesto De Martino is right in criticizing both the law of participation—which according to Lévy-Bruhl governs primitive mentality—and the "communion of all the living" with which Cassirer theorizes primitive feeling and which impedes a differentiation of nature from man and thus all causal articulation of nature itself. "In all these cases, what is merely a moment of the magical existential drama, the risk of not being-there, is abstracted from the concrete relation to the other moment, the redemption from this risk, and is crystallized and typified as 'mentality', 'psychic structure' and other such concepts."[188] In fact, De Martino conceived the anguish that leads primitive man to formulate magical symbols of exorcism as "the will to be-there as a presence vis-à-vis the risk of not being-there."[189] "For a presence that collapses without any compensation, the magical world has not yet appeared; for a presence that has been redeemed and consolidated and does not perceive the problem of its transitoriness, the magical world has already disappeared."[190]

In this oscillation in which primitive man lives—an oscillation perceived in the moment of its occurring, of its becoming, of the endeavor to consolidate one's own presence progressively—De Martino offers a method for understanding the magical world without using the categories proper to a much more advanced view of the world and of knowledge. He again criticizes Cassirer's deduction that the characters of myth lie in the powerlessness of mythical thought to formulate the symbol of an external reality, exactly because this reality is not external but appears to be immediate to the primitive imagination, because from this modern standpoint one cannot realize the passing nature, the striving after a goal, of the action that the primitive individual works, which is the only way he can become part of a true historical dimension.[191] The inadequacy of our present-day historiographic criterion in interpreting the magical world consists in the fact that "Hellenic-Christian anthropology and the anti-magic polemic ingrained in our civilization have created an abyss and have determined discontinuity; hence being-there now seems to us to be *always given,* given to man by nature." If on the other hand the magical world is conceived as that sphere in which being-there must be conquered, in which it is the *mediated result* of magical-symbolic activity, being-there itself appears as a cultural realization which in the age of primitive ignorance of oneself, the age of the effort made to come into one's own against the risk of "presence," became part of the history of our civilization.[192]

There are two contradictory aspects to De Martino's thesis. On the one hand, the magical world is able to orient itself autonomously and has its own epistemological categories of the knowledge of reality. On the other hand, in that world there is a risk of the presence that is lacking in scientific civilization, as it has been overcome in Western philosophy through Descartes's "I think" having become the stable nucleus of being-there and above all through Kant's transcendental apperception. "As long as we persist in judging the magical world through traditional categories, we will conceal from ourselves the drama that is proper to it; no wonder, then, if in that guise we deem that there is no drama there, but only the negative, which cannot have a history. But if we judge the magical as movement and development through the supreme form of the transcendental unity of self-consciousness, what before lay hidden will be revealed immediately—the audacious acts and conflicts and developments connected to the dramatic will to establish and maintain themselves as guaranteed presences in a world of defined things and events."[193] However, transcendental apperception must not be conceived in its historical nature, as Kant presents it, as a *given* being-there, incapable of development and becoming and at bottom incapable of having a history. In that case the historicist commits the error of counterposing the modern age to the magical world as if the latter were hermetically sealed in its inexplicable and irrational reality. Today the elementary being-there of the person, based on transcendental unity, accompanies us as something unmediated in our cultural life and prevents us from recognizing the time when this was not so and the constitutive being-there was still an object to be gained. De Martino sees in Kant's doctrine of transcendental apperception a further possibility for development, in the risk that even it represents for the person: "This risk crops up when the person, instead of conserving his autonomy with respect to the content, renounces his duty, allowing the content to assert its existence outside the synthesis, as uncontrolled *elements,* as *data* in an absolute sense."[194] Not even the determined presence of Kant's synthesis can establish itself as a datum or remain outside a historical process. This simply means "the metaphysical hypostasis of historical formation; . . . But no sooner has the limitation inherent in our present-day historiographic consciousness been overcome, and the magical world is discovered as a form of civilization in which the being-there of the person emerges as a *mediated result,* than there is an extension of consciousness and one learns of one's preceding limitations: being-there now shows itself to be what is really is—something 'given to me in human history,' a cultural resource that has been gained by passing through struggles, dangers, defeats, compromises, victories and lastly as a decision and choice that still live in every decision and choice we now make."[195]

De Martino thus seems to feel that a recovery of the historicity of the magical world is possible only in view of the person's gaining stability and of a transformation of the objective datum into self-consciousness, into the productivity of being-there. Though he criticizes the metaphysical postulate of transcendental apperception as a limit of a historiography that bases its own interpretative methods on this postulate, it seems that De Martino himself is unable to avoid regarding the Kantian "discovery" as a cornerstone of present-day historical consciousness. He interprets it as an acquisition of our certainty of presence; however, he is also obliged to deprive it of its character as a cornerstone in order to keep the historical dimension open to the understanding of the magical world and to its right to have a place in the becoming of our awareness of being-there. He reinterprets transcendental apperception in order to account for historical continuity.

Warburg's position is slightly different. For him the risk of presence is a constant factor in symbolic expression—in magical rites and astrological science as well as in ancient and Renaissance figurative art. The rebirth of ancient forms is made possible in the struggle between medieval forces and Renaissance forces in fifteenth-century man. Artistic expression is the expression of a struggle to assert one's supertemporal identity in a period of historical conflict. The pathos of consciousness seeks in the ancient expressions of pathos a formula that can stand for its position in the new world, which per se does not have the strength to abandon the ancient.

Warburg says the universality of symbolic forms is manifested in different contexts—not because of an endeavor to emancipate oneself from the sensory or from the purely expressive, but in order to give vent to an ever latent energy, to a dissatisfaction and to a spirit of initiative that cannot be definitively resolved but that lead to continuous variations on a constant theme.

The singularity of the position assumed by Warburg in his 1923 lecture lies in the fact that as long as he sees the process of symbol formation in primitive man's attempt to create the tools of a superstition that will placate the anguish caused by his confrontation with the sensory world, he remains within the framework of the concept of an age in transition; that is, that particular moment in human history in which at the base of self-consciousness lies the uncertainty between two opposing poles—presence as a datum and the event that threatens it, the power of the abstract consequentiality of logic and the demon of becoming which appears casual and with no knowable rule. One might say that Sassetti's personality was divided precisely between the elements of a consolidated cultural world with which he was acquainted and the risk Fortune created for his awareness of that world and for the material wealth that was the mark of personal power. But no sooner does Warburg begin to delineate the release from the state of risk by means of High Renaissance spiritualization, and then through scientific thought, than he adheres once again to that scheme of continuity in progress that seems to contradict the sense he attributed to the concept—which is dubious per se—of an age of transition. In the 1923 lecture he explicitly affirms: "Human culture evolves toward reason in the same measure as the tangible fullness of life fades into a mathematical symbol."[196] In reality his intention is to show the "change from real and substantial symbolism, which appropriates by actual gestures, to that symbolism that exists in thought alone."[197]

Side by side with this wholly Cassirerian conception of historical progress that evolves toward emancipation from the sensory, and of the mathematical symbol as the terminal stage of this progress, one perceives a note of nostalgia for the "fullness of life," because Warburg in his many years of study determined life as that anxiety-ridden but supreme synthesis of conflicts in which man found the most precise expression of himself and of his nature—Renaissance civilization. The mathematical symbol marks the triumph of reason over superstition, and succeeds in defeating the sensory and its character of transition and becoming; and yet life expresses itself here, just as it does in the historical process itself. "In the movement which we call cultural progress the being which claims our submission and was so prodigiously near, withdraws from our grasp and becomes in the end an unseen and spiritual power."[198] He observes that when the technical explanation of cause and effect replaces imagination, the primitive fears of humanity dissolve. "Man loses them," he says literally, and then adds: "We should be loth to decide whether this emancipation from the mythological view really helps mankind to find a fitting answer to the problems of existence."[199]

The modern-day Icarus and Prometheus who invented the lightning-rod and the cinema are the fateful destroyers of our sense of distance that threaten to precipitate the world back into chaos. The cosmos has been destroyed: "Myths and symbols, in their struggle to establish spiritual bonds between man and the outside world, create space for devotion and scope for reason which are destroyed by the instantaneous electrical contact."[200] The world of science and technology in Warburg's opinion is not a cosmos worthy of human nature and its vitality and spirituality. If our first impression, upon reading this lecture, is that Warburg has arrived at a theory of the symbol and hence of art as something transitory, something still linked with expressions of passion that must be overcome in evolution by more abstract symbols; if at first it seems that he has forgotten that passage written in 1920 in which logic and magic were the terms of a polarity, where he said that magic "destroys" the space created by logic—in the end we must admit that the lecture on serpent ritual is a coherent meditation permeated by harrowing irony.

The spirituality with which Dürer sublimated the effects of Saturn in his art (which also consisted of the fatigue of scientific measurement) and with which Luther rejected astrology in the name of newly restored authentic Christian faith, that spirituality which also marked modern man's great victory over superstition, does not seem to have resolved the relationship of man's consciousness with the world, despite the fact that the demons have been eliminated. The scientific system does not offer a satisfactory answer to the needs of our presence and its inalienable feeling of risk. Therefore, looming in the background of this faithful reproduction of a progressive and evolving view of humanity is the rebirth of anxiety and fear.

Warburg certainly had not forgotten that if the Olympian god of form emerges from the primitive demon, the god continuously gives birth to the demon of superstition, which determines man's submission to irrational forces and to chaos. But his historiographic style had driven him to seek the contrasting forces of an epoch and the manifestation of the image in the dynamic actuality of these forces as the expression of the victory of one over the other and of the formal dominion of everything that, in becoming, has no form.

The drama of historical consciousness was expressed in an admirable synthesis by a novelist who was a contemporary of Warburg. In Thomas Mann's *Joseph and His Brothers,* Jacob's overwhelming grief over the disappearance of his favorite son, young Joseph, whom he thinks has been torn to pieces by a wild beast, takes on the form of a meditation on the nature of history. Jacob lies prostrate and nude, his head covered with ashes, his body filled with sores from self-inflicted wounds. And he terrifies his faithful servant Eliezer with his thoughts about God, which due to suffering have taken on sudden and desperate lucidity.

He begins by defending his capacity to prognosticate, which should have saved him from the blows of destiny, with which he thought he was on almost personal terms. Foresight must concede to man the possibility to avoid ocurrences he had foreseen in his meditation. Destiny sees man's reflections and exclaims: "Are these still my thoughts? They are the thoughts of man, I like them no more." "But," Jacob continues, "what shall become of man if forethought no longer avails and he feareth in vain; that is, he feareth with reason? Or how shall a man live if he can no longer rely on things turning out differently from what he thought?"[201]

The father had feared that God would put him to the test by depriving him of the object of his doting love but, aware of his weakness, he had also believed that God would spare him a test of faith that for him was unbearable. Now his eyes behold the menacing presence of a crazed God who forgets what he owes man and how much of his power and grandeur lie in the theological meditation and creative imagination of his creature. "Sin not, Israel!" warns Eliezer, who is already frightened. But Jacob must go all the way with his rebellion; this man "with strong feelings" must give vent to the paths his thoughts take in order to understand his dramatic situation. And so he comes to a sad and bitter conclusion: "God hath not held the pace" in his compact with man.

He has not held the pace with man in the work of sanctification, in the reciprocal respect of the pact He and man had made, but has "halted behind, and is still a sorcerer."[202] In the most tragic moment of his life, which for that matter has been a series of suffering and relief, ups and downs, Jacob rediscovers that in the depths of the God to whom Abraham, the man of Ur, had given a spiritual form that met the needs of his religious anxieties, there lay the savage primordial demon. Jacob is unable to dominate this demon, but he can refuse to submit to it at least in feeling. The delicate historical tissue that linked him in conviction to the world of his forefathers is lacerated, and now Jacob refuses to believe that the mythical sage Eliezer even knew Abraham at all and that he had also been his servant, or that "the earth sprang toward him," as the legend has it. Now he must cling to reason and let the truth go naked.

Later, when suffering has taken on the aspect of resignation and habit, and all the archetypal forms of the myth and of superstition that Jacob had passed through are overcome, he imagines he can be united with Joseph again by going down to fetch him from beyond the tomb or even by generating him afresh by means of magic. At this point a more stable and definite consciousness enters his heart and his anxiety-ridden line of reasoning. "Life and love are beautiful; but death also has its good side, hiding and preserving the beloved in the past, and in absence; so that where once there were care and fear there is now perfect calm."[203] "Death, after having restored, preserves." Joseph is now inviolate, time no longer affects him with its traps and lures; unchanged, eternally young, he is protected from the disturbing vicissitudes of life.

But Joseph is not dead. He follows his destiny in the land of Egypt, is no longer part of the tribes of Israel, and thus breaks out of the mythical scheme that had bound him to his father. So Jacob is unaware even of what experience had demonstrated to him: just as his "dearest bliss turned to illusion and trickery," likewise his "sorest anguish," "as long as there is measure for measure," is nothing else but deception and illusion.[204]

Mann's story is a most intense expression of the significance of the historian's awareness, his difficult position between the "utterly profound certainty" of the past and the feeling of life which is a continuous and inexplicable succession of changes.[205] And as a historian, Warburg had to acknowledge progress at the very moment in which he had to reject it. Acknowledging progress meant accounting for an evolution through which the forms by which a civilization expresses itself are in conflict and the one dominates the other. Rejecting progress meant once again plunging into one's duty as a historian, this time to affirm the power and ever-live energy of forms, even though the forms are apparently obsolete because they are rooted in a permanent conflict that acts in the primordial darkness of the human soul but that is never really redeemed from temporal becoming except by negating and destroying a substantial part of itself. In the eyes of the scholar who rejects the principle of evolution and penetrates the conflict—in itself nontemporal—of the age of transition, the past is not concluded time whose relationship with the present is from antecedent to consequent, but is an eternal present open to all possible conclusions of the manifestation of a vital energy which in its primal nature is truly timeless. The present cannot dominate the past and cannot define it through its own categories of thought. It can only understand it by employing the historical virtue of memory in which symbols, those tools of idealization in our relationship with the world, are permanently imprinted. If modern means of communication, as Warburg believes, upset the sensory relationship between consciousness and the outside world by doing away with distance, they threaten the very structure of the symbol, neutralize its faculty of acquiring self-knowledge, and undermine the bases of memory and of the vital connection with one's history.

Death struck Warburg while he was working on a "picture atlas," a sort of compendium of the images of humanity where even those of the twentieth century, through the media of journalism and publicity, would find their rightful and uncontradictory place.[206]

Historical research reveals the essential character of being-there in its relation to an unfathomable becoming, which generates uncertainty in determining which direction human life is incessantly driven toward. If, however, one loses the sense of the question "where does it come from?" and hence the relationship with that bequeathed space lying between the two darknesses—the origin and the end—that go to make up history, existence in time will be all the more precarious and senseless. It may therefore be said that Warburg in this sense never abandoned the basic conviction that the formidable struggle undertaken by the Renaissance and its best minds to conquer the highest expression of humanism, the serene restraining force of meditation, so as to repress the demoniac imminence of the unknown, was ever and always for him the most arduous but most fecund battle the modern world ever waged to gain total self-knowledge.

2

ERNST CASSIRER

The Renaissance as Conciliation

Aby Warburg's Renaissance belongs to the interpretative tradition associated with Burckhardt, both because of the individual's characteristic of imposing his political and artistic will to expression and because of the revived relationship to antiquity which was taken as a starting point for an incomparable new outburst of cultural life. Like Burckhardt, Warburg also tends to isolate this epoch in the broadest historical context and to make it an exception, a situation all to itself in which ancient motifs of civilization converge and tradition and the rejection of tradition engage in a formidable struggle with alternating outcomes that are not always clear-cut but always prove to be extremely valuable for the history of civilization.

Burckhardt viewed the Renaissance as a splendid cultural unity, and as such attached particular importance to it, almost isolating it from the course of history so as to seize upon only its essential peculiarities.[1] The concept of an age of transition with which Warburg indicates the brief artistic flourishing from around the middle of the fifteenth century to the first decade of the sixteenth, presents that period in the same isolated framework, where the relationship with the preceding age is one of opposition and polarity and the relationship with the following age is veined with doubts and uncertainties. In his treatment of the "transition," however, one is aware that the historical position of the epoch is different from Burckhardt's and in a certain sense in contradiction to it. The solidity and unity of Burckhardt's view—the worth of which cannot be contested *in toto* even by Huizinga, who overturns that interpretation—takes on nuances and is filled with shadows in Warburg. The vigorous individualism revealed in Sassetti's personality is still fraught with traditional motifs, medieval piety, and Christian faith, with which and sometimes against which Renaissance man leads his existence, at times to take comfort in that certainty, at others to justify his will and determination to deviate from it.

The very revival of antiquity, which Burckhardt tried to place on a lower level with respect to the authentic initiative and originality of the Italian quattrocento, is accentuated by Warburg in the importance he attaches to the pertinicity of the classical symbolic form and to the influence it worked—because of its inner energy—on Renaissance consciousness. The latter thus appears to be divided between a fascination for the imitation of the ancients and the pathos that was regenerated through that contact with its origins. This pathos also addressed itself to its own position in the world and sprang from uncertainty and from a recognition of the limitation, as well as the dignity, of knowledge; it stemmed from extreme scholarly skill as well as from an awareness of the ability to maneuver within precise limits. Hence it was pathos engendered by irony, not by a sense of happiness or perfection. It is interesting to note how Warburg's proximity to Burckhardt is sometimes transformed by the above-mentioned factor into a no less solid proximity to Huizinga's point of view.[2]

Warburg certainly cannot be considered one of those scholars—the Nietzschean continuators of Burckhardt—criticized by Huizinga, even though certain characteristics of a metaphysics of art, such as the will to cosmic reunification so typical of Nietzsche's and Schopenhauer's speculation, have been noted in Warburg.[3] Warburg's quest for a universal foundation for the aesthetic event in that age of transition in which all the creative faculties were striving for the perfect form, has no relationship whatsoever to making a myth of the Renaissance or to the theory of the superman. On the contrary, we have noted in his writings a tendency to sometimes negate that "heroic" feature of the Renaissance which vice versa emerges in Burckhardt. Although he acknowledges heroism in the struggling and striving to transcend antitheses, Warburg is always ready to recognize Renaissance man's giving way when faced with his impotency, or his search for compromises by taking recourse to classical authority or to the still solid medieval tradition as well as to the promptings of Northern realism and the tremendous power of faith in the influence of the stars and Fortune.

One must not confuse the nature of the hero—who asserts himself as a model of adoration and comfort owing to his ideal triumph over adverse forces, as appears in some of Nietzsche's considerations on the Renaissance—with the nature of the genius, more suitable to the historical-aesthetic dimension in which Warburg carried out his research, who asserts himself by means of rigorous intellectual effort and profound self-knowledge and also through the sense of discovery of the immanent formal laws that mark out the confines of his world. The aesthetic sentiment, which Burckhardt noted and described so admirably in all manifestations of Renaissance life, for Warburg consisted in the desire to seize upon those tools most appropriate for controlling the vast domain of the senses through the notion of measure, which was the most vigorous and stimulating lesson taught by classical antiquity—that prodigious philosophical, scientific and artistic heritage of the Greeks and Romans.

In 1927 the Warburg Library published Cassirer's *Individual and Cosmos in Renaissance Philosophy* as one of its *Studien*. This work was the result of years of study on the philosophy of symbolic forms and was—both in the dedication to Warburg on his sixtieth birthday and in its aim—an homage to the Warburg Institute whose activities Cassirer had participated in as a philosopher but above all as a man of learning receptive to all types of historical research. In 1910 he had written a long treatise on the Renaissance that later became the first volume of *Problem of Knowledge*, his inquiry into this problem in modern philosophy. In this early work, as in the long introduction dedicated to Descartes that Cassirer had used as a premise to his doctoral thesis on Leibniz in 1902, the tendency to work in terms of a unitary monograph on ages of thought rather than on individual thinkers was already evident. The conception of a long, painstaking inquiry into the problem of knowledge from the Renaissance to the present stemmed from an idea of historiographic unity that remained with Cassirer up to the time he was preparing his last lessons at the University of Göteborg and on into his stay in the United States. If *Problem of Knowledge* has an incomplete nature and the third and fourth volumes do not seem to fit in as parts of a unified and harmonic whole, this is not due to a lack of a basic concept dominating and running through the entire work, and perhaps not even to the fact that the work was interrupted many times and that the last volume ended up being published separately and posthumously.[4] This incompleteness of Cassirer's oeuvre is also a characteristic of his *Philosophy of Symbolic Forms,* to which he had intended to add a fourth volume on aesthetics.[5] Although there is a completeness to the individual subjects dealt with, this work betrays his intention to delve more deeply into, and gain more command of, the various disciplines and individual scientific and research methods. Cassirer's tendency to strive for an all-embracing knowledge of history was never realized, partly because of his many didactic and scholarly commitments, but also because of the intrinsic difficulty such a task entailed.

Conceiving of the history of philosophy in terms of cultural history and of the organic development of a totality of thoughts and data with a definite aim—a positive increase in knowledge which in growing fulfills its original purpose, its tendency to completion—lends a definite mark to the course of history in Cassirer's exposition. Yet it also can deprive the single phases and cultural milieus of that perspicuity he sought in his evolutionary and progressive view. Here the unilinear time of the event, which is always receptive and pressing forward, seems to be taking a sort of revenge on the attempt made to bend it and delimit it within a logical and historiographic framework. The tendency to make the level of thought and of the knowledge acquired (or the symbols that express that knowledge) adhere to the chronological level—not out of an expository need, but out of the two levels' need for intrinsic correspondence—is in itself contradictory: it assumes it can reduce to a stable, permanent, and conclusive meaning what is incessantly becoming and continuously rupturing the nature of duration, circularity, and logical relationship between the beginning and end of sense and meaning. Although he is quite receptive to history and its particularities, its characteristic multiplicity of levels, Cassirer never ceases to search for a basic motif that resounds in every detail and symbolic form and is always a limpid chord, never a tormented dissonance.

But the unity he strives for and creates with such admirable dedication and optimistic sureness is not sustained by a sufficient and persuasive theoretical basis. It is a unity grounded upon Kantian authority and scientific conceptuality which he never adequately questions, considers a problem or examines thoroughly. On the contrary, he abandons himself to it as if it were an inalienable certainty.

Cassirer's enthusiasm and admiration for the thought and research of Warburg and his colleagues led him to rewrite his interpretation of Renaissance philosophy in a shorter form. Bringing to bear what he had both learned and taught at Hamburg, he reformulated his ideas on the epoch that was the center of the Warburg Institute's interest, the focus of its speculation on historical forms. Therefore, if *Individual and Cosmos in Renaissance Philosophy* is connected to the viewpoint of the first volume of *Problem of Knowledge* and faithfully reproduces its expository pattern and frame of thought, it also presents certain novelties in new fields of research, or at any rate fields viewed from a different critical angle, in Cassirer's discussion of the Renaissance.

In the dedication to Warburg that opens the essay, Cassirer clarifies the nature of his work as a contribution to a school that "embodies the idea of the methodological unity of all fields and all currents of intellectual history."[6] How deeply he felt this ideal of the methodological unity of knowledge as his very own, and how the impetus of this feeling naturally prevented him from noting the differences—not only the nuances, but the different principles and results too—between himself and Warburg's school emerges from that work, taken both as a whole and in its individual parts, in the obvious influences and inspiration that could not but have stemmed from that milieu. In fact, the "intellectual structure" that had led to the library's basic unitary principle was not based on the conciliation of opposites or the linear unity of differences that Cassirer considered the task that lay before the scholar of culture; rather it reflected (and still reflects) Warburg's attempt to present the antitheses at work in Renaissance consciousness. And those very polarities are reflected in the arrangement of the library. They are presented not in terms of a possible resolution, but rather in a "stance" of reciprocal gauging of strength between the poles—each of them appearing in the arena of conflict, as it were, in the total integrity of its sources and development and yet always implying and alluding to its opposite. The methodological unity consisted in juxtaposing spheres that remain antithetical, such as magic and science, and yet which, in moving backward in their history to their origin in antiquity, continuously refer to intermediate milieus and fields that once again lead to that antithesis and to its right to alternate continuously in accord and discord.[7] The splendid arrangement of material in the library is accomplished out of an inexorable necessity: the volumes are ordered like tesserae of a mosaic whose pattern must be reconstructed, as if a guiding hand were constantly leading the reader to some distant, invisible goal.

That must have been Warburg's view of memory: the appearance of the facts and thoughts of the past in a closely knit pattern. But memory must have been viewed more in terms of the primal energy that generated and distributed these facts and thoughts in this way, an energy which abolished the very concept of the past by perpetuating the vitality, fecundity, and fulfillment of the past in the present. Once time has been abolished and the circle of connected meanings has been established, memory can range into ever more recondite areas and re-create its own time which now, instead of destroying, conserves and increases the patrimony of a culture.

The fact that Cassirer was so enthused by this impression of "methodological unity" and hence of rigor in research and in the discovery of historical facts and the connections between them, is quite understandable, given his vision of culture as connected and significant knowledge. In the case of Warburg and the arrangement of his library, this methodological unity consisted in making constant reference to those primary documents of Western civilization contrived in the pathos of their origin and in the highest forms of classical culture. Cassirer, though, felt that human knowledge was to be apprehended as a unity of development and occurrence, a process of growth that extends into natural time and finds the univocal sense of the whole anew in every cultural event.[8] However, rather than unity, in Cassirer one can speak of a univocal direction which, while referring to the totality of knowledge (that is to say, something self-contained), also professes to be a path leading forward—and in thus doing naturally generates contradiction.

Therefore in describing the historical picture of Renaissance philosophy, Cassirer views the correspondences of Warburg's memory with utter trust and at the same time restates his own unshakable faith in the unilinear course of thought that, on the basis of medieval tradition, creates the tools of the evolution toward the modern age. And it is precisely Cassirer's manner of treating the theme of the relationship between the Middle Ages and the Renaissance that openly betrays the coexistence in his thought of the two levels described above. The first is Warburg's teaching of a connection between different areas and milieus which by their intimate nature can never be confused with, or reduced to, one another; the second is the passage of every opposite into the other opposite, the contrariety of elements being resolved in a continuity between them. Cassirer's considerations develop on these two levels—both in his own consciousness and in their conceptual and historiographic formulation—without ever being able truly to coalesce. This results in a singular "double standpoint": he has thoroughly penetrated Warburg's method and theory, while at the same time he openly contradicts them more than once in the theoretical nucleus of certain of his deductions as well as in his general formulation.

In *Individual and Cosmos* there is already a typical disagreement with the first volume of *Problem of Knowledge* that in its outlines is still very much a part of Cassirer's historic scheme. This difference concerns Burckhardt's judgment of the Renaissance, which in *Problem of Knowledge,* a work with a much more philosophical approach, sounded different or attenuated. In *Individual and Cosmos* there recurs a critical tone regarding the Swiss historian which cannot fail to be surprising in a follower of Aby Warburg. While seventeen years earlier Burckhardt was quoted in a manner that clearly revealed Cassirer's total agreement with the great nineteenth-century cultural historian,[9] now the philosopher always quotes him in a critical manner, though showing the utmost respect for his fundamental oeuvre. This attitude is more evident and noteworthy at the beginning of the book, when Cassirer makes a methodological clarification. Preparing to face the problem of Renaissance thought, and hence of philosophy, Cassirer must justify his entire research vis-à-vis the clearly negative judgment Burckhardt had made of this aspect of quattrocento culture in not considering philosophy a "constitutive moment" of the general spirit of renewal that "animated the time," as it was still totally bound to medieval theological speculation. Cassirer feels that because of his thesis Burckhardt was obliged to limit his overall view of the epoch in not acknowledging the connection Renaissance religiosity had with the cultural totality of the time and in not adequately justifying this stance. In fact Burckhardt did not even consider philosophy a part of the entire intellectual current of the time, and according to Cassirer one cannot judge if it was understood even in the Hegelian sense of "spiritual essence of the time."[10] At this point the recognition of method is brought into the picture, as it should help to explain this gap. In fact one might say that "in any conflict between those who do historical research and those who write the philosophy of history, the decision must always go to the historian, since every speculative connection must submit to the 'facts' and recognize in them its limits."[11]

In Cassirer's view this criterion is inadequate for understanding and clarifying the historical event should that event have a negative or contradictory nature. The impossibility of marking out a clear-cut boundary between "philosophic and religious issues" in the Renaissance led Burckhardt to ignore the philosophical documents of the period and to leave this nucleus of persistent medieval overtones indeterminate amid the general revival of life and will. Burckhardt set Renaissance man's instinct to turn to direct practical activity and to act immediately upon and change reality against pure Scholastic theological speculation. And yet in the actual life of the age that very spirit of rebirth betrays a tendency to fuse "theory" with "practice," those two aspects of life that Burckhardt separated, whereas according to Cassirer the two moments are "constantly coalescing and interpenetrating."[12]

In this passage the motifs that will be compared and will conflict throughout *Individual and Cosmos* are transparent: the historical-cultural method that distinguishes and separates in order to grasp the significant detail, and the need for a direction premised by the research itself, which in *Problem of Knowledge* had been enunciated as a hypothesis of an inner continuity of thought, postulated as a purely a priori idea, which must guide the historiographic investigation.[13] At the very moment Cassirer reaffirms the contraposition of the Renaissance and Middle Ages, along the lines of Burckhardt's intentions and Warburg's thesis, he already tends to dissolve this contrast into a coalescence, a turning from one of the poles to the other. This tendency returns in the discourse on individualism, which Burckhardt had proposed as the supreme characteristic, the basis of distinction between Renaissance and medieval man. Cassirer criticizes Burckhardt because he noted only one aspect in that process of individualization: the subject's setting himself vis-à-vis the object in a way that was absolutely inconceivable in the Middle Ages.¹⁴

On the contrary, one must realize that this transformation did not take place in opposition to the preceding age, but precisely from its standpoint, as Cassirer points out in his long exposition of Cusanus's philosophy.¹⁵ What determines this philosopher's optimistic and conciliatory position is his theory of the *coincidentia oppositorum,* the resolution of opposites in the very thought that poses them, and that difference between finite and absolute by which the former can never reach the latter but where consciousness of the difference is tantamount to a mediation of that very difference, which is thus ideally eliminated.¹⁶ As is the case in *Problem of Knowledge,* the entire analysis made here of Cusanus's oeuvre, which is viewed as paving the way to modern thought and as having every right to be considered part of Renaissance culture, is carried out according to a criterion of distinction—in the still Scholastic and unitary pattern of that speculation—of the "polarities" that typically come to light there and represent its novelty.

Cassirer grasps the divisions that only now emerge clearly and that in turn concern the separation of theology from Scholastic logic,¹⁷ Platonic from Aristotelian philosophy,¹⁸ and the authentic Platonic sources from the constrictions placed upon them by the great influence of Neoplatonism.¹⁹ In this type of historiographic analysis there are echoes of Warburg's thesis of polarity, which is insisted upon with a new awareness compared to *Problem of Knowledge*; but there is also the influence of Panofsky's studies of Dürer and of his relationship with the Italian Renaissance, an influence that recurs insistently in *Individual and Cosmos.* The criticism of Burckhardt aims at justifying the ample treatment of Renaissance philosophy as being a rightfully integral, even essential, part of the culture of the age and at the same time sets out to be an acknowledgment of the broader, more problematic view of the epoch established by Warburg; yet it also clearly reveals that ambiguity of levels on which Cassirer's thesis is developed. Here in fact Cassirer skillfully grasps the negative essence of Warburg's teachings on the Renaissance, the link with medieval traditions which in Renaissance consciousness does battle with the new existential view seeking to come into its own. He does not, however, limit himself to verifying this struggle between past and present. Rather, he overturns

Burckhardt's thesis of a more clear-cut contraposition of the Renaissance and Middle Ages, so that the conflict whose outcome was uncertain has now become a positive transformation based upon medieval tradition.

This tradition projects its fecund light upon quattrocento speculation and gives rise to innovating energy that will be conducive to new developments and new accents on those solid premises. But this means that the motif of immanent conflict so dear to the Warburgian experience falls by the wayside, and one no longer understands where the struggle and opposition that engender energy and striving lie. So Cassirer has to shift this moment backward in time, to Petrarch's *Dialogues,* where old and new engage in a battle that is as manifest as it is unresolvable. He explicitly asserts that that intimate battle between opposing spiritual forces, personified by Cicero and St. Augustine, that Petrarchian torment of the soul, disappeared with Cusanus, in whom one already finds a balance of forces, a stable outcome.[20] In doing this Cassirer modifies Warburg's entire view of the Renaissance; according to him this age was not the expression of a live, working conflict, but the resolution of a preceding state of conflict. And yet the entire analysis of Cusanus's thought is based upon the criterion of the distinction between conflicting forces (such as the unconditioned and the empirical world) which are repeatedly noted in *Problem of Knowledge.* These forces are animated by a new energy that reveals the mobile, fluid condition of symbol formation, the creativity from which the new formulas, the new language, and the concepts of modernity are about to spring.[21] But in the Renaissance this distinction becomes an ontological difference between finite and infinite, the absolute and insurmountable contraposition of the sensible and the intelligible, not in the medieval manner of the Neoplatonists, but in the sense Plato himself intended.

One often encounters the theme of *chorismòs*—separation—in Cassirer, who sees in this concept the distinction between Renaissance thought and medieval metaphysics in the recovery of the original Greek text over and above Neoplatonic mediation,[22] as well as the distinction between Renaissance Platonism and modern Platonism.[23] Quattrocento Platonism, both in Cusanus and in the Florentine Platonic Academy, is characterized by the polarity of man and the world, mind and nature; however this polarity "is not allowed to become an absolute dualism of the Scholastic-medieval variety. For the polarity is not an absolute, but a relative opposition. The difference between the two poles is only possible and conceivable in that it implies a reciprocal relationship between them."[24] This motif, which Cassirer undoubtedly understands in connecting Cusanus with Pico della Mirandola,[25] seems paradoxical only if it is taken per se, objectively; but its necessity and clarity immediately come to the fore if one takes the standpoint of the self, the knowing subject. "In the free *act* of willing and in the free *act* of knowing, those things are conjoined which in simple *existence* seem always to be fleeing from each other. For both the power of distinction and the power of unification are properties of these acts. They alone can distinguish to the highest degree without, at the same time, letting the things distinguished fall into an absolute *separation*."[26] With his characteristic ability Cassirer immediately connects this type of speculation, which embraces the entire Renaissance, to modern philosophic idealism, to Leibniz and Hegel,[27] after having subtly noted all its links with medieval tradition. In Bovillus's *De sapiente*,[28] he finds, once again juxtaposed in an exemplary manner, the old and the new, the schematic-allegorical order of the macrocosm and microcosm, and the consciousness of the distinction between substance and knowledge and between world and object, which is viewed by Cassirer as already decidedly Hegelian in orientation.

The separation of theory and practice was the object of Cassirer's criticism of Burckhardt. It is here transcended in a way that tends to give to the Renaissance nature of practical action—and of the individual's intervention to change his relationship with the world—an intellectual foundation in the thesis of the *coincidentia oppositorum*, of the cognitive act as a force that divides and at the same time unites, the thesis of the acquiring of wisdom as subjective understanding of the principle that sustains the whole. Renaissance philosophy is viewed in the light of the idealist theory of the cognitive act that disconnects and unites again, the act intrinsic to the subject as a possibility—by means of reflection—of departing from pure identity and pure diversity, to establish itself as the reason for all reality since it is at once identical and different. In this interpretative key, which is the strongest element in Cassirer's analysis, one can recognize the cause of the contradiction (pointed out above) in Cassirer's propensity for conciliating Warburg's thesis of polarities and discord in the Renaissance with his own unshakable conviction that those contrasts are already resolved in the philosophy of Cusanus, in the complex oeuvre of Ficino, and in Pico's and Bovillus's singular thought. In other words, these contrasts are already accomplished syntheses whose link with the Neoplatonic-syncretic tradition is transformed, by contact with the original ancient texts, into the language and conceptuality by then typical of the modern age. Cassirer could not note distinction and opposition without discerning the reconnecting, creative element—the one that draws energy and impetus for a new expressive, symbolic, and conceptual unity from the splitting up of forces. This actualist concept presents two difficulties. One consists in the problem of how to adapt the ideal a priori act to the course of history that develops in time. The other concerns the moments of separation and reunification, which at first are regarded as reflecting one another and then are viewed historically as successive to one another. The necessity of the historical task, which demands that even what is conceived as timeless must become temporal, becomes in Cassirer a necessity of the concept itself. It would seem that in his opinion thought must "unfold" in time and possess a temporality; it must be able to generate itself and hence be a generator of time.

In the section of *Individual and Cosmos* that deals with astrology and magic in the Renaissance, a section greatly influenced by Warburg's thought, Cassirer makes an observation that demonstrates how thoroughly he understood that thought, at least on a level of his knowledge as a philosopher and historian. When he analyzes the various degrees to which the astrological conception of the world was overcome—that is, the negation of astrology and its transformation into a new method of research into nature and the cosmos—Cassirer clarifies the concept of the "continuity of this process," which "does not imply that the systematic succession of thoughts is represented and reflected by a temporal succession. We are not speaking of a continuous temporal 'progress' that leads in a straight line to some specific goal."[29] In fact, the old and the new, as Cassirer tends to demonstrate here, "continuously merge with each other"; if contrasting motifs mingle in Renaissance thought and sensibility, there is no correspondence between the passing of empirical time, its linearity, and the development immanent in the criticism of astrology.

The new and the old oscillate in the actual occurrence in thought of the themes which, only after continuous and alternating conquests and regression, become typical configurations of culture: "These typical configurations make clear to us the immanent forward movement of thought, which by no means necessarily corresponds to its temporal, empirical course."[30] Renaissance thought places the attainment of a new form before the actual content.[31] Just as language, partly by having recourse to the original texts, renews itself, so do symbols, the expressive formulas of an energy and an ancient sensibility that are now superimposed on medieval content and crystallize it, taking a new direction as concerns taste, the sense of life, theoretical aims, and the concept of nature. The typical configuration is the product of this Renaissance struggle between new forms and traditional content, and it is the expression of progress that is not chronological but immanent in symbolic activity itself.

These same historiographic principles are to be found in Warburg's research on Botticelli and Sassetti, where they are expressed with greater emphasis on the revival of antiquity through recurring symbols. But besides Warburg, there is another personality who appears in this context—Erwin Panofsky, who had dedicated years and years and numerous essays to speculation on the apriority of artistic creation and on the problem of historical time.[32] The relationship between Cassirer and Panofsky is one of reciprocal influence; the art historian had drawn inspiration from the philosophy of symbolic forms, and the philosopher had deepened his historical considerations through Panofsky's studies of the concept of idea and perspective. With regard to the idea of historical time, Cassirer had embraced Panofsky's thesis that there are two related aspects in historiographic research. On the one hand, the symbol is freed from temporal bonds and depends on the logical apriority of the cognitive process and the creative imagination. On the other hand, the historical datum is understood in a temporal succession, and time is viewed as the final point of reference for the historian studying symbolic creation in its concrete manifestation.

In Cassirer's mind, however, temporal succession and systematic succession have a higher stage of synthesis. In fact, he thinks the development intrinsic to thought tends to a rectilinear becoming, so that he sees an ideally historical level on which the pathos formula progresses. He seems to create for himself a broader general view on the particular phases of symbol formation that corresponds to a "simple plotted line" that leads from the philosophy of Cusanus and Bovillus to Leibniz and Hegel. In this general view of the particular problems inherent to the various epochs, there is included a theme central to Cassirer's speculation on the history of philosophy as epistemology, as German cultural history from the Reformation to idealism,[33] and in the analysis of the Renaissance. This is the theme of the relationship between necessity and freedom,[34] between form and content and, in the case of the symbol, between idea and image and between the creative activity of the mind and its result. In Cassirer's philosophy of symbolic forms this central relationship develops more and more in an assimilation of the two terms of the relationship itself: the symbol is the formula in which intellectual activity is basically explicated. The symbol must therefore have a dynamic constitution that is always becoming, in continuous striving after mediation, synthesis and the result. However, it must also have a stable constitution, it must be the result itself in that it is the bearer of the history that intellectual activity has developed in temporal succession. The symbol is thus historicized each time, but always as a force and hence as becoming. In *Individual and Cosmos,* which follows Cassirer's research on language and myth, this formal-transcendental character of the symbol emerges continuously as a pattern of historiographic analysis in which what is apparently consolidated—medieval tradition—turns out to be charged with tension, and what is apparently becoming—the modern spirit of the Renaissance—comes to a halt and is consolidated in typical symbols and "new and yet ancient" formulas.[35] The result is that continual shifting back and forth in relation to the temporal sphere and to the caesuras that are historically imposed upon it—which is a characteristic of the volume on the Renaissance and marks its wealth of intermingling and the difficulty in ascribing to it a univocal position as regards both Warburg's school and idealistic, progressive thought.

In reality Cassirer lets himself be influenced by the prudent intentions of Warburg and his disciples, and by the notion of the pathos formula that he himself adopts[36] in order to interpret Fortune, myth, and astrology in a manner that turns out to be quite different from the original method used by Warburg's school. The Renaissance transformation of the medieval symbol of Fortune is a sign of the new relationship individual virtue has with blind fate. "There is no real break with the philosophical past; but a new dynamic of thought announces itself, a striving—to speak with Warburg—for a new 'energetic state of equilibrium.'"[37] With Rucellai and Sassetti, Ficino and Pico and Machiavelli, this striving takes on the nature of the ancient *virtus* and of a "heroic passion" in the certainty of being able to lead the course of Fortune where one desires.[38] The profound "discordance within the soul," the "new uncertainty" of Renaissance faith, "compared to the certainty and comfort of the medieval belief in providence," "signifies a new liberation."[39]

The same occurs in Cassirer's consideration of myth: in the long and fine exposition of Lorenzo Valla's thought concerning the relationship between divine prescience and free will, one notes an aspect peculiar to humanism as it was viewed by Warburg's school. A theological and philosophical problem is clothed in an external form, an ancient image filled with meaning; Valla offers a concrete embodiment of the *concept* through the myth of Apollo and Jupiter, in which Apollo represents divine foreknowledge and Jupiter divine omnipotence. Cassirer notes: "Ancient myth now receives a new role; it becomes the vehicle of logical thought."[40] In another passage at the beginning of the discussion of the subject-object problem in the Renaissance, there is an interpretation of myth that is quite removed from the one given in the 1922 essay on Platonic aesthetics.[41] Taking up Plato's thought as the expression of a philosophy of the soul bound to a cosmological and mythical dimension of the determination of being, Cassirer acknowledges that in the later dialogues the concept of the soul has lost all the mythical-primitive constitutive elements of orphic origin and has become only a symbol of that cognitive process and of the function of unification the psyche has in *Theaetetus*.

But myth survives in this new symbolic capacity to express the characteristics of becoming in opposition to those of being; the language of myth serves to describe what cannot be grasped conceptually, the temporally conditioned and the nature of the changeable and fugitive.[42] Whereas in 1922 myth proved to be essentially a heritage of the ancient mixture of philosophy and religion, now it is acknowledged as having a creative value that is used consciously by Plato to delineate a situation of dynamic exasperation that eludes the grasp of the concept. Certainly the long study on symbolic forms leads to this new formulation of the problem of myth in Plato, as a means philosophy has of lending form to what by definition cannot have form, thus setting itself—in an absolute manner and without any possibility of convergence—against the pure world of ideas. Here myth is viewed in its stage of transition to the philosophic symbol. It has become a symbol and therefore no longer has its substantial nature of objective reality that is independent unto itself; it has changed into a tool of expression and language. Such a change must have had something to do with the psychological sense which according to Warburg the symbol had as the issue of an expressiveness of the depths and of those conflicts and uncertainties that drive humanity to ascribe a stable form to its fears and fantasms, a sign that can evoke psychic forces and at the same time dominate them.

Starting from the character of symbolization that the myth takes on in Plato, Cassirer makes striking use of the theme of the soul and the road its concept has taken up to the modern age. *Identical* and *different* merge in the myth of the soul in *Timaeus* and "ideal differences of significance become converted into ontological differences of being and of origin."[43] Therefore, what in the intellectual endeavor in *Theaetetus* and in epistemological determination had become pure symbol—the soul as a transcendental unity of knowledge—reappears in *Timaeus* in its archaic capacity and is thus handed down to the speculation of posterity. The Aristotelian *nous* is therefore an objective being and Neoplatonism makes it a permanent reference point in the general hierarchy of powers. Last, Averroism offers the systematic formulation of this concept in the absolute unity of the intellect, which abandons every principle of subjectivity and individuality.[44] But the systematic conclusions drawn by Averroism, which clashed with the principle of subjectivism in Christian faith, were opposed with determination in the thirteenth century, especially on the part of Thomas Aquinas, on the basis of the thinking self as a fact, as an empirical function of thought. The personality of the believer, who is at the center of religious life, is a constitutive principle indispensable to intellectual exercise.[45] "To understand the transformation that takes place with the beginning of the philosophy of the Renaissance, we must keep in mind this opposition, this tension, which already existed in the medieval system of life and learning."[46]

The subject-object relationship as it is understood in modern philosophy begins precisely with humanism and in the criticism that Petrarch had already made of Averroism. Cassirer sees no coherent thought in Petrarch, but rather an instinctive, passionate, and hence more valuable defense of individualism and the personality, a defense that was to continue to carry weight in the Renaissance in a singular combination with Neoplatonic elements and with Scholastic Averroism. In Cassirer the value of the individual, so characteristic of the new cultural trend, does not consist so much in the different way of conceiving existence compared to the Middle Ages, but above all it is given a philosophical foundation in Cusanus's psychology, in the *principium individuationis* that is a relationship of proportion between body and soul, between sensible and intelligible, and also in Ficino's theory of Eros, which initiates modern theodicy, the modern manner of conceiving the sensible as an essential part of the mind.

In Ficino's Christian mysticism Cassirer sees the transcending of the absolute separation and immobility of the intellectual concept, which is now placed in the sphere of contemplation. Cassirer does not dwell upon the many incongruities in Ficino's thought, the intricate syncretism he was led to by the enormous cultural patrimony that he himself sometimes had difficulty in dominating. Pantheistic vitalism was in Cassirer's view only a marginal aspect of the Renaissance that was transcended by humanism and, what is more, bore in itself the germs of this very overcoming. The general Renaissance tendency to conciliate all the currents as if they were turning toward the formulation of a modern concept of the subject is most strongly felt in the transition—which in Cassirer's opinion is so evident, but which on the contrary is so problematical—from the Neoplatonism of the Florentine Platonic Academy to the artistic and naturalistic practices of the epoch. Hans Baron criticized this point in Cassirer's work, pointing out both the inconsistency of the link between Cusanus and the Florentine Academy thinkers and the clear-cut separation between philosophy and scientific research during the Renaissance.[47] The twofold nature of the artist, bound to the world of the idea, the pure form, but also to the need to realize it concretely, as was explained by Panofsky in *Idea,* is viewed by Cassirer in the broader philosophical context dominated by the theory of Eros, and he draws from this twofold influence the view of a unitary Renaissance both in its theoretical formulations and in its aesthetic nature. Here too Panofsky's viewpoint, limited to the artistic sphere and to the revolutionary solution given there to the problem of the intellect-sensibility relationship, is expanded by Cassirer to take in all aspects of the epoch. Undoubtedly he had been attracted by Panofsky's brilliant formulation of the problem of perspective and of Renaissance artistic form as the bearer of a new concept of space which only in seventeenth-century geometry was acknowledged and theorized. Cassirer wanted to reweave the historical picture into a broader realization of details, all of which converge toward the idealistic view of reality.[48]

The thesis of the artist as mediator between the polar opposition of the elements of being in this part of Cassirer's work presents itself in turn as a "syncretism" of Panofsky's interpretation and the idealist theory of history.[49] The same method of inquiry is to be found when he deals with astrology and magic. Like Warburg in his essay on Luther's age, Cassirer also sees the Renaissance freedom of the spirit opposed by dogmatic medieval theology and demonologic Neoplatonism.[50] The pagan world had handed down to the Renaissance not only the symbols of reason and creative power but also those of prognosticating magic and of the myriad demons that had populated the Hellenistic cosmos and even the Christian Middle Ages. Ficino's ambiguous relationship with astrology, his desire to attain free will for the erudite, and his belief in the causal determination of the influence of the stars, is the most explicit and anguished proof of this. And yet, in the works of different philosophers he examines, Cassirer singles out a genuine naturalistic motif. It consists in the fact that the Renaissance conception of astrology is an emancipation from doctrinal theology[51] and in the new Renaissance individual's belief that the erudite person was free to choose at least the *direction* to be taken by his own existence, which is under the ambivalent influence of a star.[52]

In 1910 Cassirer's judgment of astrology was basically negative, since he felt it conditioned the individual and was the undisputed faith for the entire epoch.[53] Now, after having become acquainted with Warburg's interpretation and having expanded the concept of polarities, Cassirer still sees superstitious fear in astrology, but he also acknowledges it as a means of lending a necessary order to the cosmos. It thus appears to him to be like a naturalistic view that studies the relations and correspondences between the many parts of the universe—a sort of "rational" astrology.[54] Demoniac causality could not but submit to scientific causality, since Renaissance ethics did not strive for man's bondage to the demon, but rather to a privileged position for him so that he could take in the positive aspect of the demons and make it part of a cosmos viewed as a living organism. The principle of correlation, which governs the image of the microcosm,[55] marks the passage, the common feature, between necromancy and modern science. Magic appears as "the active side of the knowledge of nature; what this knowledge theoretically recognizes as related, as belonging together, magic actively connects and leads to a common goal. . . . [It] supports, like the industrious servant, the operative forces of nature."[56]

Both Warburg and Cassirer found Franz Boll's *Sternglauben und Sterndeutung* (Faith in the Stars and Astrology) to be a fundamental text for the distinction between cosmological mathematics and magical practice, both of which were of Eastern origin and taken up and mixed in the religiosity and scientific curiosity of the Renaissance.[57] But whereas Warburg views the survival of demonology and superstition as a constant danger which threatens even the learned person—the philosopher—and binds him to a terror-filled determinism, Cassirer sees the very will of Renaissance man, his striving after a known goal, to which the various theoretical and empirical currents of the time lead, as marking the progressive defeat of demonology.[58]

Cassirer is in perfect agreement with Warburg's studies of Dürer and Luther which interpret the High Renaissance's emancipation from traditional demonology as the fruit of a new spiritual tension, rather than as the result of the new concept of nature that was slowly coming to the fore. This at least partly contradicts the thesis of Cassirer's historical description, which complies more with the criterion of considering quattrocento thought as having a primary function in science and art rather than intellectual independence based on the problematic and contradictory nature of the many traditions that merge therein. Cassirer thinks that the independent development of science and art in the Renaissance marks a defeat for metaphysics and its freedom-necessity antinomy.[59] Warburg did not fall into this misunderstanding typical of those who see in the author-creator subject a principle of free will. His Renaissance was certainly individualistic and pursued a form of freedom, but it was an individualism charged with tensions. It tended to acknowledge an objective world that medieval tradition still offered it and which antiquity handed down with all the authoritativeness of its perfect forms; but at the same time the independent vitality and energy of the Renaissance continuously undermined this world. If the concept of an age of transition implies a "before" and "after," in Warburg it takes on a meaning of nontemporality that aims at fixing Renaissance character in its polarities, which persist and are hence rendered objective and eternal, the constitutive elements of the human psyche and sole bearers of that struggle that marked the greatness of Renaissance works and was also their intrinsic twofold meaning.

Cassirer's Renaissance is the triumph of the modern spirit which, for the most part, is already realized in it despite, or perhaps above all because of, its opposing elements. Warburg's Renaissance is humanity facing a cosmos that has lost its compactness and coherence, and the endeavor to find a less anguished abode therein. Warburg perhaps did not have time to meditate thoroughly on the results of that endeavor, but he must not have been far from concluding that if one wants to view the Renaissance as the beginning of the modern age, the latter must always see in the former the original motives of its unhappiness and uncertainty, just as the Renaissance, with scholarly tenacity and passion, did with respect to antiquity.

Symbolic Form and Time

The history of art, myth, religion, and language, the history of every phenomenon that manifests man's spiritual creations, can limit itself to gathering facts according to their chronological sequence—the common rectilinear development of antecedent and consequent. The only relation between facts a history of this kind would take into account is the purely temporal one. The result would be the continuous loss of the material gathered, which would not be subordinated to a principle of unity or any other established law of order, but would be subject to the sole principle that one spiritual content disappears to make room for another one. If there is no investigation into the complex meaning that every product of spiritual activity subtends, or into its origins and the profound connections through which it arises, is formed, and takes on life, then there is no total insight into its correlations with the other facts and the whole thus loses its core of consistency. Cassirer opposed ideal becoming to temporal becoming;[60]

in pure flux one must identify the being proper that constitutes each single phenomenon and, vice versa, one must find in the unitary being of the phenomenon—which Cassirer conceived as a network of relations—the very thought of its becoming.

Every interpretation of the world—be it artistic, mythical, or scientific—has at base an activity of the mind that creates worlds of images. The idealistic presupposition that in Cassirer informs the research into these different worlds is based upon the principle that the real is always determined by the way it is ideated, both through static images and intellectual symbols expressing pure relations.[61] The solution to the problem of symbolic forms chosen by Cassirer is therefore of a metaphysical-speculative type; that is, it seeks to "understand how the concrete totality of particular forms develops from a single original principle."[62] He thus sets a complex system against the simple progressive deduction of symbolic forms and thereby expresses his method of inquiry: "The unity of an intellectual sphere must be determined and assured not by starting from the object, but only from the function lying at its base."[63]

In Cassirer the concept of the phenomenon is, at least originally, modeled on the Kantian one: the object presents itself to consciousness in the formal bonds that suit it; it is a construction of consciousness that only in this way appropriates the real and fixes and determines it in forms. The analysis of the mode in which this occurs must therefore precede every discourse concerning the object, since only in this way can it be grasped from within the relations that constitute it and hence in accordance with its unity with the activity of consciousness. One must therefore grasp the object at the very moment of its birth in consciousness.

Cassirer describes the spiritual world as divided by an abyss at whose margins lies, on the one hand, the object, the "thing of nature," whose basic characteristic is permanence, duration, and being, and on the other hand consciousness, which is marked by the flowing of sensations and perceptions, and hence by time, which is perpetual change, continuous death and rebirth. This drastic division would appear to be unbridgeable and would constitute the antinomic nature of the mind if there were not a median phase that fills in the abyss and determines the convergence of duration and flux, being and becoming. This median phase is symbol formation. Consciousness—pure time—is endowed with a particular creative power that produces images. Cassirer says that the basic connotation of the object is permanence, and that of time is flux. He does not clarify whether the creativity of consciousness is a sign of its identity with itself, which would be the permanence of flux, so that one can only try to interpret this spiritual force in the light of what is in his writings. Time, conceived as the continuous passage of perceptions, seems to find in the object a link with permanence and thus a possibility of transcending the level of the transitory and of establishing itself in terms of duration—symbols. Symbols participate in time but, being complex forms that transcend pure flux, they fix the object in a duration, in a network of stable relations that constitute their characteristics and determine the objective world. This latter can be known only through symbols, which in turn, springing from time, preserve the vitality of time; they are not permanent signs, but change with the changing of the totality of spiritual conditions that determine the states of consciousness.

The symbol's relationship with time appears as one of duration, permanence, a stopping of flux; and yet time continues to impose flux upon symbolic forms. This occurs because the symbolic forms are never totally separated from the sensory, but remain connected to it through expression. What remains is the activity of consciousness, which obeys certain laws; but the results of this activity change in time. Hence the results cannot be judged in themselves but their becoming must be reconstructed on the basis of the universal laws of consciousness.

Cassirer also establishes the norms of change in symbolic forms. Consciousness, this fluid and vital becoming without pause, produces forms that become more and more complex through the need, intrinsic to the creative act of consciousness, to rise above the sensory world and find its basis of duration in a more stable objective world. Thus, simple sounds and elementary utterances become increasingly abstract relations, giving rise to the history of language, to the quest for a unity more intrinsic to the character of the object and more emancipated from the conditioning that the phase of mere temporal succession in sensibility imposes.

The farther the object moves from the fragmentariness of the sensory experience, and the closer it gets to that extreme and perfect form that guarantees the duration of consciousness—the concept—the more stable and articulated the symbolic form becomes and the more consciousness regulates its own being and is enriched with increasingly objective relations. "What distinguishes empirical reality, the constant core of objective being, from the mere world of representation or imagination, is that in it the permanent is more and more clearly differentiated from the fluid, the constant from the variable."[64] Let us note here in passing that mathematical symbols, those that belong to the scientific phase of the historical course of symbols, manifest the maximum separation from the sensory. What is more, in Cassirer's opinion they are sometimes pure abstraction, so that it seems that modern science represents a terminal stage in symbolic activity, the one reserved for pure concepts of function and relation, which gives rise to a series of difficulties that will be discussed later.

The symbol, however, is still made up of sensory elements and traversed by time. The intuited object is fixed in the symbol as if the mind were temporarily dwelling in the object and vice versa. To paraphrase a famous idea of Plato's, one could say that just as the time fashioned by the Demiurge was the mobile image of eternity, so in Cassirer the symbol is the lasting, permanent image of time.

Cassirer's conception implies an interpretation peculiar to Kant and, conversely, the theory of order and function that should replace substance and being at the base of the universal principles of knowledge. Since each of Cassirer's theoretical formulations, even the most abstract one, is always accompanied by, and interwoven into, a historical view of the development of philosophical theories in thought, the theory of order or relation or function also conforms to a point of view; consequently the concept evolves from the primal thought of being—which is the starting point of philosophizing—by elaborating the idea of function. The same original relation between being and thought in Parmenides reveals the need to emerge from being's identity with itself and to set it in relation to the other. Relationship, order in multiplicity, and being-function instead of being-substance are the natural evolution of thought that abstracts more and more from the immediacy of the sensible in order to find the formal foundation, the network of connections that holds the manifold together and that constitutes the original spiritual essence.[65]

The symbolic form is therefore possible because there is established in the movement of consciousness a network of relationships, an equilibrium of meanings that goes to make up the lasting image: "'things' and 'states,' and 'attributes' and 'activities' are not given contents of consciousness, but modalities and directions of its formation."[66] Just like the categories that regulate the formation of language and myth, the categories of the scientific mind are not understood by means of their immediate objectivization. The thing-word distinction occurs only in the mind and cannot be presupposed in a substantial sense to the functions that determine it. "This is a question of taking symbolic expression in its broadest meaning, that is to say, as an expression of a spiritual entity through numbers and sensory images."[67] What matters to Cassirer is defining a principle that can determine symbolic form as a "self-contained and unitary" fundamental process. In order to be investigated in its entirety, symbol formation must possess a universal character that goes beyond the circumscribed field of its immanent use in myth, religion, and art.

"Historically we can easily see how the concept of symbol only slowly becomes ripe for the breadth and universality of its systematic meaning." The universality of the symbolic process is therefore not equally manifest in the various areas in which we encounter symbols. Cassirer wants to say that objectivity greatly determined by its limits and its original laws is made possible only by the pattern of reasoning that lies at the base of modern science. Becoming completely independent with respect to the empirical subjectivity of the senses,[68] that pattern supplies us with the tools needed to probe the functional validity of the symbol. At the base of every analysis of the formation of articulated images lies the idea of a priori structures of knowledge which operate ideally on the data of consciousness according to precise laws of connection. Therefore Cassirer feels that the symbol is that whose form unifies the multiplicity of sensory experience in accordance with relations of space, time, and causality which only now, having reached a highly evolved stage in the logical determination of cognitive principles, can be explained in all their implications and in the various domains with which they are historically linked.

Cassirer has no doubts concerning the legitimacy of attributing characteristics proper to scientific knowledge to the diverse spheres of the symbolic, because he believes in the continuous progress of symbol formation and in the unfolding of the universal in history through successive stages of evolution in the creative faculty of consciousness.

This creativity is in turn not totally spontaneous but determined by a course from the most simple—identified as what is more closely connected to the sensible, the temporary, the purely mimetic and analogical—toward what is more complex, that is to say, more abstract and more conditioned by the ideal, intellectual sphere. Thus the more complex course transcends the immediate to form itself through an ever more elaborate and precise chain of mediations.

One may very well ask whether the scientific conceptual means is suited for probing the prescientific world or the poetic world, whether the a priori structures of knowledge deduced according to the critical method can really establish certain world views in which the notion of space, time, and cause is much more fluid and not restricted within the limits of the quantitative and of measure. Cassirer's oscillation in this regard is characteristic. He does not contest the intrinsic validity of the mythical or religious world view; on the contrary, he attests to its total coherence in the conditions in which it came to the fore. On the other hand, he feels that those stages in man's relationship with the world are still too undeveloped and not yet able to realize the logical self-consciousness that the modern age already possesses to the utmost. We must therefore consider Cassirer's interpretation of mythical thought or of the structures of language to be subject to the scientific world's criteria of thought, as if myth and language were attracted by this latter sphere, included in a scheme of consciousness in evolution toward the preestablished goal, scientific knowledge and the subject-object relationship as we today understand and experience it.

The symbolic form's degree of perfection and refinement is a measure of the truth of the spiritual worlds to which it belongs.[69] This fact highlights the relationship between symbol and object, so that the more evolved the symbol is, the more clearly it represents the relation of consciousness to the world; furthermore, the symbol turns out to have a degree of evolution, that is to say, the object is increasingly adapted to the subject. "'Symbolic form' means every energy of the mind through which a significant spiritual content is bound to a concrete sensible sign and is closely attributed to this sign."[70]

The relationship between the form in which the symbol manifests itself and the content that it expresses is so close as to resemble identification. In fact, that form is the sole mediation possible between consciousness and the objective world and, what is more, content can be meaningful only through the image it takes on in the symbol.

The universality and necessity of the symbol are therefore explicated by means of two particular functions. The first is the free creativity of consciousness that fashions mediations between itself and the objective world—that is, it molds the object for itself in conformity with the principles of its innermost constitution. The second is the flow of time and the passage of every content into another content, so that the symbol also represents the order of time expressed in terms of duration. Furthermore, for Cassirer the symbol is the immediate connection of sensory elements with intellectual ones. Intuition cannot be released from the way the real is thought, that is to say, from the placing of our *I* in relationships of space and time, succession and memory.

How then can there be an initial moment in the symbolic process in which the image is still fused "immediately" with sensory intuition? How can the continuous creativity of the mind and the inevitable mediation of thought permit an immediate, unmediated stage in the cognitive process? In order to keep faith with this thesis, Cassirer must believe that the act of thinking and the formation of the symbol are originally the same thing, that is, that there is no ideal precedence of the former over the latter, as he seems to indicate in many other parts of his oeuvre. The initial and primitive phase—in the first formulations of sounds that engender language as well as in the manifestation and acknowledgment of the demon from which the deity will evolve—is characterized by the fact that consciousness has not yet elaborated the mediations, the links, that constitute the symbol and govern the objective synthesis of the sensory manifold. The problem of *immediacy* can be expressed in the following terms: the intuition of the space we move in is connected to a particular relationship with the surrounding world; it is therefore a sensory intuition interwoven with the flow of images in consciousness. In Cassirer this intuition cannot be a priori, because otherwise the bond primitive expression has with the pure cognitive act, which is still totally sensory, would not be immediate, but would already be mediated by intuition itself that is understood as pure form and thus as a framework through which the datum of sensation is organized.

With regard to "empirical thought," which Cassirer sets against mythical thought and which he nevertheless lays at the base of this latter, the critical meaning of the concept of perception is stressed: "In truth, however, what we call the world of our perception is not simple, not given and self-evident from the outset, but 'is' only insofar as it has gone through certain basic theoretical acts by which it is apprehended and specified."[71] By virtue of "a *relationship of pure judgment*," impressions are articulated and assigned to different "*strata of signification*," and this process gives rise to the concept of space as a sort of "intuitive reflex of this theoretical stratification of signification."[72]

Here one notes how Kant's pure intuition of space and time—which lends its order to the multiplicity of experience that the transcendental categories work on without taking anything away from the independence of sensory intuition—becomes in Cassirer simultaneously the sensory, disorderly immediate, pure impression and "intuitive reflex" that simply mirrors theoretical activity, like the return of the sensory impression to space and time after the categories have rendered them intelligible through intellectual connections.

"The transition from the world of the immediate sensory impression to the mediated world of intuitive, particularly of spatial, 'representation,' depends on the fact that in the fleeting series of indifferent impressions the constant relations in which they recur must gradually assume an independent character by which they are differentiated from the perpetual flux of sensory contents."[73] The fundamental activity of the categories, which are always present in the formation of the object, and which, according to the central thesis of the philosophy of symbolic forms, "must be at work wherever a cosmos, a characteristic and typical world view, takes on form out of the chaos of impressions," this absolute cognitive act is defined "little by little" in a "transition" that is revealed in a temporal experience, in a "history."[74] Here the relativity of objectivization is theorized. This function of consciousness—which is primal and, as we have seen, is an activity based on consciousness itself, the function of meaning—is differentiated according to the direction that leads from sensory impressions to the meaning attributed to them by the mind. Only in this way does Cassirer think he can explain the diversification of meanings in which reality is understood, and the evolution of symbolic forms through the relationships that constitute "the framework of objectivity" and that are perceived only gradually. There is thus a continuous shift from what is objective with respect to what is subjective in the progressive formation of experience and of its relative theoretical foundation. Yet how the same theoretical act takes on different aspects vis-à-vis perception, and how it actually changes the relationships of perception and of the image with the object, remains a problem that will never find a solution intrinsic to the act itself before the occurrence of the pure phenomenology of language and myth, and thus of impressions, feelings, and fantasy.

In Kant, on the contrary, the datum of consciousness can never be immediate, because otherwise it would not be a flux and not even assigned to a flux, but would be fixed in a formal identity and prevented from moving in a succession. Succession itself is in Kant a transcendental structure—which it would make no sense to call "immediate"—that is rather intrinsic to a synthesis of the flux and permanence of consciousness.[75]

Cassirer does not clarify that complex relationship between datum of consciousness, or sensation, and its arrangement in the structure of sensibility and intellect. That ideal precedence of the structure over the datum (despite the fact that it is impossible, as regards knowledge, to assign a precedence of the apriority over the phenomenon which, the moment it arises in consciousness, reveals the ordering action of the structure), which exists in Kant and removes the "immediately," has disappeared in Cassirer. In effect, in Cassirer the only ideal element is the creative act of consciousness that has an ideal sense of stability in the flow of impressions. In Kant the intuition of space and time is an organizational principle of the multiplicity of experience, but in Cassirer it once again presents itself with the characteristics of the immediate, which is able to organize itself only in a *successive,* even *progressive,* moment of the consciousness's creativity—the *Formbildung* (creation of forms).

If the symbol experiences a phase in which it is a simple *imitation* of the datum of consciousness and is therefore related to its immediacy (for example, in the onomatopoeic phase of language, or in mythical intuition, which in fact is called immediate), this means that the symbol is not originally a form of knowledge of the object but is such only in becoming, and it is problematical whether, as the product of a creative act of consciousness, it can then be completely introduced into that totality of mediations given by the categories. In establishing the symbol's degrees of immediacy—which per se is contradictory—and its dependence on the sensible, Cassirer contradicts his Kantian presupposition whereby there is an a priori sensible framework of knowledge.

Cassirer says we cannot search for the sense of the symbol by starting from the object taken as substantial—not because the object as a thing in itself cannot tell us anything about the form that expresses it, but because the object itself, being at one with the creativity of consciousness, is the fruit of symbolic activity and is its history, as it were, not its structure.

But he overlooks the basic fact that an immediate coincidence of the symbol with the datum of perception does not account for its history, and that the immediacy expressed in this fashion does not justify the need for mediation, that is, for relation. Nor does he stop to think that if there is mediation, then its character cannot be wholly ideal but must be structural to the datum as it manifests itself, and that pure intuition cannot be confused with sensation, and even less with perception, in a generic a posteriori. In his idea of the symbol evolving in time and history, Cassirer deprives himself of the a priori concept in the Kantian sense and reduces the concept of the transcendental to a creative force, a vitality of the thinking subject. How such vitality can be bound to the laws of thought, which are in turn conceived as the product of that vitality, or better, are the tools one acquires only in the scientific phase so as better to determine the real, will remain an unsolved problem that arises every time Cassirer strives to make understood the transition from one sphere of symbolic forms to another. And this will make the relationship between different modalities and identities of its structure incomprehensible and the original connection between subject and the world particularly fragile.

The History of Symbol Formation as a Broadening of Kant's "Copernican Revolution"

In his study on the evolution of the symbol Cassirer sets out to broaden the "Copernican revolution," that is, transfer the new subject-object relationship established in Kant's philosophy to worlds of thought in which precisely that relationship is questioned and interpreted differently.[76] At this point we can begin to verify how the initial terms of this broadening are quite unstable and contradict critical philosophy itself.[77] The broadening is thus understood as a transcending of the critical bases in order to contaminate them with the concepts of the flow of consciousness in time, of vitality, and of the mind's creativity. The very fact that symbolic expression gains in spiritual content the more it detaches itself from sensibility reveals the nonaprioristic and nonstructural character of sensibility, which in Cassirer's opinion is rather the datum of sensation, the immediate encounter with the object, something different from the mind, almost a world of nature extrinsic to the laws of thought despite the fact that sensibility plays a fundamental role in the constitution of the symbol. Here there is absolutely no trace of the purely formal character of sensibility in Kant or of the ironclad necessity that connects it to the intellect and that shows, precisely in this, that it is not wholly passive but rather an active force in defining phenomena.

Because of this deviation in Cassirer's thought, the symbol seems at times to be the primitive product of consciousness which coincides in any way and in any manifestation whatever with our knowledge of the object. At other times, however, it seems to commence at the point where language or myth begin to operate as functions and systems of relationships and no longer out of mere imitation and analogy. Thus the symbol here—as a product of consciousness—is not an original definition of the object, but the product of successive changes in the adaptation of consciousness to the object. It would therefore be better to distinguish the two levels of Cassirer's theory. First, there is the symbol as a spontaneous manifestation of the relationship between consciousness and the world—and whether this is immediate or mediated is not irrelevant, as Cassirer believes; quite the contrary, certain problems arise exactly over this point. Second, there is a conception, an idea, of the symbol which is the recovery of every type and modality of symbolic imagination from the standpoint of all the intellectual implications related to expression. Thus, according to Cassirer we have a concept of the symbol in the light of which we can legitimately analyze every totality of symbols of the mind that history presents to us.

The idea of progress does not manifest itself only from within a single symbolic sphere, but also in the transition from one sphere to another. For example, Cassirer considers artistic form *another* spiritual dimension with respect to language and myth. In fact, from the outset it is assigned a level of symbol formation more advanced than the preceding ones: "The *first* phase in artistic creation is totally differentiated from every type of 'imitation.' ... This is a question not of the pure succession, the simple historical series, of modes of concrete artistic representation, but of fundamental moments of this latter which are manifest in every degree of their development and whose differentiated relationship and dynamics in correlation with the style of each epoch, can be determined."[78]

Artistic form is thus intrinsically different from all the other forms from its first manifestation.[79] *Style* is the goal in the development of artistic subjectivity—in keeping with a pattern of Goethe's: "It is the highest expression of objectivity, not the simple objectivity of being-there, but that objectivity of the artistic spirit."[80] Thus there is an objectivity that is the continuous creation of the mind, as opposed to one that "simply exists," that is to say, to an objectivity leveled down to the pure evidence of being-there and of the existence of things.

"Being-there" objectivity is apprehended by the senses, it is "immediate," whereas "creative" objectivity is the fruit of the evolution of the mind in the progressive acquisition of an increasingly well-defined relationship between itself and the image it created. The creative function of consciousness molds the world of images that belongs to every spiritual totality of symbols and each time sets itself in a particular relationship with it which determines its degree of objectivity; and it is this degree of objectivity that Cassirer intends to investigate in every cultural sphere.[81] The awareness of acting in this relationship and the meditation upon its own creations and determinations belong to the nature of consciousness. It is this self-meditation, this "conscious energy and critical power," that sets the new form free from the old one; this is how myth gives way to religion and how the content of mythical images is transcended by the new spiritual content of religion. The change in images is contemporaneous with a change in the relationship of consciousness with images, and hence with an evolution in the content of the images themselves.

The condition of this transcendence is implicit in the constriction the symbol determines for consciousness, the limits it imposes. The mind's transition from one form to another must therefore be understood as consciousness transcending its symbols each time. On the other hand, the cognitive process leads to the increasingly profound understanding of the symbols consciousness itself uses in order to gain knowledge: "In knowledge, too, the *use* of hypotheses and principles precedes the *knowledge* of their specific function as principles."[82] Therefore in those phases of culture in which the meaning of the symbol remains obscure to knowledge, it is understood in a form that is still semimythical, as in magic and astrology. According to Cassirer, wherever substantial value is given to the symbol there is a mythical stage of knowledge.[83]

Cassirer again distinguishes between image content and ideal content. The form the image takes on, its stable connotation, refers to an ideal meaning; it represents and at the same time limits it, binding it to the world of the sensible and of perceptible form: "In mythical and religious consciousness there is on the one hand absolutely no differentiation between the image and its signification, and on the other hand a permanent tension between the two." The artistic image, however, possesses in itself, as intrinsic to itself, the ideal content. It no longer keeps man enveloped in demoniac tension. Bondage to the image is overcome as art matures. "Here the image has definitively emancipated itself from the world of action and suffering in which the mythical-religious world view had enclosed man."[84]

This thesis of the symbol, which in art would take on a totally different value from that in language and above all in myth, is verified in Friedrich Vischer's essay "Das Symbol." There is a correspondence between Cassirer's distinction between image content and ideal content and the twofold meaning Vischer attributes to the word *image* as a representation of something sensory that also serves to express something thought and conceived. In these two meanings the image is presented first directly and then indirectly.[85] Vischer takes up the Hegelian theme of the symbol's incommensurability; the sense image appears simple as compared to the totality of the manifold conceptual phases that correspond to it. Even if the sensible is elaborated conceptually, the incommensurability remains, because this conceptual elaboration creates new, puzzling connections and the properties of the image become more and more inaccessible to intellectual control. In Vischer —as in Cassirer—the bond between image and meaning indicates the symbol's mode of belonging to the different spheres of human spirituality. This bond is not a thing, Vischer says, but an act of the mind that determines the relationship.[86] In *Philosophy of Symbolic Forms* Cassirer also states that "content and expression become what they are only in their interpenetration; the signification they acquire through their relation to one another is not outwardly added to their being; it is this signification which constitutes their being."[87]

According to Vischer, the symbol is not free in religion and myth, since there is a total exchange between image and signification. Cassirer would say that the ideal content continuously shifts into the image content, and vice versa, and that this exchange determines on the one hand permanence and on the other continuous tension. "The formation of myths belongs to the obscure and bound form of consciousness, since it does not believe in its fantastic creation in a purely poetic sense."[88] Here Vischer makes a deeper analysis of that receptiveness to the symbol which is a basic characteristic of the activity of consciousness. Between poetic and mythical fantasy there is the same difference that also determines the difference between free and unfree consciousness. "He who believes in poetic fantasy does not believe in it historically, but only that part of it that is mythical reality. That is to say, he believes in it *symbolically*. This is the appropriate word for the impression of truth that mythical images inspire in us, without however our believing in the myth."[89] The myth truly becomes a symbol in rational consciousness, and one believes in the symbol in other forms than the immediate religious one—that is, blind faith—in the guise of art, poetry, and the same mythical content one now detaches oneself from. In the evolved consciousness, faith in the myth is of an aesthetic type. An image filled with sense, it is the true symbol, liberated from its unilateral identification with the sense-datum. The ideal character of the symbol manifests itself here to the full. It conceals an illusion, something unspecified, which arises during the symbol's formation at the borderline between the conscious and unconscious. What corroborates this symbol is the supreme truth whereby the universe, nature, and the mind must be one and the same.[90]

Here Vischer delimits the function of the symbol with greater efficacy than Cassirer. The fully realized symbol is the result of conscious aesthetic activity that meditates upon its own forms and in becoming conscious also takes in forms of the past while at the same time clearly distinguishing itself from them—contemplating them critically, as it were. Naturally, in this fashion Vischer is subject to Cassirer's critique of the allegorical interpretation of myth. The myth symbolized by aesthetic consciousness loses its original and independent nature. It is no longer self-explanatory but is to be explained only in relationship with the supreme form of symbolic knowledge, totally subordinated to the evolution and emergence of this latter. In order to interpret myth as a form that paves the way for philosophy, it is not right to utilize allegory—that is, a category that does not belong to the world of myths. In Cassirer's view one must reconstruct from within mythical phenomenology the stages of development of this symbolic form, which is structurally different from, but functionally similar to, the form of philosophy because it also bears witness to a creativity of consciousness striving after one sole aim—the construction of objectivity.[91]

And yet even Cassirer must agree with the affirmation that mythical thought is unable to apprehend pure ideal signification.[92] In myth the form of the image is immediately coincident with a content of reality; the evocativeness that arouses sensible emotivity and produces myth is one and the same with the mysterious entities that are thereby revealed, and this identification is so strong, its power over the imagination is such, that the intellect cannot distinguish being from the representation of being and thus adores both with equal awe.

Drawing upon Hegel's treatment of the symbol in *Aesthetics*, Vischer makes a distinction between the obscure and clear symbol.[93] But whereas in Hegel's view there exist only the two forms—unconscious and conscious symbolism—Vischer introduces an intermediate one which he calls the "symbolism of form" or "interior symbolism" or, more precisely, "empathy." This is a necessary act of the mind in all phases of the creation of symbols and only the way it is explicated changes, more or less consciously. The act of empathy is the one by which consciousness is immersed in nature and acts as if its vital energy were moving within nature.[94] Empathy is therefore related to the phenomenon of symbolic expression in its totality, which Vischer tends not to distinguish from pure form taken per se, liberated from the very sentiment of form. In Vischer, as in Cassirer, art belongs to this intermediate domain of symbol formation in which the association of concomitant representations, thanks to an inner process, shifts imperceptibly into conscious unity.

Vischer's analysis is closely connected to the study of the complex phenomenon of the beautiful which, arising from a contact between subject and object, presents itself as an interaction of several acts. The process of artistic consciousness is therefore an evolution differentiated into a multiplicity of states of consciousness—at once psychical and intellectual. The sensation of pleasure, for example, is interpreted as an increase in the general life sensation; fantasy is connected to memory, so that an image of the object through imaginative representation remains in the soul even when the object is lacking.

"Empathy grasps the object from the interior toward the exterior; it sets itself in it *centrally* and places the sentient self in its forms just like in a piece of clothing, or rather, as if it were part of its own body."[95] The relationship between imaginary sensory impressions and representations of a spiritual kind, which Vischer sets at the base of one of the most important symbolic expressions (the imitative one) is a symbolic, but at the same time intimate, type of connection in which the spiritual is really perceived in the physical and vice versa. Imitative expression is wholly unreflecting; it is the physical result of the action that a spiritual content works on sensation. The second component of the beautiful is harmony, which is the order consciousness confers upon imitative expression; it is the unifying act of this intermediate type of symbolic activity which on the one hand is bound to the sensory object and on the other is pure creativity of the functions of the *I*. Thus in Vischer's opinion, the symbol is essentially empathy; the subject enters into the object and from it takes on, in different forms and at different stages of development, an expression and an image. Furthermore, it turns out that even everything inorganic and impersonal is manifested in the symbol as an actual preliminary stage of the mind.

In his brief essay Vischer considers all those problems which—in his opinion and in keeping with the history of the concept of the symbol that matured in the post–Hegelian school—concur to form that complex and articulated part of spiritual creation: symbolic activity. Since he limits himself for the most part to aesthetics, the symbol appears there in all its distinct phases—even in the final, totally free phase that Vischer identifies with allegory—conditioned by artistic expression and the states of consciousness connected to it.

Cassirer broadens the subject matter of research and the notion of the symbol so as to take in all fields of expression. "The problem of the symbolic can be taken in such a broad sense that in the end it does not belong to any single spiritual field but is rather reduced to a systematic nucleus from which all philosophical disciplines stem."[96]

The problem of the symbol—whether it is apprehended in the immediate coincidence of image and reality in the mythical world, or whether it is part of the theme of the aesthetically beautiful, divided within itself into the sensible and intelligible at once, or last whether it is formulated as a dialectical necessity to penetrate the logical-formal world—underscores the basic polarity of being. This polarity is experience as well as an ideal point of reference, the multiplicity of facts sensibly perceived but also unity in the rule of the apperception and organization of those data. The entire world of the mind is defined and revealed, represented and made unitary, in the concrete, tangible symbol. The relationship of theory with the image is valued with greater awareness and more directly in the scientific sphere. At the height of the objective determination of thought, the use of categories is not given once and for all, but is subject—as is the case with every form of the mind—to a gradual evolution from the particular to the universal, from the individual case to the general. Consciousness pursues its broadest, most objective unity in the creation of the scientific symbol, where it can really grasp the object in its duration and not in the flux of sensations or in the partial and unilateral views of the mythical world.

From the outset Cassirer states that a description of cultural epochs, which are scrutinized as the process of the expression of spiritual links throughout history, can be effected only by starting from a theory of the symbol as the sole mediation possible between consciousness and the object, as the transcending of the immediate and of an interpretation of the immediate, and as the attainment of stability and unity in the determination of the sense-datum.[97] He rejects the traditional distinction between the physical sciences and the "sciences of the spirit" because it is inadequate for reconstructing the forms of thought he calls prescientific.

He tackles this theme of the historicization of myth precisely in the preliminary research he made for his analysis, "Conceptual Form in Mythical Thought," written in 1922. Both science and history, being historiography, move in the same sphere, that of logical knowledge. "Pure historical logic cannot give us a general idea either of the totality of these modalities related to the mythical world or of the essence that distinguishes them from one another. In fact, it belongs to the same dimension of mathematical logic, from which it wants to differentiate itself, however."[98] Neither science nor history help to explain the difference between the sphere of logical-scientific knowledge and other manifestations of the spirit, and they cannot reveal anything about the structure of radically different spiritual worlds. In the spirit's "ideal creation" of the world, independent forms are distinguished that constitute self-contained *totalities* whose regulative laws exist in particular spheres. In order to be explicated, there must be an "amplification" of logic, a different comprehension of the synthesis of the manifold that is achieved through these forms. The distinction between exact sciences and historical sciences becomes purely academic and actually tautological when one attempts to determine and distinguish spheres of spiritual reality that do not yet belong to these categories.

The mythical world is therefore called *Stufe,* a "step" in the evolution of consciousness and in the becoming of its manifestations, a fundamental, self-contained stage in the course toward science.[99] To objective determination in keeping with laws of scientific thought, Cassirer counterposes a mythical theory of knowledge still arbitrarily connected to the identification of the image with the thing and to a substantialistic notion of natural causality regulated by rules of the imagination and not by categories of the intellect. The spatial-temporal ties of mythical experience are of an extrinsic nature, they do not transcend the simple manifestation of objects; in mythical consciousness there is no awareness of the ideal nature of reality. The universal laws of change do not operate there, as will occur in the scientific world, but the modality of the relationship between consciousness and the world is bound to the sphere of the magical and to a totally concrete view of time and space, which are divided and regulated from the outset by conditions imposed by sensibility and perception.

There is a methodological distinction here; in myth it consists of distinguishing and assimilating things for their nature per se that makes them exactly as they appear to be, while in science distinction and similarity are conferred by thought.[100] It was astrology that took the first great step toward building a cosmic order that could keep the smallest parts of the universe in a cohesive whole. This was the decisive move from the notion of a fixed form of the whole to a rule of becoming, from a congruence of the several parts in the whole which deprived the part of its individual definition, to a determination of the part in keeping with the rule of the whole conceived as infinite relatedness. Cassirer asserts that the thought of causality contains within itself, at all events, a purely intellectual synthesis,[101] and he goes on to state that causality is an intellectual *explanation* of "ideal mediation" between phenomena and consciousness, that *middle term* that constitutes the concept of law in modern physics and that is lacking in the mythical world view.

The mediation that myth establishes between the subject and things is imaginative, and not yet intellectual. In conformity with its alleged Kantian formulation, the possibility of interpreting experience causally should be offered by a structure common both to sensibility and to the intellect, a structure from which one may start as if from a *primum* of every possible objective acquisition. In describing the phenomenology of the cognitive process, Cassirer affirms that the concept of cause and effect must "schematize" in intuition; that is to say, it must create for itself a spatial and temporal correlation, as if the schema—prompted by the concept's need to be represented—were to enter into the picture to place the concept in relation to intuition. Space and time remain alien to this conception of the schema as unresolved elements; therefore sensibility and the pure category of intellect are also alien.

Although he is convinced in a Kantian manner that causality must make experience possible in the schema of time, Cassirer does not manage to explain the different modality of mythical causality which, in fact, risks breaking away from intellect and shifting into sensibility without conferring an inner changeability to the structure, which then turns out to be at once an organizational principle of the changeable and itself subject to change. It is not enough to say that this structure is first and foremost a mere function of knowing and thus operates variously in the different modalities, since Cassirer establishes the laws of the changes in function only by invoking a diversity in the general structure of the principles of knowledge. When the category of causality is made to act within each totality of cultural experience as a function of that very experience, causality, because it lacks a structural relationship with sensibility, shifts precisely into that substantiality that Cassirer tries in any case to view as resolved and annulled in function.

Cassirer admits that even magical and mythical thought have something to do with a schema otherwise completely resolved in intuition. This is a schema whose direction is determined not on the basis of the primacy of the concept of time, as in Kant, but rather on the primacy of the concept of space understood as that which, determining the contiguity of things, also determines their belonging to one another.[102] By "Kantian primacy of the content of time" Cassirer evidently means privileging a principle of movement, as in the objectivization of scientific thought, neglecting to scrutinize more closely the meaning time takes on in the constitution of the Kantian schema.

While scientific space is resolved in relationships of forces, mythical space is the result of fixing forces in a concrete and clearly visible space.[103] The sense of the course from myth to science is thus fixed in the mind's need to free itself from the immediate sensory view, which is fragmentary, temporary, and transitory. It seems that when faced with a sense-datum, the mind experiences a sensation of otherness that cannot be reduced to its need for unity and identity; it knows quite well that in sensation, taken for itself, it is destined to shatter. This self-defense on the part of the mind vis-à-vis experience is evident in Cassirer's critique of astrology, whose concept of law leads to fate and hence to man's incapacity to determine becoming, whereas the modern concept of law establishes an ideal necessity as a primal and fundamental form of thinking,[104] and thus reconstructs a sphere of experience possessed in its entirety.

And yet when in *Language and Myth* Cassirer affirms that the course from myth to science is a transition from an intuition of totality to differentiated individuality, he admits that mythical representations are for the primitive consciousness the *totality* of the real. "But for the mythmaking consciousness these separate elements are not thus separately given, but have to be originally and gradually derived from the whole; the process of culling and sorting out individual forms has yet to be gone through."[105] Not being able to discern a universal law in the particular, mythical thought connects the single fact to the notion of a whole organized in a fixed, immutable, and eternal manner.

But instead of acknowledging in this procedure the activity of "involuntary thought" (as Usener called it), thus denying that philosophy can clarify the object of mythology, Cassirer views it as a process of schematization, basing his phenomenology of myth on presuppositions bound to epistemological conceptuality, and he considers the "spontaneous feeling" that engenders the figure of the deity as originating from the "ordered and continual activities of mankind."[106] It is clear that in Cassirer's opinion man intervenes in the event with an act of will and thus regulates it in keeping with his own desire and need. Here a very strong psychologistic element is superimposed on the ironclad rule of an evolution of consciousness. And the deduction of an epistemology of myth, rigorously modeled upon a similarity with the principles of scientific knowledge, avails itself of an anthropological type of phenomenology—which undoubtedly means an enriched cultural patrimony but no longer allows the philosophy of symbolic forms to adhere perfectly to an alleged universality of the system.

Along this line even the constant reference, either openly declared or understood, to Hegel's *Phenomenology of the Spirit* falls away. Where Hegel sets the beginning of science in sensory consciousness, Cassirer in fact proposes setting the beginning farther back, in mythical intuition. Since he views sensory consciousness already as an elaboration and abstraction of the datum, he identifies pure sensation, which he calls immediate, precisely with mythical intuition. It is here that the origin of science must be sought, since it is the primitive links that consciousness still obscurely establishes which will engender its true awareness of itself and the position of its relationship with the object. By setting this origin back in the history of the mind, Cassirer introduces a discontinuity in consciousness, which passes through a period of obscurity and a subsequent illumination in which the motif of will and having to be appears in the formative stage. On the other hand, he openly states that his analysis of myth depends upon necessities intrinsic to scientific consciousness itself, which thus attempts to regain a lost origin, something intrinsic to its very nature. At this point science takes in myth into its realized system and explains it through its own modalities. Science, however, must acknowledge its origin in a phase that it itself declares is obscure, "preconscious," and undetermined. It is unable to explain completely the transition to its present phase, so that the obscure phase makes its disturbing presence felt in the depths of the very structure of science, fixed in schemes that are different and that yet claim equal validity and legitimacy as far as experience is concerned.

In myth and science the categories must be the same in nature and quality, changeable only in the *modality* in which they are employed; but Cassirer in the end does not succeed in explaining this different modality except by means of "the dynamic of the life feeling," an act of passion.[107] If there is an act of passion at the base of the mythical configuration, the mythical form appears irreducible to interpretation on the part of discursive thought. Logic could never grasp the passion intrinsic to the first impulse of the mythical fact. Cassirer gets round this difficulty by observing that the life feeling nonetheless finds correspondence in pure intuition that lies at the base of every apperception of experience. Therefore the mythical world possesses the tools of spatiality, temporality, and numerability, which however are quite distinct from the tools of the scientific world. The faculty of differentiating in this case gives rise to mythical thought as well as to logical thought. If Cassirer sees the nature of mythical intuition in primordial division[108] and declares that the totality of consciousness is manifested in the symbol precisely because it distinguishes and separates in it, we must acknowledge that the identification between object and substance in myth can take place only when consciousness has already been opposed to the world and an effort has been made to transcend it in the symbolic form. Despite the attempt to set the origin, the beginning, of the history of the spirit farther back, precisely in myth, as a phase that precedes consciousness of the relationship with the object, Cassirer continues to find there the faculty of distinguishing; that is to say, it is nevertheless consciousness, which he cannot define as unconscious and obscure without exposing himself to the same treatment he so often reserved for Bergson—being accused of mysticism.[109]

If mythical thought is considered unable to apprehend pure ideal signification,[110] we must once again ask what the symbol is and why it is formed in its complete ideality only in the scientific world. We have seen that the category does not remain the same in myth; later we shall see that perception has a value in myth totally different from the one it has in science and that even the symbol—the primal function, the center of orientation round which the system of knowledge takes on form—has in myth a nature different from the one it assumes in science. It is understood as a spontaneous manifestation that the mind is able to grasp and explain only in the scientific phase. The symbol, which should always represent the result of the mind's self-awareness, and which is the source of knowledge, because without it there is no mediation between subject and object, has a history marked by a period of obscurity and unconsciousness, after which it becomes clear and receptive to consciousness. Here again one fails to understand what the motive of the passage from one modality to another consists of; nor is it clear what it is that determines the necessity of the symbol if it is not a primal means of acquiring objectivity.

The Symbol's Becoming and Consciousness

The "drama" of the symbol having an insubstantial foundation is "played out" in the third volume of *Philosophy of Symbolic Forms*, entitled *Phenomenology of Knowledge*. Here Cassirer, having arrived at the sphere of logic, faces the various problems and themes discussed in the preceding volumes that now appear before him in the light of scientific determination. While he founded the origin of language and the complex formation of mythical thought on the immediacy of the sense-datum, which as such is raised to the rank of substantial element, in the foundation of theoretical thought he affirms that simple sensation is not immediately given, but is "the expression of a theoretical supposition."[111]

Emancipation from the sensory takes place when the latter is no longer interpreted as the starting point and reference point, but as the result of a theoretical postulation which in its articulation establishes the object without any residue of sensibility and thus explains perception itself as a network of relations and as the effect of a particular attitude of the mind. In myth and in the first scientific formulations the empirical datum was pervaded with substantiality, but in science its functional aspect is recovered.

This aspect does not refer to an external reality to be organized but is the fruit of an inner organization of consciousness itself, which sets the datum in a situation that is legitimated a priori. In this way perception takes on its connotation of "function of knowledge," that is, "hypothesis," only in the scientific phase. As with the category of causality and with space and time, in the evolution of symbolic forms perception is at first something which it then no longer is, because it has become something else. It is not part of a structure but is each time the result of an interpretation. Thus, on the one hand, it seems there is an immediacy, which only subsequent theoretical elaborations demonstrate is transparent and a result of mediations; and, on the other hand, these more developed conceptual elaborations are in turn the result of the distinctions and identifications of a substantial nature that the mind makes in mythical space and time.

The motive of the passage from one symbolic form to another is essentially based on the meaning that the activity of consciousness takes on in the constitution of the symbol. The myth is the result of this activity and is therefore consciousness continuously placing itself in a different relationship with, and in absolutely real opposition to, the world. And the *I* "can contemplate itself only in this kind of projection."[112] One can therefore see that in the externalization of the image—that is, in the symbol—consciousness understands itself because it is objectified in reality, and by analyzing this latter one can understand the culture in which it operated. The symbolic form is the expression of a certain culture and it is the means for acquiring self-revelation: it is the primary tool of knowledge.

Cassirer asks whether symbolic forms represent the deepest content of consciousness, or whether they do not rather represent its continuous impoverishment and set an insurmountable barrier between consciousness and reality. With respect to the entire content of consciousness, the representative and symbolic cannot be conceived as original if it must set itself against pure perception of which it is only an ideal, subsequent, and very precisely limited reconstruction. Cassirer's answer to this problem partly eludes its intended purpose: "Without language or the other symbolic forms, we would grasp only the narrowness and opacity of sensory consciousness."[113] Since this latter is a continuous flow of data, conforming to it means being lost in that variegated and incessant world of unorganized multiplicity against which Kant erected his epistemological thought. The symbol makes that world manifest in the light of unity and relation. It conceals and at the same time reveals the creative energies of consciousness; it is the sensory foundation in which consciousness, in articulating itself, recognizes itself. "Only through form and its mediations does the pure immediacy of life acquire the structure [*Gestalt*] of the mind."[114] But the process by which one moves from immediacy to mediation, and by which mediation, in its ideal nature, continuously verifies reality, proves to be established only by the creative, inventive intervention of consciousness itself.

In symbolic signs existence springs from the meaning they take on for consciousness. While in natural symbolism the sensory content refers to a content not given immediately, in ideal symbolism consciousness creates the sensory signs themselves and by means of this spontaneous act strives for the attainment of being.[115]

This striving for a goal, the teleological character of acting, justifies history for Cassirer. The "spiritual unity of meaning" in the last analysis "must be established not in a generic and causal but in a teleological sense—as a direction followed by consciousness in constructing spiritual reality."[116] We must recognize in this finalistic process the passage from myth to science, where a self-contained totality that is also fully explicated within itself—the mythical self-sufficient being, which manifests itself as a total view and organic action of all spiritual forces—once again opens itself to the broadest totality of science. The partial directions (one might say "curves") of consciousness in every symbolic determination are related to a fundamental "rectilinear" direction toward rendering explicit the content of consciousness and the complete independence and freedom of its ideal being. The intervention of consciousness in lending form aims at the basically pure forms of scientific thought, and it is here that the rectilinear direction of the process is split in an incongruity: the categories must exist before formative activity and as functions must be its base, and yet they are the result of a slow metamorphosis of the sensory into the ideal. Cassirer's particular concept of being as what is essentially twofold and affected by a primal relatedness leads him to this determination of structure and of reality as at once the subject and the product of the subject's activity, the object and the reflex of the object's influence on consciousness.

In the introduction to the first volume of *Philosophy of Symbolic Forms* Cassirer criticizes Hegel for building the evolution of the human spirit onto the truth of the logical principle. But Cassirer likewise conceives the evolution of consciousness as aiming at the predominance of the logical over the sensory, because the latter is entirely and ideally determined in the former. The autonomy attributed to the sphere of myth, language, and art is a self-sufficiency relative to the attainment of scientific knowledge and of ideally determined objectivity.[117]

Cassirer poses the problem of whether the symbol, in its varied uses, conserves its basic function or rather does not become a mere word.[118] This is a question of determining whether the specific form, which the symbol takes on in the various spheres in which it proves to be efficacious, will allow one to maintain the principle of the unification and synthesis of the different modalities of meaning. Since the process that regulates the formation of symbols is rooted in sensibility and in the relationship that the various tools of knowledge have with this sensibility, one must broaden the investigation into the role that sensory experience assumes every time and into how it is determined and constituted. Cassirer observes that here this sensory experience is not chaotic matter that is shaped differently each time.[119]

In the phenomenon as it presents itself to consciousness, matter and form prove to be inseparable: the material and the formal coexist in sensation from the outset. The problem of sensibility and of the formal ties intrinsic to it therefore arises again each time we want to find out the difference in perspective and meaning each cultural sphere has in presenting its own characteristic symbols. "It is necessary to define the sensory as bearer of the significant."[120] In the third volume on symbolic forms Cassirer criticizes sensism and positivism in the light of the formal character of sensation: "It is the expression not of a fact, but of a theoretical supposition. It is in no way immediately given, but is postulated—and it is postulated on the basis of very definite preliminary concepts, which are themselves constructed."[121] Cassirer here takes a step forward in the explanation of the sense-datum as a meaningful entity compared to the analysis made of the formation of language and myth. Only by considering perception from a particular conceptual viewpoint can one judge its origin. Perception is recognized as having a contemplative nature that was already manifested in prescientific thought in the faithful mirroring and reproduction of the relationships consciousness has with the "external" world. The symbolic function of giving coordinates, this ideal act of meaning, is already interwoven in perception and is the primal order in which phenomena are manifested to consciousness in the datum.

Just as at the beginning of his considerations on the symbol and its formation, here too the problem of the origin of symbolic activity—that is to say, the problem of the stage of differentiation that must be intrinsic to every particular moment of consciousness—eludes Cassirer's analysis, since in his historical discourse he is more attracted by an aprioristic, *set* distinction between formal universes, each of which is constructed according to a certain *direction*. The difference is no longer examined in terms of the results of a necessary evolution of consciousness, but lies at its foundation; on the basis of this difference one must judge whether the pure form of sensibility, which acts in each of the stages, is equal in all of the formal universes or whether it takes on different characteristics in each one. The differentiated process from elementary to more complex forms is therefore internal and does not lie only in the historical course in which the various symbolic forms are interwoven and follow one another, but also lies within the very formation and evolution of the symbol.

In the prescientific (or, as Cassirer later calls it, prestructural) world there is a bond of identification between expression and sensory content: a substantial meaning corresponds to an expression and the sensory immediately reveals the meaning to which it refers. In this connection, Cassirer criticizes the concept of empathy, which fully expresses the type of relation but does not explain the cause. There must always be an objective content that transcends the limits of expression; language must show us an intrinsic relation to being and being's "consisting in itself" in such a relation. This is what Cassirer calls the "representative function of the symbol," which is followed by the meaningful function that is suspended in the "free ether of pure thought" and released from the sensory. It is "pure and abstract order." The elements of the relation thereby established cannot be grasped in themselves, they have no value outside the relation.[122]

Cassirer indicates the three levels on which the symbolic form operates, the place where its position with respect to the different spheres of stability can be identified. In these three stages the symbolic form passes through the sphere of being and the sphere of meaning that conforms to being. One would be led to think of the symbol moving along a "simple plotted line" whose various stages it must express each time, since it is its manifestation and transparence in sensory consciousness. But this simple plotted line is of such a nature that it itself—that is, the reality of the expressive and cognitive functions—moves together with the symbol, which passes through it. This alone is the duty of the symbol: to signify the changes in being or the different modalities of the function. Naturally, from such a standpoint it is impossible to construct a unitary pattern of symbolic meaning. If on the other hand the simple plotted line, the teleologically determined level, of consciousness making itself explicit, could be conceived as stationary, it would no longer explain in any way the differentiation and evolution of symbolic form. Expression, representation, and meaning are the image's peculiar spheres of stability, and in the passage from one to the other history evolves from one symbolic sphere to another, while the symbol remains more or less in one or the other in conformity with its greater or lesser distance from sensory intuition. Cassirer gives over the attainment of the pure sphere of meaning to modern mathematics and symbolic logic, which establish a system of pure relationships that is totally freed from all bonds in intuitive existence. Here the subject has disappeared, or better, it has been entirely assimilated into the relational and functional nature of the objective world of science.

The role of intuition is no longer that of referring to the thing understood in a substantial sense; intuition is completely reabsorbed by the system of relationships that goes to make up the object of experience as it is understood in modern science. Space, which gave rise to language because of the need to indicate the subject's position with respect to the external world, is not the physical-ideal space expressed in increasingly abstract symbols. Spatial meaning in the earliest linguistic expressions is still sensible and material, since space itself is not part of a permanent structure but is a setting in a relation that concerns a sensibility still considered entirely a posteriori. Space is distinguished from the concept of space as it is determined in mathematical physics.[123] Here we need only quote the comparison Cassirer establishes between mythical and aesthetic space, which are basically similar in that they both constitute a vital, concrete space: "There is no universal and stable intuition of space; space draws its specific content only from sensible order, in which it takes on form."[124] The relationships of order, in which the sensible takes on form and is organized, determine space and time. However, order is a relative concept. Therefore there is no *form* to unitary and unifying space; rather there are distinct conceptions of it.

It would seem that Cassirer, in broadening the Copernican revolution, wants to take intuition from its pure formal sphere and make it become a part of the evolutionary historical process of the mind. Intuition's predominance over meaning is therefore a prescientific stage of the mind in which symbolic activity is not yet emancipated from sensibility. Upon closer scrutiny this contamination of Kantian epistemology, which Cassirer himself calls Platonic, appears to be wholly arbitrary. In fact, time—which in Kant is the most internal and essential structure, not only of the cognitive process but also of the very nature of the subject and hence of the unitary foundation—cannot be made into a level on which the evolution of the mind is revealed and on which the different forms become truly extrinsic to one another. Expression, representation, and meaning are the fabric of symbolic structure, and at the same time one expects to verify the concrete passage from one to the other in history. The unitary development in the historical process is rendered dubious by a failure to demonstrate the diversities, whose problem Cassirer feels he can solve by having the modalities of being manifest themselves variously to consciousness. He does not explain, however, how it is possible for a system of relationships to hide and later manifest itself in keeping with different modalities.

Cassirer attempts to construct a model of unitary development, a system of evolution, for all forms of culture by taking each of them back to the ideality of epistemological functions. If there is a part of sensibility that is active, producing images that adapt the datum of perception to the spiritual content, these images or symbols are always partly sensible and partly intellectual. For Cassirer this is the new relationship established in critical idealism between sensibility and intellect.[125] And yet sensibility's contribution to the production of symbols decreases as the latter are transformed from mythical, religious, and linguistic symbols into pure intellectual ones. This is why sensibility plays no structural role in the constitution of the symbol but is only functional to its historical evolution. It is a role that is transcended in becoming because it cannot be constitutive of the unity of consciousness, since it is only its ideal and negative stage, expressing a reality to which it does not belong.

But how can time be both the internal fabric of forms and the level on which they develop? The difficulty Kant finds himself in his *Analytic of Principles* is that one cannot give a purely conceptual determination of time. Kant attempts to create a transcendental dimension as the only one capable of defining logic in time, because he posits it "within the bounds of possible experience." He bases it, that is, upon the a priori nature of sensibility and even of "sensation in general," that ambiguous element of sensibility which is, as it were, a symbol of the thing-in-itself and of the passage in consciousness of "transcendental matter." The difficulty is that if time must be the foundation of self-consciousness, if it must be the principle of the synthesis of representations and the mean between categories and sensibility, it must be something permanent and thus can no longer flow. As a structure it cannot admit that time as flux passes through it.

In Cassirer the problem of experience never materializes. In his view sensibility is a posteriori, the fragmentary and mutable. Ideality is not the demonstration of a "transcendental truth" that in its structure must be able to precede "empirical truth," which in turn must at every moment necessarily manifest the order of the former, but is a historical acquisition of the mind and proceeds from undeduced empirical reality to a conceptual awareness of the empirical; ideality is a self-criticism of consciousness during the flow of time, and not a criticism of the becoming of consciousness. This leads to a continuous lack of clarity in the concept's relationship with the sense-datum and in the relationship of consciousness itself with its history, which is partly dominated by the symbol as a functional constant in the mutable elaboration of the real and partly involves the symbol itself, which changes relatedness each time, almost as if there existed spheres of the real-in-itself that determine its validity and system of relations. Cassirer's conception of sensibility is connected to a sort of residue of substantial reality as it was understood in the prescientific world. Being bound to perception as an immediate datum also means being bound to an existence per se of the object of perception, and it is precisely the symbol that is constituted on the basis of this connection. The ideality of the symbol contradicts the origin of the symbol.

This contradiction does not exist in Warburg's thought. In fact he viewed the symbol as the bearer of a twofold ideal meaning. On the one hand, it originally represents the possibility of lending a fixed, nontransitory form to the conflict between consciousness and the chaos of the indeterminate external world, and it reproduces itself every time it is necessary to exorcise the irrational turmoil of life. On the other hand, the symbol does not conciliate the polarity that generated it, for this latter continues to have the same effect on whoever contemplates the symbol, because the very moment the polarity liberates creative imagination, it binds it to a preestablished scheme.

The process of idealization that Warburg observed as a feverish endeavor in the early Renaissance and that he saw come to fulfillment in the great sixteenth-century artists, consists in a supreme intellectual effort to wrest from the image its relationship with tradition and yet develop its primitive power in the individual's new and independent consciousness of his destiny. Taking recourse to a permanent essence of the image corresponds to the need to remain within the sphere of sensory expression, which can never be fully resolved in pure abstraction, since concrete experience is a constant datum that cannot be transcended. Creative power is realized instead in a meaningful variation of both the historical course it takes and the movement to which it is subjected because of the tension that dominates it.

In Warburg's view the history of images is a history not of changes in meaning or evolution, but of variations achieved by an inventive capacity which, far from reconciling polarity, reproduces it constantly and thus transmits the primal creative energy. This energy runs out only by losing awareness of its relationship with the world and thus by its memory of itself becoming obscure.

In Cassirer the apex of the symbolic process lies in scientific concepts, where the symbol expresses the real in pure relations and translates the categories into the function of continuous movement in contrast with the static nature of the relations established by mythical thought. In Cassirerian terms this should mean that consciousness has constructed symbols that are wholly appropriate to its flux, that its creation coincides with its movement and that it therefore has total knowledge of itself in its nature of continuous flux. In the beginning there should be consciousness's indeterminate becoming which, in evolving through successive imperfect determinations, succeeds in achieving its becoming in the purest manner—by means of relations of order without any contact with the sensible. Therefore when the totality of possible experience is made available to consciousness by the rules that permit its constitution, when experience can be anticipated, it paradoxically has also become useless because the ideal coincidence of consciousness with itself exhausts this totality and hence becoming as well.

Cassirer believes that the totality of the spirit cannot all be present at the same time, but must develop in an analytical process. The beginning and end of this process "must apparently conflict," but the tension is merely that between "potentiality" simply given in the logical scheme and its full organic development.[126] Yet we cannot visualize a totality that is not simultaneous and primal. The experience of the successive acquisitions of consciousness renders the function of ideal totality problematic, since this function should be only a tool for the determination of possible experience. If it must be manifested by degrees, we must visualize it as substantiality, and there arises the problem of being which unfolds in history and which—neither examined nor defined—lies at the base of the function. If one speaks of the process of culture, one cannot do so in terms of totality because it then becomes difficult to conceive becoming that is stationary in totality.

The scientific symbols that express pure relations and are simple and abstract functions of movement evidently represent a moment of standstill and stability in becoming. Is it here in this stationary point that historical becoming comes to a halt, nullifying its connection with possible experience, or does becoming remain uncorrelated with the symbol and thus conceptually undeducible?

How can the symbolic function change its position with respect to consciousness in such a way as to become first a substantial identification with the object and then an expression of pure relationships? Cassirer replies that this occurs because of its purely ideal character, which at first is not evident to consciousness and only in the scientific phase fully manifests itself. Consciousness has not yet arisen before this totality of meaning, since it has not yet determined its own sensible object. But the mythical symbol as well is an acquisition of consciousness, which recognizes this symbol because it has created it. Thus there can be no historical epochs in which consciousness, unaware of its own activity, dwells upon transitory forms of the interpretation of the world.

The problem of modality, which is the criterion of differentiation among the various symbolic forms, arises from the outset in the formulation of this theory. In Cassirer's analysis of the symbol the result of consciousness, the effect produced by the mind's activity, is not so fundamental as is the need, innate in the mode of knowledge, to posit consciousness in relation to the world of things it represents for itself. Cassirer holds that the ideal value of the foundation of consciousness lies in its being the rule that connects the manifold in the symbol. The function that determines the development of the central categories of apprehension—that is, time, space, and causality—must always be the same and have a universal character. Its abstract universality consists in the original placing in relation and in the spiritual activity of distinguishing and unifying. But since Cassirer examines the function in history, that is to say, in the succession of the different spheres of knowledge, he must again make that universal foundation relative to the various cognitive conditions.

"The relation of the appearance to the psychic meaning that is expressed in it; of the word to the meaning presented through it, and finally of any abstract sign to the meaning content to which it points—all this has no analogy in the manner in which things stand side by side in space, in which events follow one another in time, or in which empirical changes are produced by one another; its specific meaning can only be taken from itself but not explained through analogies from the world that is made possible only by this meaning."[127] The interpretation of the original fact, which makes this meaningful relationship manifest, breaks up the union with itself; and the conferring of meaning produces that breach that lies at the origin of change and progress. "The moment in which any particular sensory impression is used symbolically and understood as a symbol is always the dawn of a new era, so to speak."[128] In order to conserve the ideal meaning of the consciousness-experience relationship, where experience is for consciousness at once action and passion, Cassirer no longer conceives the function as always equal to itself, but rather as becoming, and this becoming presents itself not as receptiveness but as a determined and sealed off proceeding that follows a necessary design and a direction preestablished in the very nature of consciousness and of its relationship with experience.

Thus on the one hand the permanent function, the origin of change, and on the other the function's effects that in their multiplicity reveal the becoming nature of the consciousness-experience relationship, are examined and juxtaposed on an equal footing. The becoming nature of this relationship proves to be ambiguously composed of permanence and change, without Cassirer's evincing a clear awareness of this difficulty or offering any further deduction concerning the simple position of relatedness. The "one-many" relation intrinsic to the nature of consciousness is conceived as primal because the "one" is not abstract but is *in* the "many"; the constitutive rule of the whole is already entirely present in the part: the instant intrinsically (Cassirer says "intentionally") refers to the different moments of time, the point is determined by the totality of positions in space, the number contains in itself the principle of the entire series of numbers. However we must note here that it is one thing to say there is a universal rule that aprioristically constitutes the possibility of experience, and quite another to identify this rule with the functions of becoming in consciousness. Consciousness would in fact be the rule, and at the same time would represent the exception of the rule, constantly differentiating itself from itself in the various modes of empirical realization of the rule. Therefore the becoming of the symbolic form is always led back to a creative activity of consciousness that is presupposed and, in the end, verified in another undeducible element; that is, in the evidence of historical change.

It is necessary to postulate a creativity in order to explain becoming, because the latter cannot be deduced from the rule. If the one is in the many because it is their structural rule and the many are in the one because they are its structure, the relationship between the one and the many is stationary, defined in the identity of one and many or in the identical reflection of the one in the other "ones": thus we fail to understand how this static situation can engender a moving and changing one.

"Logical 'one in many' which appeared with identical meaning in the most diverse stages of concretion" is "unity of the relation by which a manifold is determined as inwardly belonging together."[129]

The breach between the logical world and the ontological world is in Cassirer defined by the will to grasp the manifold not in its essential relationship with unity, but as being organized in keeping with an ideal type of unity always relative to the different connecting function of the manifold.

In the chapter on the intuition of time in the third volume on symbolic forms, Cassirer uses Leibniz's concepts to explain this fundamental conception of the "expression of the manifold in the one," characteristic of the monad, an expression that fundamentally holds true as much for the future as for the past.[130] Memory has a creative function that unites and synthesizes experiences, thus creating new data in the form of symbols. The sum of the completed experiences determines the experience present in memory. The intention of consciousness in relation to the past, the perspective in which past becomes present in consciousness, is represented here. The symbolic function of memory lies in the *reference* to the past that consciousness effects simultaneously with the act of presentation. Only in this condition can consciousness represent an experience for itself and transcend pure presentation, since presentation is perceived in the fabric of the moments that necessarily follow one another and, just as the past is already inherent in the present moment, so the present moment bears the preceding one along with itself. The perception of the present is also immediately the perception of the potentiality of the following moment. There is an "expectation" in consciousness, an orientation toward the future which justifies memory at the same time that it totally determines the action by giving it the ideal character of anticipation of the future.[131] In this sense historical time, the time of culture, takes on its full meaning for Cassirer. "Only a being who wills and acts, who reaches into the future and determines the future by his will, can have a history; only such a being can *know* of history because and insofar as he continuously produces it."[132] Here the "living impulse of will," which projects the present image of the self in a future, is associated with creative imagination.

The symbol is not only an immobile image of the becoming of experience, but it originates in a time articulated as a reference to the past and expectation of the future, and thus possesses an inner vitality that shapes both the past and future of consciousness. "Every phase of action now occurs in view of an ideal plan, which anticipates the action as a whole and which ensures its unity, cohesion and continuity."¹³³ The history of culture finds its characteristic unitary form in the expression of a "mode of vision" of consciousness which is directed as much at the past as at the future but does not always have the same relationship with memory and expectation, as it varies it from epoch to epoch, thus determining the different world views. The symbol is the reproduction of a connection originating in the time of consciousness, the connection of the succession of moments in keeping with a rule. But this ideal law of history is based upon the particular nature of consciousness, which flows in equal measure toward the past and the future, taking shape in both directions as action and will. The unitary direction toward the future is the sense of progress ensured by the aim that guides consciousness and by the ideal goal that governs movement. Progress in history is therefore based at once upon freedom of action and on the need to have an intrinsic aim.

"Only to the degree in which the spirit 'becomes,' to the degree in which it unfolds toward the future, can it see itself in the image of the past."¹³⁴ Cassirer criticizes Bergson's theory of time—which he often compares with his own—in that Bergson privileges the past more than the future, that is to say, he privileges authentic memory, recollection of the past, as a glance into the depths of the self, more than action, which in Bergson corresponds only to the restricted utility of the moment. He also criticizes Bergson for his biologistic interpretation of the *élan vital*. Yet Cassirer makes the contrary mistake: he privileges the moment of action, thus the turning to the future, basing temporal dynamics on the "will" of consciousness. So, despite the fact that many critics refuse to acknowledge this and despite Cassirer's endeavor to eliminate it, there is undoubtedly a strong psychologistic element in his manner of determining the dimensions of time. These are built upon consciousness's modality of presenting itself, first of all as pure becoming and thus as a glance directed at both past and future. In fact, while it is becoming, consciousness creates symbols, anchoring itself to a permanence of the object, which is only the function of permanence because the object in reality changes along with the necessary change in symbols. And consciousness's relationship with the time from which it becomes and with the time toward which it is projected, is manifested in symbols. As such the symbols must preserve for consciousness the memory of itself and at the same time drive it to create new forms. Evolution thus presents itself as a continuous creation of symbolic forms and at the same time as a progressive emancipation from them. Consciousness is intertwined with its own history, which symbols both produce and make manifest. Once transcended and transformed, however, the symbols remain in historical memory and are not obliterated. In fact, the level of history, though a product of consciousness, transcends consciousness itself and becomes the level of the spirit; this new level is all ideally unfolded, it suggests to consciousness what its goal should be, liberates it from the bondage of the immediate and from the limits of sensory experience and is the necessary harmony of that ideal cosmos represented in the incessant symbolic metamorphosis of consciousness itself.

Beyond change, the residue symbols of becoming remain in the past: the static forms from which time once drew its strength and vitality and which have remained to characterize self-contained epochs of history. In order to be interpreted correctly, these symbols must be viewed as a constitutive part of the spirit's becoming, one must note in them the life that is by now no longer action since the dynamic reality present in consciousness, the dynamic reality through which consciousness is called upon to judge the world, has changed. Consequently, the spirit must always be present in its ideality in order to take in those moments of the past abandoned by time which live again only by appearing in a different symbolic representation. The spirit must therefore transcend becoming, which is impossible, precisely because becoming in Cassirer's view is always becoming of the spirit.

But if the spirit becomes, what happens to mythical symbols, the momentary gods, the totems, and the mysterious power of *mana*? The past can exist only in the present modification of the symbol, in the latest representation of reality, so that it will always be impossible to understand that which is no longer, and myth will never again be accessible to our consciousness except in its present metamorphosis. The past phases of civilization, the prescientific epochs, can make themselves transparent only in the light of the concept, which simultaneously modifies them; therefore they are in themselves always opaque and inaccessible in their autonomy and self-contained signification. What are the signs that history has handed down in a form that evidently has nothing at all to do with either consciousness or the spirit as they are conceived by Cassirer? Where does the possibility of writing a history of those signs lie, without this endeavor failing because of the violence of that eternal present which is metamorphosis, the becoming of the spirit?

Or are we, in the wisdom of our world view, recapitulating all past world views, in the sense that *this* view contains them all and even maintains their proper position in time? Perhaps Cassirer really thinks that humanity has reached the final, all-embracing stage of civilization in which the history of the spirit, being fulfilled, is unfolded in its perfect clarity. But if the spirit continues to become (and how could it cease to do so?), the past will never be a "document," but will change continuously, thwarting at every moment this interpretation of the past which must continuously adapt itself to the changing color of its symbols. This Cassirerian time is truly a god that devours its children, and the pure functionality of scientific logic will never be able to replace the newborn child with a stone in order that the problem of history may be presented once again.

We have seen the contradictions in Cassirer's theory of the symbol. Although it undoubtedly contains details that are important and even essential for the reconstruction of historical epochs, the general system is vitiated by profound incongruities, by optimistic ideal impulses that are not matched by a solid unitary view, and last by attempts at conciliation that do not always make due allowance for the nature of the terms to be conciliated.

My aim has been to isolate certain works of Cassirer's written in the 1920s without setting them in relation to his works on philosophy and the history of culture before that time, that is, before he began teaching at the University of Hamburg. The theory of symbolic forms was written almost entirely afterwards, even though the philosopher's intuition of the problem had come to him some years earlier.[135]

The basic theses, which were important to emphasize here, therefore concern the origin of the symbol in the sensory expression of an ideal process, and at the same time its historical origin prior to the epochs characterized by scientific thought. The symbol is both the expression of an attitude consciousness takes regarding the senses and the meaningful expression of a totally organized and self-contained world view. Man's fate and condition in the cosmos is manifested in the symbol, but only because symbolic activity itself lies at the base of this condition, is conceived in an ideal sense, and has its own directions and modalities—so that the experience that derives from it is imprinted and determined by a precise plan of historical evolution toward an aim.

I have attempted to demonstrate the incongruities this view lapses into in its theoretical development, without dwelling on the imposing resources and apparatus, the solid historical-philosophical preparation and background that sustain it—though it must be said that these are not sufficient to solve the basic contradictions of Cassirer's view and, on the contrary, are often overwhelmed by such contradictions. These incongruities do not thoroughly take into account the activity proper to symbol formation and thus prevent Cassirer from also shedding light on the history of the symbol and on how it became the history of the spirit and its significance.

I have noted more than once how essential the subject-object relationship is to this history, a relationship which for Warburg takes on form as a relationship between subjective vitality and an artistic or symbolic style of representation. We shall see how in Panofsky's view the consciousness of this relationship, which arose in the Renaissance, becomes in the artistic sphere total awareness and the capacity to act intellectually upon that very relationship only with seventeenth-century aesthetics, with the emergence of the new idea of the artist and his work as ideally organized and inspired.

Cassirer examines the subject-object relationship in that "intermediate domain"[136] of symbolic forms. He follows the formation of the object in human consciousness through a process of idealization, a process in which the object is referred to laws and relations of a purely ideal nature by a subject who only through this intellectual and form-creating course succeeds in knowing himself and detaching himself from the pure flux of life.

In his 1930 essay on the philosophy of Max Scheler, Cassirer makes some interesting observations on contemporary thought, on the life-spirit duality that emerges in it, and on his own relationship with Hegel. The contrast between real life energies and the ideal and purely teleological energies of the spirit is rendered irremediable by the two completely different worlds in which the two energies take on form, and therefore the common task one would like to see them destined for also becomes unrealizable.[137]

The absolute difference, the dichotomy of values, in contemporary philosophy is quite removed from the aesthetic harmonization between nature and spirit effected by Schiller and from Hegel's theory of overcoming; rather it stems from the romantic antithesis between life and knowledge, a bipolarity that gave rise to a host of conflicts and breaches. In choosing to inquire into the sphere of symbolic forms, Cassirer makes a distinction between an energy of action, characterized by immediacy, and an energy of pure formation [*Bilden*] and the creation of images. The latter kind of energy belongs to a sphere that does not correspond to reality but is a world of signs, symbols, and meanings.[138] It imposes a direction upon creativity and aims at attaining a new consciousness of reality in which the subject moves outside himself and contemplates himself through the mediation of this movement. This pure formation is, in Cassirer's view, common to artistic creation and to intellectual and scientific activity.

While the spirit as it is determined by Scheler becomes gradually ontological and contains a metaphysical residue that does not conciliate the antithesis but rather stimulates it, pure form as a creative act has an exclusively formal nature.[139] In this way each form can retain its entire polarity, which is in itself antithetical, as a twofold movement and continuous exchange between forces of attraction and repulsion that constitute its energy.[140] Precisely in this duplicity of determination the act of forming and creating symbols "casts the world behind it" and erects a barrier between *I* and the world, something that never occurs in the domain of pure vitality. But it is exactly in and through this new world of the imaginary, of appearance, and of play that humanity regains the world of the real.

The profoundly aesthetic meaning of this observation of Cassirer's is made explicit when he refers to Schiller's essay "On the Aesthetic Education of Man," where the poet states that man must *only play* with Beauty, but also must play *only with Beauty*.[141] Play, as an act of pure formation in the ideal, abstracted from all reality, not only opens up the sphere of beauty, but also that of truth.

Thus in order to surmount Scheler's antithesis, one must conceive the spirit as a movement of life itself, a motion that passes from the circle of organic creation to the circle of ideal creation. The error in contemporary philosophy lies in the misunderstanding it has established as regards Hegel's concept of life as it is expounded in his early writings, but above all in *Phenomenology of the Spirit*.[142] It is singular how Cassirer here adopts Hegelian categories which are most thoroughly determined in *Science of Logic*—such as attraction and repulsion and self-mediation in appearance[143]—and, on the other hand, how he couches his philosophical discourse in openly Warburgian terminology: "The eternal pathos of the spirit is its conflict with itself";[144] every symbolic form has an inner *polarity*. This polarity reveals the true nature of human beings, which lies in a turning against itself in a self-destructive tendency, since man is a being capable of putting questions but is eternally subject to questions.

This intrinsic contrariety does not destroy the symbolic form, it does not rend it romantically, but rather creates the conditions whereby its unity can rise above the contrast and be represented externally.[145] Cassirer arrives at this concept of eternal mobility—in which the unitary result must be distinguished—through an analysis of language, which is never the same and which in usage reveals its activity and its struggle to realize change as well as to consolidate itself in entirely meaningful concepts.

Here, as in other parts of Cassirer's philosophy, there comes to light his particular sensitivity to the aesthetic aspect of symbol formation. In fact, the nature of the symbol seems to endure essentially in the domain of aesthetics, the sphere of sensory representation, which is the only one suitable for expressing the reality gained through a laborious process of mediation.[146]

It is therefore incorrect to maintain that after his book on the Renaissance Cassirer moved away from artistic subjects to immerse himself in epistemological studies.[147] His long and intense working relationship with Warburg's circle had lent a particular stamp to his original classical culture and education, above all to his profound knowledge of Goethe and Schiller, who were always interwoven in such a typical manner in the fabric of his philosophical speculation. The problem of aesthetics, understood as the theory of sensibility, worked a strong, impelling influence on Cassirer's theory of the symbol and on the historical-philosophical conflict between the different forms of knowledge that he had placed at the center of his research, as well as on the theory of the phenomenon of the beautiful from which truth transpires—a theory that followed him in his constant references to

Plato, in the studies that surrounded him at the Warburg Institute, and in his unceasing comparison with the research Panofsky was carrying out on the same subject in order to give a theoretical basis to the history of art.

3

ERWIN PANOFSKY

"Eidos und Eidolon" and *Idea*

The first volumes of the Warburg Library's *Vorträge* and *Studien* series came out in 1922 and 1923, respectively, and featured two essays by Cassirer: one on the symbol in the "sciences of the spirit" and the other on mythical thought. This shows how readily Fritz Saxl, then acting director of the institute, had perceived and appreciated the philosopher's contribution and how the subjects he was dealing with in *Philosophy of Symbolic Forms* had taken on a position of primary importance in the institute's activities. In Saxl's opinion, Cassirer's formulation of the problem of myth and of the image in history was quite in keeping with the characteristics and aims of the Warburg Library and of its founder, who at the time was in a Swiss sanatorium because of his serious, distressing illness. Saxl hoped to arrange a meeting between Cassirer and Warburg as soon as possible because he felt the philosopher was the person most fit to persuade Warburg to find the strength necessary to return to his post as director of the institute and also to resume his important research. Cassirer's solid and vast culture, the serenity and trust he inspired, his systematic and unifying view of knowledge, the calm and optimistic nature he manifested in his daily school and private contacts must have convinced young Saxl that his personality was an essential complement to Aby Warburg's prodigious knowledge and experience, which were interwoven into his tormented and apprehensive disposition and were the result of gruelling efforts to attain rationality and measure.

Saxl spent quite some time preparing the meeting, which finally took place in the Kreutzlingen rest home in 1924. It was an alternation of lucid, erudite discourses and pauses of horror into which Warburg, suddenly assailed by the obscure demons that persecuted him, often lapsed. But the visit, as Warburg himself wrote in one of those strange expressions of nocturnal happiness he sometimes found the courage to experience, was "truly successful." And in fact Warburg returned to Hamburg and to his studies shortly afterwards.[1]

It is singular and interesting to note that neither Saxl earlier, nor Panofsky or Edgar Wind later on,[2] and above all not even Warburg himself, ever pointed out that, over and above the similarity in culture and perception, there was a profound theoretical difference between Warburg and Cassirer, whose relationship had become one of steadfast friendship marked by reciprocal esteem. In fact, they seem to have taken opposing and irreconcilable paths to give a historical base to the symbol or image that would explain their evolution, change, or immutable permanence in the thought, representations, and customs of the different epochs of human history. Between Cassirer's seminars at the University of Hamburg and the meetings at the institute, and above all in that atmosphere of gloomy omens so typical of the Weimar Republic, that fundamental difference in historical-theoretical formulation was resolved by the common objectives of their research, the kinship of their goals. The two schools, of such different origin and formation, proceeded together, each with its own characteristics, in the endeavor to construct knowledge as a totality where even the apparently insignificant detail was taken from obscurity, given meaning, and continuously drawn into a broader sphere in which it could reveal its true and whole being.

The second volume of the *Vorträge*, published in 1924, contained an essay by Cassirer entitled "Eidos und Eidolon" that concerned the problem of the beautiful and art in Plato's dialogues. In this study Cassirer delineates a problem of cultural history whose object is a theme fundamental both to philosophical speculation and, more in particular, to the research on symbolic forms that Cassirer was carrying out at that time. It is the problem of the essentially Platonic nature of all art theory (or speculation on art) developed after Plato, especially after the severe ban he had pronounced, which declared art to be unsusceptible to thought. In fact, Plato's philosophy is always in some way a point of reference in any attempt to transcend that dichotomy between the sensible and intelligible that might obstruct the intellectual consideration of art since it is a pure object of the senses.

Cassirer explains the dichotomy implicit in aesthetic idealism which marked all Neoplatonism, including its influence on the art theories of the Renaissance. This antinomy consists in the endeavor to take the sensory fact that constitutes the artistic experience back to form as it is understood in the Platonic sense, without the particular manner and direction of artistic creation being dispersed into a total abstraction, the pure universal of form.[3]

Thus, in the history of aesthetic thought after Plato, Cassirer singles out a tension between the concepts of *eidos* and *eidolon*—form and image—a tension that originated in the conception of form as it is expressed in Plato's philosophy. In Cassirer's view, Plato goes beyond that sensory schematization of the concept of being that still predominated among the pre-Socratic philosophers. At that time Cassirer was firmly anchored to this thesis, as is demonstrated in his contemporaneous essay "Goethe und Plato" by the opposition between the pure myth of being in Eleatic philosophy and the notion of the first true *logos* in Plato.[4] According to the method of transcendence typical of Cassirer's historiography, one observes how Plato is the first to "raise" philosophical consideration from the sphere of pure being to that of form, understood as the ordering principle of the real. Nature is not a pure concept inherent to material things but, through the eternal order that dominates it, takes part in the domain of forms.[5] Cassirer cautions against the dichotomous view of Plato's philosophy as an idea of universal genera as opposed to the multiplicity and particularity of things. In reality it is thought, along with the unity of the concept, that must dominate every particular form. In order to do this knowledge cannot dwell on the sensory world—which is fugitive and transitory and not subject to normative mediations, and as such is dominated by contradiction—but must abstract from becoming, in which the immediate datum is always resolved, in order to reach a sphere of coincidence with itself, a sphere of the permanence of logical rule, the only one through which it can achieve the stability of true being.

Both the natural and artistic phenomenon belong to the sphere of the pure image, so one can have only a fleeting notion of them.[6] The concept of knowledge excludes from itself the concept of becoming. Only by distinguishing himself from the concept of becoming can the knowing subject organize himself; he sets the known object before himself and establishes himself in relation to it by delimiting and determining it. In his interpretation of Platonic philosophy, Cassirer, in order to avoid one dichotomy, seems to lapse into another, no less serious one: that between knowledge and being. If knowledge achieves being by abstracting from becoming, and its stability and identity lend stability and identity to being, being is determined by knowledge and even draws its essence from knowledge. But Cassirer does not offer an explanation of how one can still note a difference between them. Above all, his brief quotations from *Theaetetus* and *Cratylus* cannot, from this point of view, be legitimately set again into the context from which they were taken.

In fact it is no accident that, in starting from his method of inquiry, Cassirer sees the contrast between form and image in Plato's philosophy as a contrast between ideal form and sensory form in which the term *ideal* takes on the particular meaning of "ideally constructed," that is to say, a transcendental sense that is not natural to the very treatment of the problem of knowledge in Plato. In *Theaetetus*, the fundamental question in which in Plato's opinion the epistemological theme is to be identified, is not so much the distinction between sensation and idea, which should then be conciliated and connected or remain absolutely separate to yield true knowledge; it is rather the difficulty Plato himself encounters in defining knowledge of the different and in finding the criterion of distinction between truth and error, being and nonbeing. In the long and tense discussion in which Socrates and Theaetetus try to justify false opinion, an argumentation that is mysteriously suspended at the end of the dialogue, knowledge seems to be imprisoned in the identity and unity of being, which do not allow it to gain access even for a moment to that world of multiplicity and difference (and, as certain passages in the dialogue imply, to the world of temporality) in which judgment meets up with its validity or falsity. The contradiction between *eidos* and *eidolon* that Cassirer notes is therefore in *Theaetetus* not the opposition between two worlds, the intellect and the senses, but is the contradiction that takes place in knowledge itself when it is forced to admit it knows the false and sees nonbeing.

In this regard Cassirer makes the same mistake in his interpretation as Natorp makes when, precisely in discussing *Theaetetus*, he writes that the soul (which he translates with the word *consciousness*) is not a concept expressing substance but rather indicates the function, identical with ourselves, by means of which we achieve the determination of the sensible in thought.[7] He does not see that the doubt that animates Socrates' quest and the same perplexity in Theaetetus lies in whether it is possible for this function—which because it is unitary and identical unifies time and the manifold in which sensation is manifested—to justify false thinking, that is to say, nonbeing. It is no accident that Natorp refers to the theme of connections or relations which comes up at a certain point in *Theaetetus* (in his opinion these are what epistemological activity primarily works on) without seeing how Plato so promptly rids himself of this apparent solution by identifying the elements of the relation with the relation itself and by making the latter the entire first principle that does not admit of any distinctions into parts.[8]

After having confirmed that the image in Plato belongs to the world of opinion, which is wholly distinct from the world of thought and true knowledge, Cassirer proceeds with his inquiry by tackling participation, the concept of which is indissolubly connected to the concept of separation. "The world of pure forms places separation in the phenomenon, but not in order to judge it as total negation. The purely null could not in fact even appear."[9] Already in purely transitory and ephemeral things there appears a stable order, a relatedness that is reducible to mathematical laws. Cassirer therefore feels it is possible to follow a Platonic path toward the progressive conciliation between the domain of nature and the domain of pure forms,[10] which takes place through purely ideal mathematical order and the concept of measure connected to it. The universe is not a mixture of matter but is in itself shaped in conformity with figures and numbers. The form of time itself is viewed in *Timaeus* as an intimate connection of the becoming world of images with its stable and eternal structure, which mathematics reveals in its rules and abstract schemes. "Every becoming is achieved in the unity of time, which in turn does not flow but remains immobile as such."[11] Time is thus the moving likeness, according to number, of eternity. With this resolution the thesis of the fleeting and temporary natural image disappears, and the ordered appearance of nature in time gives rise in *Timaeus* to an apotheosis of nature itself, in which *diaeresis* is also a link with the idea and a manifestation of the idea in the image. Here Cassirer interprets the

Platonic myth by attempting to make explicit the nucleus of the theory of nature and the mystery—which is perhaps inaccessible to us—with which the mythical form clothes the meaning of the doctrine. Myth, which in Plato is mixed with true philosophical discourse, is considered by Cassirer a sign of likeness inherent in the representation of natural becoming and quite distinct from the realm of *logos*.

This view of Platonic myths as schematized by Cassirer does not agree with the one that Karl Justi formulated in his early book on Platonic aesthetics, a view with which Cassirer was well acquainted. Justi affirms that mythical expression in Plato was only apparently a means of confirming the seriousness and importance of the new dialectical inquiry vis-à-vis the traditional philosophical method of inquiry. The future art historian upheld the fundamental nature of myth in Plato's system as a complementary element, a sort of territory adjacent to philosophy that serves to confirm the results obtained by logical procedure. "Only through the spectacle of the myth of a universal culture was Plato able to make the relationship of becoming being with the eternal and the nature of the soul comprehensible."[12] Myths are not subject to philosophical demonstration; they are its representation in terms of fantasy.[13] This different meaning attributed to mythical narration is not irrelevant to the purposes of the general interpretation of the function of art and of artistic consciousness in Plato. Justi attempted to distinguish, in the magical unity of myth and *logos* in the dialogues, the elements that could lead back to an intrinsic artistic element in the very philosophy of Plato, while Cassirer explicitly criticizes this point of view in his essay, as he tends to isolate rationality with respect to legend and to find in the former the roots of that process which, from the first readings of Plato in classical antiquity, led to the so-called Platonic conception of art theory.

The contradiction between form and natural becoming was resolved through the mathematical model revealed in nature, only to reappear in Plato's position regarding art. Art shows us a "second nature" and thus offers a doubly mediated image of being that leads more and more deeply into the conditioned and the derived toward a subjectivity which in Plato's view passes over into arbitrariness.[14] Like the sophist, the artist creates images bound to the phenomenal world; both imitate reality, which in turn is already an imitation of the divine world. Plato justifies the craftsman who adheres to the ideal model, while he criticizes the artist, who creates fantastic images, apparent objects devoid of reality. "The painter's 'free' art seems to create as if from a void, and thus in Plato's view there is established in it only the unilateral dependence upon the sensory model which now, instead of being recognized as a mere reproduction, is changed into an original image, a binding norm of the artist."[15] Through art the rigorous concept of idea is replaced by the ambiguous and multiform concept of the ideal. Here lies the misunderstanding into which post-Platonic art theory fell: by taking the ideal as its starting point, it thought it could proceed along the path marked out by Plato, whereas in reality it often went so far as to deduce the original sense of the idea by starting off from the meaning it had taken on subsequently. The ambiguity of the aesthetic ideal lies in its not being at home either in the intelligible world or in the sensible world, but rather in the wavering between these two. Cassirer sets against this the Platonic irreconcilability between the unity of the idea and the artistic translation of the sensory manifold. Pure artistic abstraction from individual phenomena as they present themselves to the senses has nothing at all to do with the unity of form; it is something ambiguous and uncontrolled, the domain of dreams, irreducible to the idea and a source of the utmost mystification since it takes the similar for the true and deceives both the senses and the intellect.

Cassirer therefore criticizes Justi's thesis that the Platonic idea has an aesthetic meaning. In fact Justi stated that the attainment of the idea can be compared to the artist's duty which, subject in all its phases to becoming, culminates in the work of art, which is an eternal form, not an original and unitary one. "Thus here the examination of opinions, the coming together of the single and often contradictory parts of a phenomenon, the process from the datum to the universal, ends with the idea, which is like a conclusion that simply *is*."[16]

Cassirer rightly points out that Justi did not note the boundary between philosophy and art in Plato. For that matter Justi was well aware of having given an interpretation of Platonic theory that rather forced its meaning; but he felt it would reveal Plato's error precisely in the difference between philosophy and art. For Justi the beautiful is always only the result of artistic activity. He analyzed the meaning of that power, which in aesthetics is called ideal, as distinct from the concept basically because it is not an object of thought but of intuition.

This power is differentiated from individual existence in its striving after the whole of the content of the different species, since instead of the natural being-there in time and space it has an ideal being-there in the imagination of the people and the artist. The ideal is the striving for an extension in the material substratum that should not be inferior to nature itself, but should rather be its achieved enrichment and perfection.[17] It is no accident that this striving reveals itself above all in plastic art, and in these passages Justi bore in mind Winckelmann's description of ancient statues, especially the bust of Hercules in the Vatican Museum. This is why he interpreted Plato's expression concerning the beauty of the idea in its most concrete sense—the idea as an object of artistic activity. According to Justi, Plato's error lay in not recognizing the essence of the beautiful there where it was precisely to be found, that is, in the artistic ideal, while in Plato the beautiful is achieved only in the idea and thus in the sphere of the purely intelligible—a definition which did not fully satisfy even him. In Justi's view, there is an unconscious admission in Plato's dialogues that the search for the relationships between ideas does not exhaust the explanation of the world, which is to be noted rather in the harmonic system expressed in the beautiful phenomenon. The "pure and simple" intelligible therefore presents itself in philosophy constantly changed in an aesthetic sense.

Indirectly Cassirer wants to point out in his critique how Justi is to be included in that current of Neoplatonic aesthetics which, in forcing the original meaning of the idea, leads speculation on the types of being and on the relationships of the one with the many onto the plane of the ideal, which is indefinite and alien to Plato. Justi's interpretation is certainly wrong when he states that the idea is the achievement of a unitary form beginning with the phenomenal datum, and also when he leads the essence of the idea back to the artistic phenomenon understood ideally. Yet his complex analysis of the problem of art in Plato deserved more attention on Cassirer's part, given that the latter was no stranger to certain aspects of that inquiry. Justi erects a historical-cultural design onto his interpretation—the same design, in fact, that Cassirer uses when he schematically tracks the problem of aesthetics after Plato.

The pattern Justi follows for this construction is the Hegelian one according to which Plato's philosophy is an exact expression of the

Greek world view. According to this view, the contrasts in Platonic dialectics are the same contrasts and tensions of the Hellenic spirit, which, in recognizing the power of nature, establishes and develops a culture as the exaltation of nature and at the same time as a limit set against its infinite power (which itself is apparently indifferent to every universally human desire). The idea of number and measure that lies at the base of the cosmos reveals the deep feeling of insecurity and void and the consequent necessity to prepare a world fit for one's needs and representations in conceiving this world as the work of an essence similar to oneself.

"This desire was the one for the love of which the Greeks sought their ultimate satisfaction in a world view that would set the regularity of lovely forms and movements in place of chance, which enters in conflict with man's nature and aims, a world view that—through the reduction of forms that have become familiar to him in the sphere of art as well—would make the world equally ideal for his works and abode, as culture must really do, as long as its limited influence is predominant."[18]

Justi distinguishes two phases in Platonic philosophy. The first is the philosophic-intellectual one, which has handed down to the history of later philosophy the basic problems of the conception of the real. The second one is conditioned by the culture of its time, which tended toward the erection of the ideal cosmos and which in Justi's view is what prevents the concept from developing independently and Plato from being a pure dialectician. The image of Plato as a "bad philosopher" because he is "still too much an artist" belongs to the historical scheme whereby the development of the idea is achieved by degrees through phases of transcending in which art is considered to be in a lower stage of development than philosophy.

But in Justi this linear Hegelian scheme becomes quite complicated in his view of the meaning of culture and above all in the value attributed to art as the bearer of the supreme values of a culture and thus as the beginning and end of the organization of the world. "The historical and cultural meaning of art consists particularly in this— that it represents and offers to sensory pleasure the sustaining forces of the epoch and its abstract ideas in concrete, sensory forms that at times are only reflecting and at others idealizing."[19] Viewing Platonic philosophy as the realization of the greatest effort to form the phenomenon ideally, Justi connected this need to a struggle on the part of Greek thought against the hostile power of chance, of partial and material aims and of the finiteness of the individual, in order to rise up in a mighty driving force toward a higher and transcending unity, toward a supreme order of things. This order must answer the needs of our representation of the real. It seems that Justi uses the term *representation* in the sense attributed to it by Schopenhauer: the intuition of the thing in its being and not in its relations, which all depend on mere will. Schopenhauer also conceived the Platonic idea as representation, that is to say, as an "object for a subject," as the appropriate objectivity of will.[20] Justi drew upon this interpretation of Schopenhauer's for the basic working principles not only of his research on Platonic aesthetics, but also and above all of his idea of culture as the representation through art of intuitions that begin with the sensory real in order to encounter the ideal rules imposed upon the sensory to organize it.[21]

"Thus was born that marvelous fabric of inquiry and poetry, universal laws and musical forms, astronomy and psychology, which has endured to this day as a monument of how the world is reflected differently in man's different epochs."[22] Justi marks out a fundamental law of culture: its being inspired by isolated movements and elements to allow entire civilizations to exhaust themselves in the quest for and production of a unitary element which is handed down in history as the ideal unity of a real manifold.[23] So Greek civilization is unrepeatable, in the sense that the manifold, with which it experimented and which it identified in a unifying form, was later reproduced in more and more complex forms that go beyond that perfect order, that accomplished identification of the subject with nature as an organized cosmos. For Justi here lies the problem of the bases of that original mixture of the theoretical and practical with the aesthetic which constitutes the basic difference between modern and Platonic art theory. Unlike the former, which is concentrated in the search for a distinction between the beautiful and the true and good, with the Greeks, and above all in Plato, there is the continuous alternation of separation and reunification of the world of the senses with the world of ideas.[24] We have seen that Cassirer agrees with the latter thesis; but he ambiguously takes a critical stance vis-à-vis Justi because he sees the process of separation and reunification only in the sphere of the concept. Now this is a viewpoint one might agree with if it were not for the fact that for Cassirer the concept expressed by the Platonic idea is still contaminated by the influence of sensory elements which Cassirer—unlike Justi—does not even define.

If the theme of the beautiful runs throughout Plato's philosophy, Cassirer insists upon the fact that this is never artistic or sensory beauty, but rather that beautiful given by mathematical order and by the perfection of measure, which makes the harmony that holds the cosmos together manifest both in the sensory world and in the world of ideas. In *Timaeus* it is the concept of measure that unites beauty and truth, and in *Philebus* the concord of harmony and proportion is acknowledged as being a "pure pleasure" which however absolutely cannot be compared to the deprived sensation of pleasure. Here Cassirer introduces an observation that reveals the horizon of his thoughts at that time in his speculation on symbolic form. He asks whether it is not possible to have at least a symbolic expression of the idea, not equal to the idea but an adequate expression of it. Such a conciliation in the symbol would take place by means of determined numerical and mathematical relationships which alone give the rule of the beautiful.[25] Cassirer seeks the intermediate term between unity and multiplicity in the concept of expression and of symbolic form and probably views the Platonic idea of numbers as an anticipation of those mathematical symbols that for him signified the highest degree of expression— through images—of the concept.

At this point the value of the image frees itself from the sphere of art and becomes a sign of an activity that concerns pure knowledge as well.[26] Thought must necessarily be translated into images, and since this transfer of the idea to words is always inadequate, Cassirer finds here the drama of the necessity of the sensory which affects the dialectical thinker and forces him to modify and mediate continuously through images the pure significance of the true. For Cassirer, this mediation of the *eidolon,* which in Plato has nothing to do with numbers and on the contrary has a totally negative accent, must be understood positively as an ineliminable stage in the attainment of the highest philosophic knowledge.[27] Here the notion of a progressive historical scheme comes into play, where the concept tries to make its way in its expression of itself through increasingly precise images of its system of relationships and internal links. There takes place in this process a singular exchange between the concept that operates by means of a knowledge of the system of relationships and the sensible that determines it and changes its original connections, which become more and more "adequate" to the knowledge of phenomena. For Cassirer and his philosophy of expression, the concept becomes along with its symbol and there is a continuous mediation inherent to the totality of the knowable. In light of this thesis he sees in Plato's expression—which is aesthetic *malgré lui,* contaminated by myth and artistic form—a still unrealized liberation of the concept from the immediate influence of the sensible, and he interprets the severe judgment Plato makes of artists as an attempt to overcome the deep impression that art, not yet reduced in terms of pure philosophizing, made on the Greek philosopher's personality and individuality.

With this interpretation the mythical discourse also appears to be an art that Plato himself cannot do without, since in the likeness that is manifested therein it is possible to make perceptible the true that thought strives for. As a heritage of speculation that by now belongs to the past, myth is considered the sign of an unrealized overcoming of the sensory image against which Plato fought in vain. Plato's system does not even admit of the possibility of a philosophical aesthetics, and yet precisely this system has generated the premises for the development of an art theory.[28] In fact every subsequent justification of aesthetics is built upon the foundation of the Platonic theory of love. Every *eros* is a creative *eros,* every force in human beings is a generating force and humans cannot create ugly things, only beautiful ones. "In art too a genuine *generating function* is at work which is figurative *representation.*"[29] In Plato love was inspired only by dialectics, but with the Neoplatonic thinkers this theme is developed in doctrines that tend to interpret the concept of creative energy as a mediation between the sensible and the intelligible.

Despite the fact that Cassirer, as opposed to Justi, keeps art and idea in Platonic philosophy clearly separated, he still notes the justification for a defense of art as a means of knowledge. The inner necessity of philosophic expression in its individuality, from which the drama and tension of that thought are generated, is viewed also as a necessity of the universal course of history which makes the becoming of the spirit emerge from the contrast. Cassirer thus no longer accounts for that ambiguity, which he had criticized in aesthetic idealism at the beginning of his essay. Now he uses the contradiction and negation between Plato and Neoplatonism to create a fertile ground on which the philosophy of art and the evaluation of artistic expression in terms of positive creativity and a process toward the attainment of the concept and the idea have every right to develop.

Two directions of thought do battle in the brief essay "Eidos und Eidolon," which grew out of a lecture Cassirer gave at the Warburg Institute: the will to total mediation between the different moments of history, so that every experience is intimately necessary to the development of the whole; and the open struggle between contrasting theories in which nothing becomes except through opposition and contradiction, through the creation of authentic ruptures which the historian can only scrupulously record and acknowledge, forgoing any attempt at achieving harmony between the former and the latter, which is impossible in this case.

Cassirer's lecture at the Warburg Institute had paved the way for subsequent developments of the theme of Neoplatonic aesthetics and the interpretation of the various art theories that in the Renaissance had arisen and multiplied in its celebration of the revival of antiquity. "Not only did the Renaissance take shape through the most profound understanding of Plato, but later on as well all the great epochs of artistic creation and reflection on art returned to the Platonic doctrine of love as the true speculative construction of all artistic form."[30] But Plato did not think along these lines, Cassirer affirms: the art of love was for him the art of dialectics. And it is singular that, in recognizing this, Cassirer is not willing to revise his interpretation of Platonic philosophy as still subject to sensory expression and hence still not free from the imprint of the manifold and multicolored world of reality. His thesis of a philosophical aesthetics which, taking the ideal as its base, builds upon the philosophy of Plato in which it sees its own origin in such a way as to interpret Plato in the light of the ideal it has invented—a thesis Cassirer used rightly to criticize Justi—now turns against Cassirer himself. He formulates the theory of the symbolic form as an ideal mean between the sensible and the intelligible, already finding in Plato's dialectics the beginnings of this research, and at the same time he interprets Plato as a step in the process of the constitution of the symbolic form in which this latter had not yet been grasped in its purity. Justi and Cassirer thus make the same mistake of viewing the idea as an attempt at systematic abstraction from the totality of phenomena or as an incomplete theoretical realization of the conceptual links that are still dominated by sensible elements which are not reduced conceptually.

And yet Plato himself, in *Theaetetus, Parmenides, Sophistes,* and *Philebus,* excludes from philosophical reasoning the manifold given in sensibility whose evidence has no need for a foundation and, with extraordinary and unique tension, investigates the possible relationships of being in conceptual links. Plato's effort to build an ontology correctly is alien to the world of the sensible; in this respect Plato is interested in the destiny of phenomena, of finite and becoming things, only in that their pure evidence drives the activity of the intellect to investigate the nature of being that does not change and to see whether in being a manifold may be articulated according to a certain relationship and a certain measure. Perhaps it is this last point that suggests to Justi and Cassirer the view of a progressive abstraction of the idea from the sensible, whereas for Plato the problem is to understand what the image of the sensible is, the image in which all the contradictions that must not enter into the idea appear.

As for the question of the symbolic form that Cassirer sought in the idea of number that mediates between the world of the manifold and that of ideas, it is opportune here to point out that in Plato's view the most suitable means for measuring being—despite his doubts and hostility regarding the written works of philosophy, as can be seen for example in his *Epistle VII*—is precisely the word.[31] This is demonstrated by the nimble, rapid-fire conversation in the dialogues that contain a complex and articulate round of concepts and that, as in a mystery, hold together the meanings of a logic of being in a single phrase—something that only an elaborate and arduous writing style could otherwise achieve. *Parmenides,* for example, is perhaps the most evident demonstration of this. In the space of a few pages the old philosopher of Elea emancipates himself from the traditional doctrine of ideas, reducing it to a mere nothing together with that world of the sensible with which the doctrine in some of its derivations thought it right to have dealings. Then he lays down the hypothesis of the one and being and of the relationship with the many, and with a vertiginous and almost incredible deduction keeps together in a few efficacious remarks the difficulties that for centuries before and after Plato assailed whoever touched upon these problems. What symbolic form is more abstract, and most coherently and essentially exhausts every dimension of the real or the object, than the one Plato found for his philosophy? Cassirer seeks a course of the symbol in formation through language, myth, art, and science, in a progressive emancipation from the sensible, and he does not realize that not even Kant succeeded in totally freeing "sensation in general," that is, the pure possibility of experience, from the imprint of the senses; nor did he manage to formulate a hypothesis of a connection or definitive exclusion between what he calls "transcendental matter" and the object, its thinkableness.

In his book on Plato, Paul Friedländer rightly hoped and called for an overall study of the interpretations of Plato in the course of history.[32] Such research might shed light on those contradictions engendered by Platonic philosophy, whose original energy has each time been both imprisoned and developed in one doctrine or another, so that an approach to Plato's text always proves to be mediated from opposing positions, each of which takes in only one aspect of Platonism and more or less consciously either takes possession of it or fights against it. Plato, a philosopher who delved into every supposition in order to find its foundation, is almost always interpreted by means of either Platonic suppositions or opposing ones.

The stimulativeness in Cassirer's essay lay in its having regarded this distance between Plato and Platonism in one of its most apparent forms, art theory, which was the one that most aspired to knowledge of the nature of sensations and images. In this work he asked for a thorough verification of his thesis (for that matter, this was not the first time he had made this suggestion), which meant entering into the details of the various aspects of the history of aesthetics so as to offer a total picture of it in a Cassirerian perspective.

This invitation was accepted by Erwin Panofsky who, explicitly taking his cue from Cassirer's essay, devoted himself to an analysis of this question in a book that came out as one of the Warburg Library's *Studien* in 1924: *Idea. Ein Beitrag zur Begriffsgeschichte der älteren Kunsttheorie*, whose English version is entitled *Idea. A Concept in Art Theory*.

Two themes in "Eidos und Eidolon" inspire Panofsky's work. One is how the history of art theory has altered the original Platonic doctrine. The other, connected to the first, is the idea's transformation into the ideal, a transformation Panofsky observes above all in the passage from the Renaissance to Mannerism and Classicism. In *Idea* there is a mode of reconstructing the history of a concept or an image by following its development, not through a progressive scheme but in the oscillations, changes in direction, and reformulations that the concept or image has manifested over the centuries. In Cassirer's view there is an ideal evolutionary pattern in history, so that it is the history of the spirit, and sensibility accompanies it in its appearance but is never truly opposed to it, and progress is a course with an aim and is hence unopposed. In Panofsky's view on the other hand—and for that matter in Warburg's as well—the most important thing is to verify the different historical positions that are constantly struggling with one another. Often these positions emerge from this struggle through differences and variations—as if in the conflict of opposed tensions something in the original idea were changed, or as if the theory's proceeding in time, or the image's surviving the deterioration that time imposes, were a laborious process that takes place in matter which the theory or image in turn reproduces in freeing itself from it. Cassirer feels that the emancipation of the symbol, as an adequate image of the real, from sensibility is a destiny of human knowledge and history and that historical continuity is exalted above all in the necessary passage from one system of relations to a more perfect one. On the other hand, Panofsky, and the school he comes from, state that there is no image of the real in history that is not engendered by a more or less evident conflict with other images having the same necessity.

Panofsky does not dwell upon the question of art theory in Plato because he does not believe aesthetics exists in his philosophy. Only briefly in the introduction to *Idea* does he develop his interpretation of this question, decidedly linking himself with Cassirer's essay: for Plato there is a clear-cut separation between art and philosophy, so that art is either an imitation of the idea or it is sham and presents itself totally subject to the dominion of the idea and its conception. In a historical context in which antiquity and the Renaissance are indissolubly linked, Panofsky notes the question of idea already in the Latin Platonic philosophers, for example in Cicero, as the development of two aspects of the theory of ideas that were completely foreign to Plato: that of the idea as a representation or inner model of the human spirit and that of the idea being in the thought and works of the artist as its privileged seat.[33] Already in these brief statements, though, one notes a barely perceptible difference between Panofsky and Cassirer. While Cassirer does not judge Plato's ban on art and artists, Panofsky begins with an interpretation that could well be considered quite close to Justi's: "Plato, who established once and for all the metaphysical meaning and value of the beautiful, and whose doctrine of Ideas has become ever more important for the aesthetics of the representational arts, was nevertheless unable to do full justice to these representational arts themselves."[34] And again: "Plato applied to the products of sculpture and painting the concept—utterly foreign to their nature—of cognitive truth (i.e., correspondence to the Ideas) as a measure of value."[35]

Panofsky does not say that Plato's dialectics was not pure, but admits for a moment that the philosopher almost arrived at an art theory, claiming to dominate it entirely through the idea or to abandon it as the path to error and falsity. But aesthetics cannot leave the question of the sensory unsolved, and so Plato was wrong to entrust it to the pure conceptual model. So Panofsky is connected to Justi's thesis whereby Plato noted the idea of the beautiful where it does not exist and did not look for it where it has its legitimate place—in art. Yet from the outset Panofsky clearly covers a domain that necessarily is not the same one that Cassirer dealt with and that will determine the detachment of his line of thought from Cassirer's, despite the fact that the art historian is always concerned about affirming his accord with the theory of symbolic forms and with the inquiry regarding them.

Panofsky operates in the sphere of history and art, the two disciplines that converge in the point of becoming, that is, in the appearance of the sensible manifold. The complexity of his oeuvre, at times even the abstruseness of his "path to history" and his interpretations of the artistic object, always consists in the endeavor to construct a theoretical, unitary design as a conceptual tool so as to gain access to that plane of evidence and factuality that the historian of culture must reduce to significative connections. And the propriety of this endeavor of Panofsky's lies in his never abandoning, not even in the most abstract schematism, that problem of the sensible which lies at the base of artistic expression, which because of its nature merges with temporal becoming and which therefore should constitute an irreducible obstacle to conceptual dominion and to pure explanation by means of connections.

The second question in which Panofsky departs from Cassirer, albeit in a purely unconscious manner in *Idea,* is the one concerning the passage from the doctrine of ideas to the interpretation that has been given of it since antiquity. In fact, while Cassirer makes every effort to see already in Plato that ambiguity between idea and image that is the principle of the development of modern art theory, Panofsky sets aside Plato himself, who in an incontrovertible manner separated art and philosophy, and directs his attention to the interpretations of Plato and to how they appropriated the concept of idea, changing its meaning and signification *from the very beginning.*

"Classical antiquity itself had transformed the Platonic concept of 'idea' into a weapon against the Platonic view of art, thereby preparing the ground, as it were, for that of the Renaissance."[36] The example of the line that Panofsky will take throughout his book is given in Melanchthon's quoting from Cicero's *Orator* in the passage which affirms that the forms of things are eternal in the mind of the artist. Panofsky sees in Cicero the premise of a concept of the essence of art similar to that of the essence of the idea and contrary to Plato's. This anti-Platonic conception originates in Cicero's compromise between Plato and Aristotle and in the tendency in antiquity to consider art inferior to nature in that it is pure imitation, and superior to it as well in that it "confronts nature with a newly created image of beauty."[37] Art, being able to dispense with the model perceived by the senses because it is an autonomous creation of the artist, rises from the sphere of empirical reality and at the same time is mixed with the idea, removing it from its sphere of pure form and from its philosophical and metaphysical essence. Panofsky notes already in Aristotle the thought that Neoplatonic speculation will use to interpret the Platonic idea as an ideal of artistic creation. In the seventh book of *Metaphysics,* Aristotle says: "Things are generated artificially whose form is contained in the soul."[38] Then, a few pages farther on, he states: "Thus obviously there is no need to set up a form as a pattern . . . ; the thing which generates is sufficient to produce, and to be the cause of the form in the matter."[39]

By means of these quotations from Aristotle, Panofsky points out the transcending of the concept of imitation, which no longer has any place if the act of shaping and constructing is conceived as the "entrance of a definite form into a definite substance."⁴⁰ Neoplatonism therefore owes a great deal to Aristotle when he theorizes both a substance willing to be formed and its actual reduction to a form. Although one must also consider how the Neoplatonic philosophers noted in matter a residue of negativity which, while it makes its way toward the idea and the highest good, still remains as absolute passivity and obstructs complete formal determination, in certain degrees of knowledge it totally blocks it and produces that return to the corporeal and the formless which Neoplatonism considers the ever self-reproducing fall of the soul into the lowest spheres of being.

In Plotinus the idea of the artist is identical to the *Nous*; it is an act of intellectual vision superior to mere thought. In this sense Plotinus's aesthetics can be understood only as a confluence of Plato's and Aristotle's philosophies. As opposed to the irreducibility of sensation as a material datum to pure form, Plotinus exalts the battle art is waging for the victory of form over the formless.⁴¹ The concept of the potential, which allowed Aristotle to take all negativity and privation back to the sphere of form or predisposition to form, is lacking in matter as conceived by the Neoplatonists; this matter is totally inert, indifferent to the attraction exercised by form, which as such is a separate essence in the Platonic sense, while on the other hand it has the power to determine the formless, at least as a striving for the ideal, even though it is impossible to realize concretely. The Renaissance conception of sculpture as the liberation of the idea from matter is rooted in Plotinian aesthetics rather than in the original Greek conception in which there is no material residue in the final realization of form.

But if works of art are the manifestation of ideas, their every aim and autonomy are conditioned by the ideal transcendent model to which these works of art always aspire—an "unattainable" goal, because they are impeded by the resistant matter which they use to carry out their "sublime task."⁴² A significant aspect of this art theory is that one can gain access to theoretical truth through the beauty of the art work as well, but only if this latter creates a new object from an inner vision instead of imitating the given object. Panofsky lays down the premises of his analysis of art theories in the Neoplatonic and the later medieval contaminations of the philosophy of Plato and Aristotle, as well as in the contemporary theologizing of the concept of idea in patrology, mystical theology, and Scholasticism. There is also the presupposition of that disagreement between a conception of the idea as immanent to the divine spirit and, later, to the spirit of the creative artist, and a more strictly Aristotelian theory of form that impresses itself upon matter as its absolute determination, where matter is conceived as a necessary substratum of creation.

In the Middle Ages art was in no way independent from theology but was rather a product intrinsic to "divine cognition" that grew out of its conceptual horizon and merely reproduced it.[43] St. Augustine viewed art in a Neoplatonic fashion as the image of that supreme beauty present only in the divine idea, an idea which for that matter for the Christian philosopher still had a Ciceronian meaning of eternal form that is a model of everything that lives and dies.[44]

This attempt at a historical liaison between pagan thought and Christian theology might have been more explicit had Panofsky grasped the intimate essence of the passage in the *Confessions* (10.34) that he quotes as a demonstration of Augustinian aesthetics. This passage on artistic beauty, which St. Augustine views not only as a pale revelation of a superior beauty but more than anything as an impediment to the contemplation of God and to a healthy and sober Christian way of life, conceals much more genuine Platonism than Panofsky would like to admit.

Leaving aside the basic motivations, which are moralistic in a different religious sense with respect to Plato, the words "I resist the allurement of my eyes, lest they entangle my feet by which I am progressing on Thy way," and those concerning the persons who abandon themselves to the attraction of the senses and "become devotees of their external products, while abandoning internally their own Maker and annihilating the things made by Him,"[45] are directly derived from the tone of the *Republic* and other passages in Plato in which art as the creator of nothing leads one away from the virtuous path of knowledge. In these words one even feels the Platonic pathos in opposing a fascination that is too great and too dangerous for man's equilibrium, as he must find true pleasure only in intelligence and in the intellectual domain according to dialectical rule, which is the rule of truth. The difference is that the motif of the seduction of the worldly and exterior is transformed by the early Christian thinkers into the motif of the fascination of pagan culture, which must be defeated in the name of the City of God, where the impersonal intellect that sees the true relationships between the genera of being becomes a personal divine intellect that the imperfect essence of the believer yearns for.

More than in St. Augustine, this Christian striving for a renewal of culture—a renewal that takes place through an idealization of the present task—is felt in one of St. Jerome's letters, when he narrates a dream he had while in a feverish state. The saint, brought before the "tribunal of the judge" of the heavens, is accused with the following terrible and revealing words: "Thou art a Ciceronian!" It is the pain of the lashes he receives as punishment and the "flame of conscience" tormenting him for his sin of pride for having again experienced the impulse to enjoy the lovely and refined pagan culture, that drives St. Jerome to ask for forgiveness and to repent. He vows never again to look with sense-perceptive eyes, and an inner vision opens out to him, a vision grown from the need to abandon a criterion that is judged to be purely aesthetic and to glean the truth from what is coarse.[46] This destructive fury against pagan culture, of which Tertullian is one of the most violent examples, this will to subvert a civilization, is a basic cause of medieval indifference to independent aesthetics as an autonomous construction of an ordered cosmos.

Panofsky could also have noted how the process of intimate idealization of the pagan become Christian as described in these passages of St. Augustine—like a blinding necessary to replace one truth with another that has a different basis—produced that transition to a transcendent dimension which will constitute the limit and true obstacle to every later attempt at concord with reality. That "projection of an inner image into matter" that Panofsky identifies as the medieval conception of the work of art,[47] is much farther than his careful study would like to admit from the true sense of the Platonic idea and of the convergence of form and matter in Aristotle. If we are still formally in the sphere of classical thought, whose energy alone could furnish the tools to the new doctrine, the rupture with those theories is deep and irremediable. Sensory reality is no longer a datum that rational tension faces by imposing its rule, and it is no longer what form is always immanent to; now it is obscured, set aside by means of blinding, replaced by an ideal that takes on form in an inexact and imprecise approximation of perfection in which it is virtuous to believe and infinite abjection not to believe.

One can thus understand why the Renaissance appears to be divided between an attempt at recovering the Greek concept of measure in the meticulous, and already scientific, analysis of sensible reality as a depository of order and an interiorization of the idea. The latter is the light of consciousness yet always only a "certain idea," infused by divinity in the soul of the artist or created by the mind of the genius but always difficult to reduce to concepts, the fruit of the oscillations of time, dominated more or less unconsciously by an uncertainty regarding objective order.

Panofsky sees the opposition between medieval and Renaissance thought in the new subject-object relationship that is established when the concept of imitation takes on a positive, practical meaning in being the direct imitation of truth. This is the task of the Renaissance artist and theoretician: to reproduce visible reality as faithfully as possible and at the same time improve upon it in terms of beauty and formal perfection.[48] Art theory as a science arises in response to the problem of how nature is to be observed, imitated, and corrected, and one feels the need to possess a knowledge of nature as suitable as possible in order to be able to build and paint better. Precision and beauty are the two criteria that guide the artist to the discovery of mathematical and pictorial formulas as tools for reproducing reality. And yet a problem in artistic creativity "could not become apparent to Renaissance thinkers since they considered the nature and behavior of the 'subject' as well as the 'object' to be determined by definite rules either valid *a priori* or demonstrable empirically."[49] Thus the discipline of art theory was "at first almost completely independent of the revival of Neo-Platonic thought" of Ficino and his Academy. Here a combination of Plato and Plotinus, of Arab natural science and Scholasticism, was effected. Only later on did this give rise to a true speculative theory of art; but at the time it could not be of any fundamental value for a "practical and rationalistically oriented theory *for* art" such as that of the early Renaissance. Leon Battista Alberti led the phenomenal, empirical conception of beauty to victory—the same conception that Plotinus had fought against and that Ficino himself fought against, although the latter's struggle had implications that partly differed from those of the father of Neoplatonism. According to Panofsky a *non*-metaphysical conception of the beautiful loosened the bonds between beauty and good and thus introduced that autonomy of the aesthetic experience that only at the height of the modern age took on its true meaning.[50]

It is strange, if not downright contradictory, that a theory of art as a study of reality and its measurements should produce a doctrine—the aesthetic one—which Panofsky himself (thus following Cassirer) feels had developed more in terms of the ideal as understood in the Neoplatonic sense than in terms of modern experimental science and its laws. Undoubtedly making art a discipline necessary for an exact knowledge of nature, as Leonardo da Vinci wanted, meant removing it from the sphere of the contemplation of the inner idea and taking it within the limits set down by objective knowledge. Generating what is beautiful means increasing natural order by means of rational, mathematical order that is partly taken from the observation of nature itself and is partly the fruit of an intellectual search for absolute laws. But already in Galileo this procedure becomes a privileged characteristic of the exact sciences that rejects art as being imprecise and unfit for promoting the acquisition of true knowledge. Panofsky's attempt to set the origin of the aesthetic sphere in the already Renaissance concept of a logical apriority—hence a scientific, modern origin in the sense of the Kantian foundation of science—seems to fail at that moment in his essay where he shows how the classical and idealist tendencies alternate, fight against, and even influence, each other in the theoretical treatises and in the artistic currents themselves up to Impressionism and Expressionism.

The Renaissance contradiction concerning art consists of an increased influence of the theory of ideas in a markedly metaphysical sense that corresponds to art theory retreating farther from its "originally practical goals and unproblematical premises," and of an increasing adherence to these goals and premises with a corresponding decrease in the transcendent value of the theory of ideas.[51] Yet the distinction between these two tendencies is much less drastic if we closely follow Panofsky in his research, because from one standpoint the idea of beauty—both in Alberti and Ficino, the two protagonists of this polarity—is clearly dependent upon experience. Even for Ficino, for example, visible, perceptible beauty is the bearer of that invisible, superior ideal of the beautiful to which we are invited to ascend to contemplate in the realm of the spiritual. In Alberti experience must equally be the abode of the beautiful, even though its real idea does not wholly originate in sensibility, because otherwise one could not improve upon nature and the foundations of the artist's creative power (which in Alberti moves in harmony with nature itself) would break down. It is this necessary concord between idea and experience that marks the as yet unrealized distinction between subject and object, a distinction that will be effected by the theorists of the age of Mannerism for whom the validity of the laws of artistic creation is placed in reality by the subject.

The greatest difference from the Middle Ages is that the doctrine of the beautiful appears in the early Renaissance as a spiritualized form of the selection theory whereby beauty is achieved "by an inner vision that combines individual experiences into a new whole."[52] Ancient thinkers "had not identified the 'Idea' with the 'paradigm' (παϱάδειγμα) obtained by choosing from among the most beautiful things. They had conceived of Idea not as a compromise between the mind and nature but as that which guarantees the mind's independence of nature. But Renaissance thinkers understood the Idea concept in the light of a fundamentally novel attitude toward art which identified the world of ideas with a world of heightened realities" whose essence was to transform "the concept of the 'Idea' into the concept of the 'ideal.'" This came about, according to Panofsky, by stripping the idea of "its metaphysical nobility" and bringing it into "a beautiful and almost organic conformity with nature."[53]

Panofsky places the ideal for the Renaissance artist and theoretician in an intermediate sphere between the idea, which is the creating subject, and the rule that lies in nature. This is a mediation between the opposites—whose antithesis had not yet been conceived in the Renaissance—of genius and rule or genius and nature. It is therefore a privileged area of "compatibility" that "secured freedom to the artistic mind and at the same time limited this freedom vis-à-vis the claims of reality."[54]

Panofsky seems to attribute to this reciprocal limitation and measuring of strength between man and nature a character essentially different from that notion of the ideal that Cassirer thought had derived from an incorrect interpretation of the original meaning of the Platonic idea. In Cassirer's opinion, the transcendent and metaphysical sense of the idea is transformed into the transcendental value of the ideal. The ideal then takes on shape in the subject, becomes increasingly independent within it vis-à-vis the sensible world, and ends up being the true and only determination of objectivity. Panofsky takes up the terms of the question as it had been posed by Cassirer, but he does not remain connected to that scheme of the foundation of symbolic activity inherent to the subject. Rather, he interprets the Renaissance as an age in which measure is an intermediary between the subject and the object, and the power of the ideal is kept within rigorous limits. These limits consist in a rediscovery of classical antiquity that respected its original texts and authority, as well as in a link with the observation of nature and the concrete practices of art in which the object was not viewed as a problem.

Panofsky's all-embracing view of history—whereby there are many threads in the design that subtends the differentiation between epochs and that in order for the connection to be complete and meaningful no detail can be ignored—leads him to quote from Giorgio Vasari's theory of design as a "visual expression and clarification of that concept which one has in the intellect, and that which one imagines in the mind and builds up in the idea."[55] Here the idea originates in experience and is interpreted by Panofsky as that intellectual synthesis of the sensible manifold, which for him is the highest realization of the "conciliation" between mind and nature. Yet we discover already in this example from the late Renaissance the possible source of that replacement of the concept of Idea with the notion of Design that was to be a characteristic of Mannerist art theory.

The unity of the inner and outer world through the laws of measurement ignored the mind-nature antithesis. In Mannerism, however, this dualism was explicitly faced and harmonized by recovering the metaphysical sense of the idea as an inner inspiration of the artist who sees reality through God. Mannerism, in the apparently formal rigor that is required in artistic composition, frees itself from the mathematical and stylistic rules so venerated by the Renaissance and strives for a more inventive and creative rapport with the object under observation. Panofsky holds that Mannerism returned to the Middle Ages, to that synthesis between Aristotelianism and Neoplatonism that is particularly clear in the new philosophical need to lay a solid theoretical base for artistic creation. Speaking of the late-sixteenth-century theoretician Giovanni Paolo Lomazzo, Panofsky notes that despite his aversion for mathematics, numbers, and systems, which he considered a limitation to the genius's expressive possibilities, Lomazzo sought formal rules—for example in his severe codification of expressive movement—that could offer a rational foundation for creative genius. There is thus an increasing tendency to conceptualize and systematize art in order to make it a science.[56] The return to philosophical speculation based on either Aristotelian-Thomist Neoplatonic models reflected the need to legitimize artistic production theoretically and metaphysically, since it was no longer possible to solve the new aesthetic problems in a purely realistic and normative sense.[57] "The theory of Ideas ... fulfilled the double task, first, of making the theory of art aware of a problem that had not been acute before, and second, of indicating the way to its solution."[58]

Panofsky's analysis of this philosophical speculation focuses on the book written by Federico Zuccari in 1607, *L'Idea de' pittori, scultori ed architetti* (The Idea of Painters, Sculptors and Architects). Zuccari tries to define the "inner Idea" concept that lends form to the image and, not wanting to call it either "intention," "example," or "idea," he gives it the name of Design, since he is speaking to painters. The practical representation is the outer design of that inner Design which is "an idea and form in the intellect" that represents the very object of the design.[59] Therefore, through a complex evolution in the relationship with the outer image, there arises a view of artistic creation that is ever more independent from sensory perception and that is autonomous in what is preestablished in the intellect. The artist creates through God-given ability, just as nature creates in reality through the same influence. The concept of imitation has substantially changed meaning here. It is no longer an imitation of real, self-sufficient forms; nor is it an imitation of rules and laws that stand between the concept and sensory reality. Instead, it has become an idealizing representation of the object, a creation of forms through analogy with that creative process that animates nature itself.

Zuccari made every effort to "secure the genetic and systematic priority of the 'idea' over the impressions of the senses: sensory perception does not induce the formation of ideas, but the latter (by means of the imagination) causes sensory perception to take place."[60] If it is true that "the intellect perceives only by means of the senses," the Design is "Prince, ruler and governor" of the senses and of the intellect. This speculation—which Panofsky calls Neo-Scholastic because he notes the same theological-metaphysical premises that are to be found in medieval Scholastic "trains of thought"—tries to justify the birth of the idea within that sensory manifestation, that is, artistic creation, which derives from divine inspiration that penetrates matter to determine it. And matter is conceived in an Aristotelian manner as suitable to take in form, while yet resisting it to a greater or lesser degree; and the beauty or ugliness of the finished work of art depends upon the type and quality of this resistance.

There is, however, no complete theory of the beautiful in Zuccari; it is to be found rather in the contemporary Neoplatonic authors in whom the concept of beauty is understood as an overcoming of the metaphysical antithesis between idea and matter.[61] Mannerism thus effects a double return to the Middle Ages: from the viewpoint of artistic creation, which takes place through the intercession of divine grace, and from the standpoint of the theory of the beautiful, which is connected to the realization of good and passes through Ficino's commentary upon Plato's *Symposium*. Aristotelianism and Platonism are still doing battle in the artistic schools of the late cinquecento because a concept of the beautiful that derives from an intellectual view of the idea and cannot therefore be grasped in phenomenal reality is opposed by the view of matter that is fit to receive the form. "Both the Peripatetic and Scholastic view and the Neoplatonic view agreed in that which most clearly distinguishes the Mannerist from the real Renaissance attitude toward art—in the conviction that the visible world is only a 'likeness' of invisible, 'spiritual' entities and that the contradiction between 'subject' and 'object' which had now become apparent to the intellect could be solved only by an appeal to God."[62]

In the second half of the seventeenth century, art theory turned against Mannerism and its metaphysical reflections and revived a concept of the idea taken from experience, from direct contact with reality. Yet while the Renaissance fought only to defend the concrete observation and study of nature, which it aimed at reintegrating into the classical concept of measure and law, Classicism fought at once on two fronts: against 'mannered' painting which marked the triumph of fantasy over the analysis of concrete reality, and against exasperated 'naturalism' as embodied in Caravaggesque art.[63] Panofsky cites Giovanni Pietro Bellori's introduction to his *L'Idea del Pittore, dello Schultore e dell'Architetto* (The Idea of the Painter, Sculptor and Architect), published in 1664, as a fundamental text and document of the theoretical base of Classicist art theory. Here Bellori upholds the thesis that the idea is won by contemplating nature and at the same time through the self-contemplation of the creative subject who generates original images by modeling them after those sensory ones that have not been contaminated by matter. The idea is immanent to the artist's spirit and is devoid of absolute metaphysical value—that is, it needs sensory perception in order to apprehend nature and transfigure its forms. Panofsky notes that Bellori quotes Plato in support of this theory; he borrows a statement from *Phaedon* which affirms that knowledge depends upon the acquisition of the sense-datum, but he changes Plato's meaning, as the latter held that sensory perception is merely an occasion for understanding, an occasion that leads thought to the mind, which proceeds autonomously. In Bellori's opinion, however, the sense-datum is a necessary premise for the formation of the idea, which as such manifests itself in perfect harmony with nature. Panofsky's observation may seem right if one stops to think of the great care Plato took to remove the path of the senses from knowledge, as that path is nothing but erring and disorder. However one must be careful about assuming that Bellori's quotation is incorrect. In fact the passage from *Phaedon* is found in the context of the discussion on recollection, in which Socrates demonstrates to the young and slightly bewildered Phaedon how, upon seeing sensory objects that are equal, there arises in us the recollection of the known previous quality which is perfect compared to these imperfect examples that lie before us. But this absolute equality is in some way similar to the imperfect equals if through them we are reminded of that one and thus overcome the incompleteness of the sense-datum by means of the determining power of the concept. For that matter Bellori also holds that earthly imitation is *inferior* to the model the soul has the power to evoke.

This passage brings to mind another passage of Plato's in Book VII of the *Republic* where, with the aid of the cave allegory, Plato begins to extol the virtues of arithmetic as that discipline which draws the pure matter of speculation from sensory reality. Here Plato distinguishes with greater clarity in the world of the senses: "This, then, is just what I was trying to explain a little while ago when I said that some things are provocative of thought and some are not, defining as provocative things that impinge upon the senses together with their opposites, while those that do not I said do not tend to awaken reflection."[64] Plato then rapidly introduces into his pedagogic discourse on which disciplines the Guardian of the state should practice the question of the relationship between the one and many, weaving it into the theory of the senses that awaken the need to discern and understand. "But if some contradiction is always seen coincidentally with it, so that it no more appears to be one than the opposite, there would forthwith be need of something to judge between them, and it would compel the soul to be at a loss and to inquire, by arousing thought in itself, and to ask, whatever then is the one as such, and thus the study of unity will be one of the studies that guide and convert the soul to the contemplation of true being."[65] In *Philebus* too it is the need to predicate the same attribute of many objects, and to use pure reflection to distinguish what would otherwise be confused and vainly mixed, which generates arithmetic and the ontology of the One and its relationship with the infinitely manifold, of which it is the end, the limit, the measure.

The view of the polarity of beings, and also what surrounds them and gathers them under a meaning, moves the mind to pose the fundamental question, which leads to true knowledge. The idea has always existed, but the temporal circumstance in which the soul passes through its existence is the same one in which the imperfect equals aspire to their model without attaining it, always remaining inferior to it despite the sensations' anxious striving for perfection.[66] And again, in that problematical dialogue *Theaetetus,* in the remarks in which Socrates attempts to distinguish between feelings and reasoning that lies above them in order to determine the principle of knowledge beyond the deception of the manifold that becomes, there is a moment of absorbed reflection upon the nature of knowing that returns with an almost unchanged rhythm in *Letter VII*: "Is it not true, then, that all sensations which reach the soul through the body, can be perceived by human beings, and also by animals, from the moment of birth; whereas reflections about these, with reference to their being and usefulness, are acquired, if at all, with difficulty and slowly, through many troubles, in other words, through education?"[67] Almost as if to confirm the foreboding lying in such doubtful and prudent wisdom, there follows the unresolved struggle to keep all elements of time and becoming—the vain realm of sensation—far from pure speculation, without however knowledge being able to establish itself in perfect autonomy and to be uncontaminated by the danger of that false opinion that arises everywhere to contradict it.

It is therefore difficult to affirm drastically and recklessly that sensory perception is in Plato always only the occasion for the mind to turn to the idea, as Panofsky states. If knowledge is possible, there can be no absolute incommensurability between the sensible and the intelligible. Nor can the intermediary be something ideal, as Cassirer believed, for otherwise the solution would precipitate into only one of the terms, leaving the other intact. Bellori most probably intuited this difficulty when he uttered the strange expression "contemplation of nature" and was thus closer to classical antiquity than Panofsky thought. Closer and, as we have already seen in the case of St. Augustine, at the same time profoundly different. When Bellori gives his definition of the artist's idea—"born from nature, it overcomes its origin and becomes the model of art"[68]—he sees the terrestrial creator as inspired by visible reality, which is an imperfect imitation of the model, and also by the supreme architect, the "First Maker" that the artist imitates by shaping an example of superior beauty in his soul. The idea is "measured with the compass of the intellect" and "animated by fantasy." Thus the contribution of sensibility is essential; it is an integral part of that new origin that is based precisely on a sensible origin. Panofsky acknowledges the importance of sensory affection but, neglecting the theological aspect of the First Maker's inspiration, he thinks that with Bellori Classicism gives rise to idealist aesthetics, as if there were formed in the soul of the artist in a totally independent manner the idea that is then contemplated in nature. At the same time, the idea the artist contemplates in nature derives from that model of which nature itself is an imperfect realization. Artist and nature are therefore connected by their aspiration after the model; they are two forces united in their pursuit of the idea.

Panofsky, who shares Cassirer's thesis of an ideal that in history replaced the original Platonic idea, does not see how in the "model of art" the ideal is no longer being thought of in the sense in which it was conceived in Hegelian and post-Hegelian aesthetics. The artist is not the absolute subject; he creates the work of art because he is at once faithful to nature—that is, to his model—and unfaithful to it— that is, to its imperfection. The difference between this conception and

Plato's is profound, but not in the way Panofsky believes it to be—not in the sense of ideal creation and not even in the importance Bellori attached to the sensible origin. This is rather a question of how the problem of the image was formulated. Plato would never have affirmed that the rigorous rule of the intellect could fashion sensory images superior to nature and in themselves perfect. Everything that is imitation is in Plato different and inferior because it possesses that supreme and inconceivable alteration of the idea—movement, hence time. Bellori was not unaware of Plato's negative judgment of art, and in fact he quotes it expressly and interprets it as a theory against the creators of "specters," against those who place their trust entirely in practice and nature without trying to improve upon their deficiencies, incongruities and ugliness, since beauty is reserved for the perfect measure of the Idea. This is a viewpoint one should bear in mind if one wants to embark upon that study of the interpretations of Plato that Friedländer desired.[69]

Bellori reads in Plato a polemic against the art of his time which was too naturalistic,[70] and he himself polemicizes against the excesses of Caravaggesque art and considers the artistically beautiful only that which adheres to the canons laid down by the great classical Greek painters and sculptors. A century later these same canons of beauty were followed by Winckelmann and Lessing, at the borderline of what might be called idealistic aesthetics. Only this latter will give the ideal the value that Cassirer attributes to it and with which Panofsky as well seems to agree, although only in passing. In Bellori, imagination (Plato's "fantasy") appears in a positive sense as an essential component of creativity and the junction between the intellect and sensibility because it turns into sensory images what the intellect sees and measures of the pure idea. Nonetheless, one cannot yet speak of the ideal in the modern meaning of the term, in the sense in which the subject gives it form in historical becoming as a tool of his knowledge of reality and, what is more, as reality itself, of which the subject is the total "maker." As long as the beautiful is considered the fruit of an objective measure and drawn from nature, which the artist's observation and the particular relationship in him between intimate intelligence and external participation improve upon, we cannot claim to be in the sphere of the ideal, which is independent from both the intervention of a transcendent god and from a reality truly external to the subject and apperceived through the senses.

Friedrich Theodor Vischer, one of the most well-known exponents of post-Hegelian aesthetics, the "Culture-Philistine" as Nietzsche called him,[71] offers some indication of the accomplished transformation of the idea into the ideal in his essay on the beautiful and art. He says: "The nature of the Beautiful is of a historical type."[72] Through culture, understood as the formation of the individual, there develops what is purely human, and the beautiful occurs only when man in his totality and fullness has transformed his inner essence, the secret of his soul, into an object. In the beautiful the inner content of the object is entirely penetrated so that it can be found again in external appearance too. The ideal, as the autonomous and absolute formation of the subject, has its most concrete foundation in the concept of culture, since only in a world viewed as the historical development of potential forces of the subject—a world in which the subject is the totality of the historical process—is a form of appropriation of nature itself (understood as appearance) legitimate. The ideal proper to each epoch thus becomes the whole of the forms that that epoch has developed in its different spheres of influence. The clearer the sense of the ideal is to consciousness, the stronger the sense of identity between subject and object becomes, and sensible objects, and with them images, become symbols by means of which the subject expresses its all-embracing essence.

Now all this was still alien to the seicento classicists and for the most part it was so up to Lessing and Winckelmann; thus it is improbable that the theory of imagination and idea in Bellori could have engendered an idealistic art theory. At this point in his brilliant and erudite exposition Panofsky leaves aside his careful analysis of the detail in order to gain access to a historical plane contaminated by the concept of culture as well as by that of the ideal. And precisely this concession to an ideal historical plane betrays Panofsky's tendency in that period to agree with Cassirer and his historical-ideal scheme and to build, over and above any contradictions, a continuity that aims at being consequential too.

A more coherent historical discourse is to be noted when Panofsky limits the value of classicist aesthetics to the elaboration of normative aesthetics which fought against both metaphysics and empiricism. The intermediary between these two planes consists precisely in the objective rule that has ensued from the union between intellect, which imitates the idea, and imagination, which draws from experience the elements to be transfigured in accordance with the idea.

Panofsky concludes his essay with an analysis of the concept of idea in Michelangelo and Dürer. This concept is genuinely Platonic but Neoplatonic as well in Michelangelo, and problematical and modern in Dürer, who acknowledges an individual value in artistic *ingenium*, preceding the Italians in posing the question of the genius-nature, subject-object relationship.

Commenting upon Dürer's vast and tenacious exploration of the opposition between idea and image, between subject and object, as a basic component of the history of art theory, Panofsky brings up the problem of the "thing in itself" which has always been invoked as the necessary inspiration for the work of art as the concept of the mind or of the direct influence of God so as to solve the difficult problem of knowledge and of the relationship between idea and sensation. The presupposition of the "thing in itself" was "profoundly shaken" in the field of philosophy by Kant and by Aloïs Riegl in aesthetics. "We believe to have realized that artistic perception is no more faced with a 'thing in itself' than is the process of cognition; that on the contrary the one as well as the other can be sure of the validity of its judgements precisely because it alone determines the rules of its world (i.e., it has no objects other than those that are constituted within itself). Thus the opposition between 'idealism' and 'naturalism' that ruled the philosophy of art until the end of the nineteenth century and under multifarious disguises—Expressionism and Impressionism, Abstraction and Empathy—retained its place in the twentieth, must in the final analysis appear as a 'dialectical antinomy.' "[73]

The alternation of different solutions to the problem of art-theoretical thought is of an antinomical nature and therefore is insoluble philosophically. Yet this antinomy has affected art-theoretical thought and has given rise to its very evolution. Panofsky acknowledges the insoluble nature of this problem. Cassirer's point of departure—a development of the anti-Platonic concept of idea, founded in the doctrine of ideas and led to its extreme consequences, to the point of revealing its most recondite deviations and derivations—is in the end abandoned on a strictly theoretical plane. Panofsky therefore does not view the concept as evolving in conformity with its internal logic of development; rather, he observes the historical manifestation of an antinomy, a contradiction that can be discerned in time.

In Panofsky's view the history of the theoretical formulations of the problems of artistic reproduction occurs through temporary and partial solutions that vacillate between one extreme and the other of the antinomy, and the alternation of cultural epochs can be noted in the opposition of one aspect of the question to the other. A history of the concept of idea in the sphere of artistic creation and aesthetic speculation is possible only if the original interpretation of this term is broken up into the components of its antinomy (thesis-antithesis).

The process of the various theoretical formulations is not linear, but tortuous and filled with references to preceding viewpoints, negations, and resumptions. And yet the historical analysis itself is made possible by the direction the research takes; it must in any case lead to a result in which it is possible to ascertain the difference between the "before" and "after," and therefore a real development.

In *Idea* Panofsky is bound to the historical design that leads to a solution of the problem of art theory in the ideal, which is not conceived as a thing in itself but as an object that corresponds to the laws of the artistic consciousness that lent it form. "Just as the intellect 'causes the perceptible world to be either not an object of experience at all or to be a nature' (Kant, *Prolegomena*, §38), so, we may say, the artistic consciousness causes the sensory world to be either not an object of artistic representation at all or to be a 'figuration.' The following difference, however, must be remembered. The laws which the intellect 'prescribes' to the perceptible world and by obeying which the perceptible world becomes 'nature,' are universal; the laws which the artistic consciousness 'prescribes' to the perceptible world and by obeying which the perceptible world becomes 'figuration,' must be considered to be individual—or to use an expression recently suggested by H. Noack, 'idiomatic.' "[74] In this distinction Panofsky seizes upon the legitimation for his historical construction: the laws the intellect prescribes to the perceptible world are of a universal nature and thus are not subject to development or change; those prescribed by the artistic consciousness to the perceptible world are idiomatic and thus are determined differently in a process. They are susceptible to history. This occurs because, in changing, the artistic consciousness and the perceptible world influence each other in the determination of the laws and remain in a fluid sphere that is not susceptible to a definitive determination. However one must remember that, not being able in reality to change substantially the perceptible world in form if this latter is understood in a Kantian manner as a structure, what changes is rather the interpretation the artistic consciousness gives of this perceptible world. According to Panofsky, the force of change develops in the antinomical position of the thing in itself, as if only this thing could allow fantasy to take different paths so as to ascertain the relationship between artistic creation and the thing in itself. Since the latter relationship is no longer necessary in the authentic idealistic view, it seems that that movement must come to a halt because the subject, or consciousness, has definitively arrogated to itself the rules of the determination of the object.

Were this the case Panofsky would follow the same path as Cassirer and would agree with his scheme of historical development. It cannot be denied that during that period of collaboration a suggestion of that scheme might have entered into Panofsky's historiographic analysis; but in this regard he seems to be rather undecided and prudent in fully adhering to it. The indication of this uncertainty lies in the concluding lines of *Idea,* where a distinction is drawn between historical and philosophical consideration. The former reveals to the scholar a situation of antimony which for philosophy is "by its very nature" insoluble.

The limits established by Kantian criticism upon the power that connects the perceptible world and intellect do not allow for an exhaustive theoretical explanation of the practical realizations of this antinomy. There is an irreducibility of the two spheres—one of the concept and its logic, and the other of historical facts and the connection between them. The antinomy that sets becoming in movement can be observed and become an object of rigorous analysis and infinite hypotheses of relationships, but it cannot be reduced to purely theoretical terms. It seems that at least on this point Panofsky does not accept the hypothesis of a total extension of the Copernican revolution to the themes of the history of art and culture, which Cassirer tried to achieve.

In order to understand how Panofsky arrived at the formulation of

Idea and the meaning of the expression "artistic consciousness," an expression that seems to be the center of the analogy with the intellect and yet of its distinction from the latter, we must move back in time and analyze his earlier writings and the art-historical schools from which his view of the problem derived.

The Theoretical Writings and Art History

In his brief 1915 essay, "The Problem of Style in the Figurative Arts," Panofsky makes a subtle criticism of Heinrich Wölfflin's 1911 lecture on the same subject. Wölfflin distinguished two roots of style: an intuitive form with no psychological meaning, and a content made up of the state of mind and interpretable as expression. The development of styles, for example from the linear to the painterly, or from the patch of color to depth, is according to Wölfflin caused by the pure evolution of a form quite independent of the expressive root. Panofsky criticizes this wholly formalistic viewpoint, as he feels it is impossible to make a rigorous distinction between expressive and formal phases in a work of art.[75] In particular Panofsky criticizes the formalistic approach that explains the creation of a certain pictorial form exclusively through the relationship sight has with the outside world without any link with the psychology of a given epoch. He asks: what does leading visual perception to a form mean?[76] Who or what interprets the sense-data aesthetically, if not the psyche? What Wölfflin calls an "optical attitude" is really the mind's relationship with sight. An epoch expresses itself in a given form not only because it sees a certain form in reality, but because it feels that a totality of ideas and sensations must be translated into that form. "The distinction between expressively relevant stylistic moments thus proves to be a dialectical distinction; in short, it is founded on an unconscious play upon the two different meanings of the word 'vision.' "[77]

One notes here the Kantian sense the word *dialectical* has for Panofsky; in fact he criticizes Wölfflin's arbitrary replacement of one stylistic phase with another. Panofsky does not admit of expressive "neutrality" regarding the modes of representation; he can conceive of form only as part of the expression of a content. According to Wölfflin there is total independence between forms—color, lines and surfaces—and the expressive means they take on in each epoch. But how can the psychic content come after form and be taken on by it, and above all, how would this explain the differences between epochs precisely in the choice of certain forms? Panofsky uses the term *expressive gesture* to characterize the elements an artist seeks in taking possession of a particular form, since this form is wholly inseparable from that gesture. By "form" Panofsky seems to mean that multiplicity of elements subsumed into a unitary rule through which the work of art manifests itself. One cannot read "optical perception" in the strict sense because it always reveals a world view that goes beyond the pure formal dimension to constitute a universe of contents in it. It is therefore necessary to distinguish between form and object because the concept of form is rather part of the subjective sphere. Therefore not only the modes of representation, but also the individual expressions proper to the work of art, are part of the concept of form. "The particular (individual) form is therefore an actualization and differentiation, as it were, of the general one which thus, as a potential form for a work of art, must be rigorously distinguished from the actual form of a work of art; its individual moments can be legitimately ordered in a particular system of categories."[78]

Panofsky thus delineates the perspectives of research in art history in taking into account the general possibilities of representation and their link with a certain conception of the world, with a historically defined will to choose from among the various possibilities exactly the one judged to be the most expressive at the moment. There is also an unconscious aspect in this choice, yet only in the actual expressivity of the work of art is it possible to determine its form and connect it again to the general categories of art history. Panofsky does not dwell at this point either on the system of categories that must make a historical exposition of the artistic phenomenon possible or on the "link" between the categorical order and the subject's "will" in choosing a particular form. One can already note how he strives to determine an intimacy between form and content that could pave the way for a historical consideration of art as the expression of the epoch and the unity of the spiritual forces in it that contribute to culture.

Kant's epistemological model is implicit when Panofsky rejects the notion of apriority of form and its lying outside psychic-spiritual content. It is the subject who accomplishes the unification, in the object, of his visual perception and world view. Here a new category makes its appearance—the category of the subject who chooses and of the individual's will—which is interesting to note in Panofsky's writings because it will later be a significant component of his historiographic analysis as well as of his inquiry into the theoretical bases of art history.

The essay on *Kunstwollen* (artistic intention) is the second of Panofsky's theoretical works in which he attempts to establish his art-historical research on a rigorous plane of philosophical inquiry, delineate its modalities, and establish its legitimacy. This time the source of his speculation on the artistic phenomenon is Aloïs Riegl, who was the first to eliminate from art theory and from the theory of interpretation the phenomenological character of pure external manifestation, the psychological character connected to the subjectivity of the artist, and last the character of explaining the phenomenon by means of the epoch or of the causal links with preceding artistic forms.

The term Riegl invented to indicate the center around which the interpretation and the very history of art must be oriented is *Kunstwollen*. In the various interpretations given of this concept there has been a general tendency to bring the meaning of this term close to that of *style*, in that it is what constitutes the external character of form, a "dependent variable" of the structural principles of the work of art in its entirety. Style is what changes and makes necessary the demands made on the force that operates the change in forms and on what Riegl himself calls the "dependent variable"—the direction that artistic intention takes, its goal, the "profound structure" of the artistic object.[79]

In his brief essay Panofsky sets out to liberate this still ambiguous term from the meanings that may erroneously be superimposed upon it and to define it even more explicitly than Riegl had, as the apriority, the unitary and necessary foundation of the artistic phenomenon. Artistic activity is distinguished from general historical events in that the work of art is not an event, but the result of acts that lend form to the different materials that offer themselves to this activity.[80] In order to clarify the existential conditions of the artistic phenomenon it is necessary to draw it near the object of consciousness rather than the historical fact. One must grasp it over and above its phenomenal sense and discover the root of the links it establishes with the artist's individuality on the one hand and with the outside world on the other.

The will or intention on which the result of the aesthetic object depends always takes on the nature of a decision, Panofsky says. "One may sensibly speak of 'will' only when there is no unitary impulse that inevitably imposes a certain result, only when there potentially exist in the subject at least two different representations of an aim from which he must choose."[81] Only when there are in the artist the conditions for a polarity between original creative impulse and cultural *Erlebnis* (inner experience), does the consciousness of distinction catch fire and does there begin that reflection which will determine the choice and thus lead artistic intention to a finished result.

This use of the expression *Erlebnis,* which Panofsky here dwells on with a concision that is almost offensive to the reader, deserves more attention than the essay itself sets out to make explicit. One characteristic of Panofsky as a theorist is the very rapid synthesis he makes of the meanings his age had produced and elaborated over the years and through entire schools of thought. What makes him often obscure and leads many critics to hasty generalizations and to attribute only roughly defined positions to him, is precisely his own philosophical intention, which presents us with a "hermetically sealed" and difficult product of different thought processes and constant inspiration drawn from the currents of his epoch that are reelaborated until they are hard to take in and distinguish on his level of abstraction. In the 1920 essay the use of the expression *Erlebnis* makes it possible for us to interpret the rapid and schematic articulation of the concept of artistic intention. "Inner experience" refers to Dilthey's studies on the "sciences of the spirit" and on the foundation of historical knowledge. It is a structural unity of consciousness in the immediacy of its learning relationship with the object. It is givenness apprehended in its interiority from the psychic structure, which is constituted as a tendency to penetrate the world. In fact for Dilthey this structure is endowed with a purpose which lies in the apprehended and interpreted object. Inner experience is a unity of forms and contents; it is the being-for-itself of consciousness; it is on the one hand the evident, the certain and first datum, and on the other the fabric of states of consciousness that is reflected in the object immediately and in a unitary fashion. However, since inner experience is initially a purely emotional state, the object only partly coincides with it in emotion and partly transcends it, because it is through the object that inner experience reveals to itself its structurality and links.

This is not the place for an exposition of Dilthey's epistemology, especially his theory of perception and learning, which in that philosophy is closely connected to an idea of history. Nor is it opportune here to attempt a criticism of the contradictions that emerge from this theory of knowledge, which are partly of the same nature as those one meets with in Cassirer, despite the fact that in many respects the two philosophers have strikingly different viewpoints. Here it is enough to mention the thesis according to which humanity becomes a spiritual object only in that the human states are immediately lived through and become expressions, and in that these expressions are understood.[82] This connection between immediacy, expressivity, and meaning is quite close to Cassirer's tripartite division of the phases of symbolic formation into the expressive, the representative and the significative, in which a succession of results obtained in the becoming of the symbol, rather than the constitutive process of the object, was indicated. The common point in the two theories lies in the first term: in Dilthey immediate experience (*Erleben*), which takes on a historical character, and in Cassirer expression, which, having the characteristics of a sensible "immediacy," must in turn be transcended in meaning.

When Panofsky speaks of the choice artistic intention is forced to make because a cultural inner experience works on it, he is surely bearing in mind the problem Dilthey posed of the connection between knowledge and the types that entire historical epochs develop and in which a vital unity is effected. The very concept of artistic intention and choice belongs to the sphere of inner experience since, tending to knowledge of the object, this experience expresses a psychic energy that lies at the base of every act of will. Panofsky speaks of cultural *Erlebnis* and then only of the *Erlebnis* of those who contemplate the finished work of art. It thus seems that in general he does not accept inner experience as an a priori foundation of the artistic phenomenon, the foundation on which scientific art history must be established. Inner experience is considered a perception of cultural situations that have become stratified and that impose the choice of models, forms, and types upon a more original creative force.

In Panofsky's view inner experience is taken in only from a cultural point of view and, one would say, a posteriori; it is the result of the artistic intention of different ages and is the action this intention works on the beholder by means of the artistic phenomenon. Artistic intention has a more original component than inner experience itself because, set in motion by the latter, it then chooses a particular expressive model that corresponds to a certain inner experience. There is antagonism in the artistic consciousness between inner experience and the original impulse to create and, in choosing, the intention is engendered by this contrast. Moreover, artistic intention cannot be defined in psychological terms,[83] while inner experience is a psychic structure, even though "psychic" in Dilthey has a meaning that goes beyond the pure and simple nature of the soul. In any case its psychological origin is evident in the criticism Dilthey makes of Marburg Neo-Kantianism, which considered only the intellectual side of spirituality and not feeling. In particular Panofsky repudiates this interpretation of artistic intention in a Kantian manner and sets it in an intermediary sphere between intellect and sensibility, between reflection and civilization, which makes it particularly difficult to understand this concept.

The deduction of those categories that make art history objective and in conformity with the theory of knowledge proves to be extremely difficult and theoretically problematical. There is an epistemological essence to philosophical propositions, a pure cognitive content, that leaves aside every psychological and formal determination as well as the intention of the thinker who has uttered them. This apriority must be found for art as well, and Panofsky turns to Kant to define his critical method. In fact he speaks of a "connection of perceptions," of the "pure intellectual concept of causality," of "consciousness in general." Furthermore, he mentions the method in order to acknowledge the objective validity of the philosophical proposition by means of the same data it offers. Last, he finds in the category a criterion of determination "that decides upon the 'yes' or 'no' of the unity of experience, like a reagent given *a priori* that authorizes the object that must be analyzed to account for its proper essence by means of its positive or negative attitude toward that unity."[84] The same consideration must be made in regard to the artistic phenomenon and its possible existence by searching for its immanent sense in the philosophical-transcendental nature of artistic intention—therefore not in its relations with history, the psyche or style, but in its essence as a phenomenon and in the a priori condition of its existence.

The categories that designate the form of artistic intuition are best expressed, according to Panofsky, by the opposition Riegl made between objectivistic and subjectivistic to indicate the attitude of the artist's *I* vis-à-vis the object. The necessity this kind of historiography notes in a certain historical process does not have the same value as "a causal relationship of dependence among different successive phenomena in time, but rather [is equivalent] to the unitary sense that may be discovered as an all-embracing artistic phenomenon."[85] Such a transcendental method does not prevent the more strictly historical method from operating, but should supply it with a basis of possibility, an integration that is indispensable so as not to confound arbitrarily art and artist, subject and object, reality and idea.

Naturally many approaches to the phenomenon under consideration contribute to a historiography understood in this way. The work of art, whose immanent sense must be grasped, first of all must be understood with the aid of the many documents regarding it that have come down to us in the course of time and also by means of successive stratifications of meaning that have deprived it of its original objective aspect. In understanding the work first of all in the concrete and formal meaning of its phenomenal manifestation, which leads us to its inner meaning, historiography must bear in mind the many factors that help to offer or obscure that meaning, especially the errors deriving from the interpretations of the past. "The purpose is not to establish the course of the facts genetically as a necessary succession of diverse individual data, but rather to interpret the history of the sense of this course as an ideal unity."[86]

What does Panofsky mean by "ideal unity"? It is a unitary principle of interpretation that does not note causality and succession in artistic phenomena, but points out their constant in their immanent a priori sense. "Art is not—as a present-day position that overaccentuates its opposition to the theory of imitation would tend to have us believe— a subjective manifestation of feelings or the existential occupation of certain individuals, but is rather a realizing, objectifying conflict, aiming at definite results, between a molding force and the matter that is to be molded."[87]

Panofsky's position here is authentically Kantian in its duality, the comparison between opposing determinations, or better, between something determined a priori and material to be determined which yet remains each time structurally extraneous to the determined thing. This is the Kant of that dramatic section in *Critique of Pure Reason* entitled "Confutation of Idealism." But for Panofsky the material determined and at the same time exposed to ever new determination takes on in the 1920 essay the characteristics of "historical material," "cultural *Erlebnis*," on which the intention (which is not subjective intentionality) makes its choice. The ideal unity of history is not a unity of a process and of an evolution, but a unity of the will that is expressed in the artistic phenomenon as a direction toward one or the other terms of an ineliminable antinomy. Here are the premises of the conclusions that will be dealt with in *Idea,* in which history is conceived as a field of contrasts between which every art theory moves in expressing itself in terms of will, that is, concrete creative energy that arises on the level of this conflict. The artistic phenomenon itself is ideal in that it can manifest itself and make itself quite visible in a material situation of opposition and contradiction; but it is ideal in a transcendental sense because of the endeavor to regain the image from within an epistemological scheme and an a priori structure of the artistic phenomenon.

As a sideline to these considerations, it is interesting to note that in 1920, just before his meeting with Warburg's circle (with which, by the way, Panofsky was already well acquainted) and with Cassirer, he attempted to extend Kant's Copernican revolution to take in art history by trying to deduce the artistic categories in the same way Kant deduced the pure concept of intellect. How illegitimate this procedure was in Cassirer as regards cultural forms has already been pointed out in the difficulty he had in making the apriority coincide with the historical level of development of the apriority itself. Panofsky is more coherent with the Kantian conception because he refuses to explain historical evolution as a conformity with causal links; on the contrary, he makes the historical plane a sort of matter shaped in the phenomenon, a datum that is necessary because it is real and formed in inner experience but has no inner coherence as long as it is not reduced to the phenomenon and to the object of art. Panofsky also makes a noteworthy effort not to confer any vitalistic or evolutionistic character upon creative energy, upon the force implicit in making a choice, and thus does not give in to the influence Bergson and Dilthey exerted at that time; and he also makes a considerable effort to keep the notion of value at a distance from the artistic phenomenon and the problem of history.

How Panofsky intended to make use of that method founded on artistic intention as an a priori determination internal to the artistic phenomenon, as well as on the definition of the historical course as a manifestation of the different will in diverse epochs in choosing the canons of artistic representation, can be seen in the essay published in 1921, "The History of the Theory of Human Proportions as a Reflection of the History of Styles." This work is exemplary for an understanding of the use Panofsky makes of art-historical categories and for following the course of reflection and research that leads to *Idea*. In this period he wrote another significant work, "Albrecht Dürer and Classical Antiquity," which faces the problem of the Renaissance view of antiquity and the new dimension this age took on in comparing itself with the past. These two essays, which concern at once an inquiry and a program that informs this inquiry, were written when Panofsky was already teaching at the Kunstgeschichtliches Seminar of the newly founded University of Hamburg and when he was already in contact both with the philosophy seminar in which Cassirer had just begun to teach and with the Warburg Library. The library had recently been opened to the public as an institute of studies and cultural initiatives connected to the university. And Saxl was filling the difficult position of director, at the same time acting as an intermediary between Aby Warburg (who was still at the rest home) and the daily aims the institute was pursuing with the imprint of its founder's teachings.

The choice of the theories of proportions as the subject of a history of artistic tendencies grew up in the mathematical—and hence unequivocal—essence of the study of human proportions and in its presenting itself as a "reflection" of the history of styles which is however clearer and more explicit than the notion of style and thus more suitable for explaining the nature of the concept of *Kunstwollen,* which creates doubts among interpreters.

Faced with the need for measurement, or for establishing mathematical relations, in order to reproduce the object, the various cultures and epochs established different principles and elaborated the expressive will for each case in forms and viewpoints that changed and often conflicted from one period to another. Panofsky makes a distinction between "objective" and "technical" proportions. The latter are related to a theory of proportions that coincides with a theory of construction, and they alone pose a question whose answer lies in the artistic process itself.[88] There are three different possibilities of pursuing a theory of human measurement. The theory could aim at establishing objective proportions without bothering about their relation to the technical ones; it could establish the technical proportions without troubling itself about their relation to the objective ones; or it could dispense with choice and let the technical and objective proportions coincide, as the Egyptians, and only the Egyptians, did. The problem of proportions is also connected to that of vision and of the change that body movement effects in the dimensions of the moving part and the other parts. The Egyptians were unaware of these problems because their artistic will tended not toward what is changeable, but toward what is constant; they aimed at realizing timeless immobility.

In passing let me note that it was precisely this sense of immutability that caused Plato to admire Egyptian art so much that he even considered it much more worthy than the Greek art of his time. The Egyptian figure reproduced the form but not the function of the human being, which the artist measured so as to be able to reconstruct.[89] The coincidence of technical and objective proportions did not obtain in Greek art because the artistic intention there was to vary freely the objective so as to lead to the reproduction of a figure more consonant with the artist's and viewer's vision. Therefore the measurements given in Polyclitus's canon for the human figure were more anthropometric-objective than technical and were regulated according to organic differentiation rather than to mechanical identity.

Quoting the anecdote of Diodorus of Sicily on the Egyptian moduli of applying proportions, Panofsky points out how Diodorus was clearly aware of the difference between Egyptian and Greek canons and how he efficaciously interpreted the former as a canon of reproduction or "reconstruction," while the latter needed to be confirmed for each case and thus adapted to direct visual observation. The

Greeks had to reformulate the system of measurement each time the imitation of reality required a particular foreshortening, a torsion, a detail in movement; faced with these problems, all canons betrayed their limits.[90]

In medieval art one finds, in contradistinction to classical art, a "planarity" of forms in which the "depth motifs" are only "devaluated," and not completely "suppressed" as in Egyptian art. This is an "unrestrained mobility" of forms which, though presupposing the free movement of ancient art, liberates itself from rules of imitation and reproduction and employs a purely schematic method. Panofsky distinguishes two tendencies in medieval artistic intention—Byzantine and Gothic. Byzantine is based upon Hellenistic sources and on number mysticism that leads it to choose an algebraic or numerical system of measurements which is much more compatible to the medieval tendency to schematize than the classical system of common fractions.[91] The canon of proportions reveals the Byzantine artistic intention, since it discards objective dimensions in favor of facile technical reproduction.[92]

"The Italian Renaissance looked upon the theory of proportions with unbounded reverence; but it considered it, unlike the Middle Ages, no longer as a technical expedient but as the realization of a metaphysical postulate."[93] At this point Panofsky makes an observation that also clarifies a general method of inquiry in *Idea,* which was criticized exactly on this matter by Walter Friedländer. In his 1928 review of Panofsky's book in the *Jahrbuch für Kunstwissenschaft,* Friedländer had noted an inconsistency in Panofsky's mode of expounding art-historical material; first he deals with the concepts of idea in various philosophical theories and then, beginning with the Renaissance, he considers the artists and no longer the philosophers. The critic notes that in the Middle Ages as well artists must have had their opinions on art theory and their thought must not have been so different from that of an Alberti, a Leonardo, or a Raphael. It is strange how this critique remains so indeterminate and does not cite examples that could fill in the presumed gap in *Idea.*

Actually what Panofsky is concerned with pointing out in the transition from the Middle Ages to the Renaissance is a change in the relationship between theoretical analysis and artistic practice. The metaphysical postulate, which was present in the medieval conception of measurement of the human body, "followed the line" of harmonistic cosmology and, according to Panofsky, had no relationship with art. Insofar as the purely theoretical canons had come into contact with artistic practice they had lost their metaphysical-theological nature and had "degenerated into a code of practical rules." The Renaissance, which began to accept sculpture and painting as part of the liberal arts and to conceive art as an expression of universal laws, reinvested the theory of proportions with metaphysical meaning that was fused with the artists' actual works.[94] This theory now became the necessary premise for artistic production and at the same time the expression of harmony preestablished between microcosm and natural universe, the rational foundation of beauty. The same process can be seen in *Idea,* where Panofsky notes that medieval speculation concerning the concept of ideal beauty is integrated in the Renaissance through the reproduction of the idea into lovely and harmonious images, so that the aesthetic problem of a relationship between intellectual activity and sensory perception is for the first time made explicit and becomes an object of study for the artists themselves. Renaissance artistic intention tended to legitimize and rationalize the forms of subjectivity,[95] so that it effected a fundamental innovation in the classical canons of proportion, supplementing anthropometry with "both a physiological (and psychological) theory of movement and a mathematically exact theory of perspective."[96] And here Warburg's teachings make themselves felt, albeit still implicitly, in Panofsky's discourse. Measurement and observation are reborn together in Renaissance art, but the artistic taste for the classical motif of movement is accentuated, and this movement becomes almost an autonomous category for an interpretation of this epoch.

An example of the transition from the Middle Ages to the Renaissance in the personality of one artist alone is quite clearly revealed in Dürer. Panofsky brings to fruition his profound and exhaustive 1913 study on what Dürer acquired upon coming into contact with the Italian Renaissance[97] to show how, when he arrived in Italy from his German-Gothic milieu, this great artist basically modified his view of the theory of proportions, influenced in this above all by the purely anthropometric science developed by Alberti and Leonardo. He even went so far as to pursue the study of this subject as an end in itself, so that it lost its connection with artistic reproduction, like an exclusively scientific and abstract field all to itself that could no longer depend upon any possible practical application to art.

This Dürerian episode concludes an artistic epoch of the theory of proportions, for its necessity as a foundation for art in the construction of the human body declined when the subject-artist-spectator came to the fore and prevailed upon the very definition of the object. "The value and artistic meaning of a theory that dealt exclusively with the objective dimensions of human figures set within definable limits necessarily had to depend on the importance attributed to these figures, that is to say, whether or not they were acknowledged as being the final aim of artistic activity."[98] When Renaissance subjectivism was deprived of the absolute model of classical rules and the revival of antiquity lost its value as a vehicle of imitation and rediscovery, the subjective principle triumphed over observation and the definition of objective laws and decreed the subject's accomplished independence from the object. In the seventeenth century the human figure meant very little in comparison with the "light and air diffused in unlimited space."[99]

By demonstrating the connection between the theory of proportions and the history of styles, Panofsky lends credence to his thesis—which is critical of Wölfflin—that style becomes part of that totality of forms that go to make up *Kunstwollen*. In reality he creates a history of artistic intention from the standpoint of the particular aspect of the theory of proportions and demonstrates the movement and change in style in the alternation of different historical artistic intentions. Here the principle of antinomy inherent to the historical process, which will come fully to the fore in *Idea,* is not yet explicitly stated, though Panofsky clearly abandons the positive meaning of the evolution of a form since its appearance and disappearance are observed in historical becoming without any attempt at grasping these events theoretically. Rather, one notes in the course of the history of art a constant, which is artistic intention, just as in *Idea* the constant will be the subject-object relationship which, perhaps because of its philosophical-epistemological nature, is followed in the chronological process of forms that it engendered, in a context of contrasts, negations, and recurrences.

With respect to *Idea* there is another difference, connected to the attempt to determine artistic intention in its potentiality and expressive force, which in the Panofsky of that period is to be seen above all in the totality and complexity of the subject-object relationship in the Renaissance. The Renaissance *Kunstwollen* tends toward the harmonic and mathematical perfection of forms, and its cultural inner experience is influenced by the power of the classical example which is rediscovered and renewed also and above all in its new historical dimension vis-à-vis the Middle Ages. Now for the first time the theoretical presupposition of art is sought in a philosophy and science of the subject-object, artist-nature relationship. The artistic intention of later ages, on the other hand, opts for the metaphysical predominance of the subject and searches for the principles of reproduction of the real in it. In the 1921 essay on the theory of proportions, the Renaissance is viewed as a highly vigorous moment in the search for an objective and universally valid solution to the problem of the subject and its relationship with the world, which is expressed in terms of the rationalization of subjectivity. In the 1924 essay on the concept of idea, even though Panofsky's viewpoint remains the same, the Renaissance is interpreted as agitated by the more confused and contradictory situation that obtained in the various currents of thought, that is, the different way in which the very revival of antiquity was expressed. And the contradiction engendered by the all-embracing view of the Renaissance, which is however delimited by objective rules, is overcome by more far-reaching research into the subject on the part of Mannerism and then Classicism, research in which the rule lies a priori in the subject and is the ideal and absolute model for a reconstruction of reality.

In "Albrecht Dürer and Classical Antiquity" both the direction historiographic analysis takes through the importance attached to antinomies in history and Warburg's influence on the way Panofsky approaches Renaissance works are made explicit. In this study on Dürer's relationship with the revival of classical antiquity, Panofsky singles out a series of motifs that constitute the basis of his inquiry as an art historian. He tries to answer the question of whether and how a fifteenth-century German artist could return to classical art and pose for himself the problems handed down by that art. Here the expression *historical necessity* is introduced to indicate the fact that in an epoch still unaware of the "pathos of distance," there grew up in an artist the suggestion of the return to classical antiquity and the will to examine in both theory and practice the possibilities inherent to an in-depth study of antiquity. Then there appears—and here we are in a totally Warburgian atmosphere—the term *pathos* and an interpretation of the Renaissance as an epoch attracted by the " 'tragic unrest' of the Antique before it could appreciate and abandon itself to its 'classical calm.' "[100] An understanding of the "quiet grandeur" of the *Apollo Belvedere* comes after the German artist is enraptured by the dramatic death scenes or the ever changing movement and agitation of the Maenads' veils on ancient sarcophagi. In reproducing the image of Apollo, Dürer even animated his creation with the tension and struggle suggested to him by the model, and his many attempts to lend form to that figure betray his uncertainty in the choice of new formulas which pressed upon his imagination and sensitivity and finally came into being.

A twofold mediation leads Dürer to the reproduction of the classical: his reading of an Italian poet—perhaps Poliziano—who had translated Ovid's *Metamorphosis,* and the observation of the way the Italian painters had resolved their perception of the material of ancient art and sensitivity. The Nymph, which lies at the center of Warburg's inquiry into quattrocento art, was also for Panofsky an example of how the Renaissance had taken in a particular attitude used in classical art only in exceptional cases—that of frenetic movement—and had destined it to the common representation of persons moving.[101] What allowed Dürer to depict delicate, nervously animated figures in conformity with contemporary taste at the same time that he created examples of ponderous energy was the manifold influence worked by the Italian quattrocento, which taught him both the classical style and its modern interpretation. According to Warburg's formula, fully adopted by Panofsky, the Renaissance coupled heroic pathos with the Apollonian aspect. The more Dürer increased and enriched his contact with Italian art and his knowledge of classical models and the theoretical texts on creating figures, the more he appropriated those numerous aspects his artistic will succeeded in taking in and reproducing.[102]

But mere imitation of, or thoroughgoing conformity with, the Italian quattrocento made no sense to Dürer's brilliant mind. Rather, he felt the need to interpret those images independently by means of his great interest in the historical documents that were continuously being unearthed during that time, and the need to discover an affinity among the different symbols. His creative vigor manifests itself most of all in the new synthesis of the antique displayed in some of his works, such as the version of the *Apollo Belvedere* in the guise of *Helios Pantokrator,* in which the gestural rendering departs from the original through the ideal fusion Dürer used in conceiving this image. The sun god of the classical Greeks, so worldly and splendid in his natural synthesis of agility and power, is replaced by the invincible god of Eastern mysticism until the new Christian religion replaces the cult of Mithras with the image of a victorious Christ, now become a sun understood in a moral sense, a *Sol Iustitiae* rather than a cosmological sun.

Panofsky's reconstruction of the iconological models used by Dürer in his artistic formulation of the concept suggested to him by the *Apollo Belvedere,* and now filtered through a myriad of different expressions into images of that concept, is based on the texts of classical German philology, especially those of Hermann Usener, who had been one of Warburg's teachers. This reconstruction also explicitly reveals Panofsky's adherence to the aims and formulas of the Warburg Library. Besides Warburg's influence and his thesis of the migration of images, one already notes the effect of the collaboration with Fritz Saxl and his unique way of viewing the superimposition and coincidence, in the mind of an erudite artist, of diverse cultural and cultic experiences that the various epochs have set in images, as well as his supreme effort to choose one motif rather than another in the end. Just as the Christian concept of the *Sol Iustitiae* competed with the *Sol Invictus* in the mind of late antiquity, so these two concepts competed in Dürer's imagination.[103] "Only the power of Dürer could translate this concept into an image."[104]

In the fourth section of this essay, entitled "The Fundamental Question," Panofsky pays homage—perhaps unique for its conciseness in the art historian's oeuvre—to those scholars who inspired him: Warburg, with his theses and sources, and Riegl, with his theory of *Kunstwollen* and its having become basic for an understanding of art history. The chapter opens with a quotation from Goethe on the theme of nature, which the ancients depicted in its excellence and nobility, as they possessed its most profound rules. Goethe opposes idealist art theory and sees the peculiarity of classical art in its sublimation of nature by means of nature itself, thereby resolving the conventional antithesis between idealism and naturalism.[105] It is strange how Panofsky in *Idea* does not think of using Goethe's image of nature to distinguish Bellori's aesthetics and the normative tendency of classicism in general from the subsequent idealistic phase. Two concepts are ignored in *Idea*, where Panofsky wants to consider the force of the ideal already operating in classicism: that whereby the force in every return to a classical conception of the beautiful consists in possessing the rule that serves to dominate nature and force it to assume lovely forms, and that whereby such expressive vigor is to be explained most adequately in Kant's definition in *Prolegomena* ("nature is the existence of things in so far as it is determined by universal laws") and is therefore incompatible with a notion of the ideal as the subject's power to imagine beyond simple natural appearance.

In this essay the suggestion that influenced Panofsky's historical view probably came from that attempt to construct history in conformity with a unitary, finalistic design which Cassirer had indicated in his works of the same period and was elaborating in his *Philosophy of Symbolic Forms*. But behind that contingent suggestion a much more serious influence was at work, an influence stemming from the interpretation given by Hegel, in his *Aesthetics*, of German classicism (Winckelmann and Lessing) as idealism, since it had marked out the ideal of Greek art in "noble simplicity and quiet grandeur." The Greek ideal that Winckelmann described so passionately in regard to the Vatican statues and the drawings of Greek marbles in the great Rome collections he frequented has nothing in common with the ideal that in Hegel—and in the aesthetics he inspired—is the total possession of the idea on the part of the subject. That ideal is the definition of a rule of measure of the real and is the striving for a beauty that stems from the observation of nature and at the same time from a view of that very nature in what in it is potential, not immediately perceptible, in the revealed laws of its mysterious harmony.[106]

Here one touches upon the complex problem of the interpretation of classical antiquity that Panofsky, because of his capacity for assimilation and his quickness, had viewed as fundamental for Warburg's art-historical method of inquiry. Noble simplicity and quiet grandeur had become in Warburg's writings an impassioned fever of movement, an anguished pathos that barely managed to conceal itself in the equipoise of forms, only to explode as soon as the subject reproduced allowed it to do so. Panofsky briefly mentions the conflict between Apollonian and Dionysian that Nietzsche found in Greek art, a view certainly shared by Warburg, who made every effort in his studies to find a satisfactory equilibrium between the admiration for measure and the pain and sorrow caused by excess.

The greatness of the Greeks consists most of all in their having made the most varied synthesis of the data of experience in types and images that have remained impressed upon humanity's memory and have never been totally abandoned because they are too evident to the imagination and are the repository of all possible knowledge and reproduction of reality. Panofsky accepts as valid categories in the construction of art history the pathos formulas that Warburg viewed as eternal expressive forms of the aspirations and fears of humankind to which the Greeks—according to him—had given a tangible dimension once and for all. "Thus to have captured and ordered the multitude of phenomena is the eternal glory of classical art; at the same time, however, it was its insurmountable barrier."[107] In fact typification utilizes the concept of measure that excludes excess, imposes moderation, and prohibits going beyond harmony and limit. This was not often accepted in history, and each epoch that tried to free itself from the constriction of ironclad rules either rejected or ignored the classical model.

Once again, in Panofsky's view an artistic intention is at work in history; it makes choices, appropriates models or rejects them. This intention was decisive for the Greeks as well, who had no need to choose between Apollonian and Dionysian, between divine calm and Bacchic turmoil, because their will manifested itself as a miracle of synthesis. In the Hellenic will "there is neither beauty without movement nor pathos without moderation; the 'Apollonian,' one might say, is 'Dionysian' *in potentia* while the 'Dionysian' is 'Apollonian' *in actu*."[108] Rather than an affirmation of bourgeois or Philistine banality, as Nietzsche would perhaps have called it, we must regard this attitude of Panofsky's toward the classical as a "joke" on the part of his lucid and uncontaminated critical intelligence. He was only too well acquainted with the excesses of Mannerism and Baroque art and the power wrought upon a subject by overcrowded space in Dutch painting to allow himself to be ravished by enthusiasm for classical art and its absolute rule of the beautiful. Constantly armed with Kantian epistemological determinations and with rules well within the limits of the conditioned apriority, Panofsky carries out his task as a critic in search of the constants and energies that have dominated the course of that multiform and multicolored spectacle—that is, artistic production through the ages.

And in the essay on Dürer another category finds its configuration and application: that of cultural *Erlebnis,* which comes to the surface again when it must be explained why it was Dürer who taught the Renaissance to the Germans after his apprenticeship in Italy. The Germans could not directly absorb classical art because "the Antique was not yet an 'object of possible aesthetic experience.'"[109] Northern art had developed upon principles diametrically opposed to those of classical art. While the latter tends toward the typical and is thus basically plastic and its figures contain both unity and multiplicity and are isolated from their surroundings so as to exemplify or typify a multitude of cases, Northern art developed along particularistic and pictorial lines and started off from a subjective, unilateral viewpoint. While the particular object has a representative significance in classical art and embodies the perfection of its type, in Northern art the object is a particular thing in a much vaster field, incorporated in a meaningful spatial totality.[110] The first German Renaissance did not want to merge art with the discovery of the antique which, both among erudites and humanists, took on a fundamentally antiquarian value, since the subject matter of the classical tradition was appreciated, but not from an aesthetic or formal point of view. The Italian Renaissance was an intermediary between classical antiquity and Northern *Kunstwollen.* "On the other hand, however, the Italian quattrocento shared with the Northern fifteenth century one basic premise which did not apply in the Middle Ages: on both sides of the Alps, art had become a matter of direct and personal contact between man and the visible world."[111]

It is thus the subject-object relationship, in its still nonconflictual form of independent observation of the object on the part of both the artist and the viewer, that unites the Northern and Southern renascences, despite their different cultural inner experiences, and opposes them to the Middle Ages. The subject of the observation of nature leads Panofsky to deal with the question of perspective and the importance of the studies effected in the quattrocento on infinite space and the vanishing point. The zeal with which both the Germans and Italians developed the method of perspective is the sign of a historical turning-point with respect to the Middle Ages that unites the different areas of the Renaissance in a common consciousness of the mathematical reproducibility of figures in space. "Thus, the relationship of the Early Renaissance artists to classical antiquity was dominated by two antithetical impulses: while wanting to revive it, they were compelled to transcend it."[112] In this context the fact that many Italian quattrocento artists felt the influence of Northern and Flemish art as much as that of ancient art, is highly significant. Classicizing "idealism" and Northern "realism" are often to be found in the same painting. Panofsky regards this mediating character of Italian Renaissance art as a sign not of an imitation of antiquity, but a re-interpretation of it by means of a precise artistic intention. If in one respect this intention seemed similar to that of the classical age, it also had an overwhelming interest in its own research into the sphere of images and form. The Northern Renaissance gained access to the antique and understood it only after Dürer had imparted the artistic intention and creative characteristics of the Italian Renaissance to German artists. Dürer approached antiquity only through the canons of his epoch, which he learned in Italy, where the antique had already been revived for generations; and classical art was perhaps comprehensible to him only because it "confronted him in a form altered according to contemporary standards."[113]

In the equilibrium and sureness of Panofsky's meticulous historical reconstruction, there appears, as a sideline so to speak, in brief notes, the urgency of a polemic that reveals the historical moment in which he embarked upon these meditations. Rather subtle mention is made of the question of the distinction between natural sciences and the "sciences of the spirit," a distinction not lacking in irony in that almost imperceptible way Panofsky had of being ironic. And there are respectful but resolute protests against the enemies of rationality and of that postmedieval intellectual form, that is, perspective. Rather than against Expressionist art as a whole, this attack seems to be aimed at the irrationality and anti-intellectualism that were so widespread as cultural expressions of postwar Weimar Germany. And of a similar political nature is another rapid and scornful attack leveled against the nationalism that makes certain critics regret Dürer's "contamination" of pure German art with Italian art. Panofsky considers all rhetorical emphasis alien to the historian's task, and he waxes ironical about those rationalistic critics who on the other hand "could not forgive Rembrandt for *not* going to Italy." Here again, in separating himself from the frenzy of extremism and from radical positions, Panofsky finds his proper milieu in the circle of scholars at the Warburg Institute and in company with Ernst Cassirer. Naturally he sided with those intellectuals who tried to repel the conflict that was coming to the fore in German culture by correcting its excesses as much as possible, as they were well aware that this state could only lead to a veritable catastrophe.

Artistic intention and historical necessity, historical conflict and cultural *Erlebnis*, formulas expressing pathos and the research into perspective are but some of the basic categories that Panofsky deduces through his analysis of sources and theory to lend a scientific, and not contradictory, character to his discipline. He thus aspires to construct a historical design not to establish it as an absolute law of becoming, but to offer a structure to that configuration of phenomena and spiritual products that would allow one to recover missing data continuously and that would supply the most suitable tool for fathoming the obscure and insidious "well of the past" in search of lost components and of a coherent explanation of the event. Moving backwards with respect to the normal course of becoming, Panofsky removes the different images of humanity from their mysterious migration and gathers them together; as he believes in their eternity, he evokes them from the obscurity they are hidden in and sets them in their legitimate place "in broad daylight," as it were. This is a struggle against oblivion in which the fear of life and horror of death are generated like anguished specters.

Before discussing Panofsky's new historical work, "Die Perspektive als 'symbolische Form'" (Perspective as "Symbolic Form"), published in the Warburg Institute's *Vorträge* series in 1924–25, I must mention the first work that resulted from his collaboration with Fritz Saxl, the essay on Dürer's *Melencolia I* which came out in the institute's *Studien* series in 1923. The research carried out on the iconographic material in Dürer's famous engraving—which seems to have been executed in 1514—revolves around the contrasting meanings that the myth of Saturn and the temperament of melancholy have taken on in the course of history, and on how, through the Renaissance reformulation, the Saturn-melancholy motif transmitted images, sentiments, and thoughts to Dürer that he fashioned into a new and original product in his engraving.

It is in connection with the formation of the mythology of Saturn that one speaks of what Cassirer calls conceptual structures. For the historians of Warburg's school and for Warburg himself, the conceptual structure manifested in the image of a given reality undergoes only expressive or stylistic variations in the course of history and remains basically the same. The conceptual structures that lie at the base of historical interpretation take on the value of a permanent entity. History continually refers to them and this constant guarantees the unity of a historian's analysis. What relationship is there between this constant and becoming? In Panofsky's opinion it is an a priori foundation not only of historical analysis but of becoming itself, whose permanent point of reference lies in these categories. In Cassirer's view the structures are a schema of interference between the epistemological foundation of reality and the process that has led to that structure. In each case it is at once the beginning and the result. Panofsky, however, distinguishes—both in his theoretical and historical writings—the analytical base as a structure of history from the results which, in conformity with that base, the historian verifies in phenomena. His rigorously aprioristic position thus leads him to express the doubt that total theoretical reducibility between a logical apriority and historical becoming is possible. His position also makes him cautious in his judgment of an artistic phenomenon because he knows that the legitimacy of the datum's reference to its conceptual basis is rendered problematical by the antinomical situation with which reality offers itself to the inquiry, and by an almost insurmountable difficulty in interpreting the dynamics of the facts. Yet the scheme of reference is not called into question by becoming or by the passing of time, but rather by the obscurity of the sources and the inscrutability of the paths the historian must take to reassemble the original configuration.

However there is in the work of these scholars a great faith in the potential of historical knowledge and in the value of the discoveries this knowledge makes possible, discoveries that lead to a clarification of the facts. The objective pursued is the universality of knowledge, because it is precisely in leaving no stone unturned in the paths of knowledge, in the investigation carried out in the most disparate fields, that one is certain to find, sooner or later, the detail that was lacking so that the picture can acquire unity. The detail that passed unobserved in the oblivion of the past is the missing link of a chain that in itself is not affected by becoming but remains stable, even though it apparently breaks up every time some of its parts are unknown to us.

In the particular case of the myth of Cronus, a careful analysis of its intimate structure and its character, which is not simple but composite, can explain the modes of its representation in time.[114] Just like the myth of Saturn through the gnostic-pessimist tradition (the soul's fall) and the Neoplatonic-optimistic tradition (the positive influence of the stars), the definition of melancholy is marked by a polarity of signification that leads to the multiplication of contradictory meanings regarding the same figuration. Among the Greeks melancholy is a disease, as are all the temperaments for that matter, with the exception of the sanguine.[115] But there is also a conception of melancholy as genius and virtue, which for Aristotle takes on a positive meaning. An ambiguous connotation nevertheless remains; men of genius move between two abysses—the precious, divine gift and the dangerous poison that makes their character unsteady and insecure. Genius is therefore an extreme nature with a difficult, painful equilibrium that is undermined by its falling into one of the two extremes. The conciliation was attempted also in the Middle Ages, where melancholy as a type characterized thought. Mental fatigue generates illness which is sometimes interpreted as approaching grace. In the negative interpretation of a certain iconographical tradition, however, Saturn remains the cursed star with a harmful influence. Only with Dante (in Canto XXI of *Paradise*) does it become the star of contemplation; and along with the great poet all Florentines of the early Renaissance rediscover the value of this positive astral influence upon the behavior of geniuses.

With Ficino the traditions of melancholy and Saturn merge. Since melancholy is a necessity, an astral destiny, for some people, Ficino states that one must defend oneself against it with certain rules of living. This apparently contradictory thesis is the result of a view of the cosmos as a vital unity which is the harmony of the parts in the whole. Melancholy comes from Saturn; it is a singular, divine gift, because Saturn is the noblest, most powerful star.[116] For Ficino the saturnine person is the man of letters and the philosopher who must understand the infinite possibilities open to him by the influence of the stars and must therefore attempt to avoid the unhealthy, negative side that his melancholic temperament and his celestial protector communicate to him, and enjoy only the positive side—contemplation.[117] To this end Ficino prescribes an orderly, moderate life that is rationally administered and disciplined with the appropriate habits and food; and he also advises the use of the astral magic of talismans. In astrology there is a peculiar characterization of the cosmos by which a structural element (the presence of the god-planet and the analogy terrestrial things have with it) is connected to a fortuitous element (the planet emanates influences that modify terrestrial things). A mythical anthropomorphic view is complemented and slowly replaced by a view of cosmological dynamism. A link is forged here between the analogical thought of magical origin and a scientific-causal explanation of phenomena which led to a possible explanation of life in the sense of a dynamics immanent in nature. The importance astrology had in intellectual history at the beginning of the modern age lies in this relationship.[118]

Here there is an approach to Cassirer's thesis of the "passage" from an anthropomorphic mode of thought to one regulated by the causal schema. Yet for Panofsky the causal schema remains for historical observation a viewpoint internal to a conception of the world and of nature that sinks its roots in a distant past, in the history of a latent antinomy. In Cassirer's opinion the causal schema is a point of arrival in the progressive objectivization of concepts and of their being rendered universally valid in relation to a possible experience. The analysis of Ficino's position is typical of Warburg's milieu; in this philosopher there is the struggle between the fear of the ancient demon and late Hellenistic Neoplatonic faith in the universal harmony of the cosmos in which it is possible to resist, and even make positive, a negative influence by means of an intelligent mixture of rationality and magic.

The passage to a meticulous observation and interpretation of Dürer's engraving is carried out along the lines of these premises. The means indicated by Ficino (dietetic, medicinal, and magical-astrological) in his *De vita triplici* to overcome the negative influence are to be found in Dürer's work.[119] On the other hand, the melancholy person's gesture of clasping his forehead originated in a very ancient expressive gesture whose essential meaning as a sign of grief is represented already in Egyptian reliefs.[120] However it also has another meaning; it indicates tiredness and fatigue on the part of creative thought. There are the symbols of the trades and occupations typical of the saturnine temperament as well. In the reproduction of the tools of geometry and of measurement, Dürer offers an image of the totally symbolic melancholic temperament. But here the symbolic, though imitating the expressive tradition, serves to fashion an individual thought, a subjective atmosphere, a true determination of the character over and above the type that is depicted. Melancholy is personified in an ambiguous, subjective sense, which can be understood as a melancholic disposition, as illness, and as a melancholic atmosphere. The essence of melancholy contains the essence of Saturn, whose polarity is translated by Dürer into an ambiguity of modes and expression, into artistic unity—not only spatial and stylistic, but intimate as well.[121]

This essence of melancholy is to be found in a meditation of Heinrich von Gent (quoted by Pico della Mirandola in his *Apologia*) on the nature of this temperament. Von Gent says that there are two types of men: the metaphysically oriented ones who contemplate abstract essences without a body, and those who can think only in terms of representation, when the imagination of this latter accompanies the thought, that is, when these men can *see* the thing represented *spatially*. The persons in the second category are the melancholic mathematicians incapable of engaging in metaphysical speculation because they are always conditioned by spatial representations. "We do not know whether Dürer knew of this meditation [of von Gent's], and yet we discern in his passage from the physiological-astrological to the transcendental-psychological a motif central to his oeuvre. Here we have the expression of the tragic destiny of a human spirit who sees himself hemmed in by the limits of his own inner rules, which he cannot escape from and yet wants to escape from."[122]

Panofsky and Saxl see a spiritual self-portrait of Dürer in the symbolic image of melancholy.[123] The work reveals Dürer's awareness that mathematics could not lead him to the absolute, which for him, a Renaissance artist, was absolute beauty. In 1512 he wrote that he did not know what beauty was—where for "beauty" he did not mean its concept, but its sensory appearance in the form of proportional measurements. This skepticism on his part corresponds to a Faustian type of awareness (as Wölfflin had already noted) of not being humanly able to know anything.[124] In this way the theme of not being able to know, which belongs to the old Saturn myth that in such varied forms and through diverse philosophical attitudes came down to Dürer, lives again in him in the fullness of its contradictory original nature, which a great Renaissance artistic consciousness makes evident for the first time in its entirety. The conceptual structure of the "Saturn essence" thus has in Dürer's work a manifestation of itself that is as original and faithful as it is modern and charged with all the meanings that the Renaissance was discovering about human nature.

The title of the 1924 essay on perspective is an explicit homage to the *Philosophy of Symbolic Forms,* the first volume of which was published in 1923 by Bruno Cassirer. This book, on language, was preceded by two essays published in the Warburg Library's *Vorträge* series that summarized the conception of symbolic form and of the connection between concept and myth and between symbol and "sciences of the spirit." As in the contemporaneous work *Idea*, in "Die Perspektive als 'symbolische Form'" Panofsky presents the history of a concept utilized in many different ways in artistic practice and theory. But whereas in *Idea* one notes the transformation over the centuries of the original meaning of the Platonic idea in relation to aesthetics, here an analysis is made of a category of artistic reproduction, perspective, and of its intrinsic meaning vis-à-vis the view of space typical of the various ages. In general perspective is—together with *Kunstwollen* and one and the same with it—an a priori component of artistic creativity, since through it one expresses a spatial point of view that varies in accordance with the artist's different modes of viewing objectivity.

Panofsky chooses a Cassirerian type of definition of symbolic form: "a form through which a particular spiritual content is connected to a concrete sensory sign and is intimately identified with it."[125] It is important to point out from the first that Panofsky does not say "immediately" identified, but uses the word *intimately,* which best expresses the accomplished synthesis between spiritual content—the historical inner experience, the feeling and the intention of the epoch and of the artist, that is, a direction in the formal choice—and sensory sign. Whatever the actual typology of the symbolic form may be and whatever epoch it is manifested in, it expresses the power of a mediation—which is at once of a conceptual and emotional order—between the rule that it communicates and the object it determines and constructs. It takes in an expressive need that is inalienable to Western art, whatever the conception of the world, and the will that studies and reveals it in the work, may be. If perspective was a particular object of technical study and invention among Renaissance artists, this was not because of its intimate evolutionary force tending to self-perfection, as Cassirer believes, but because of a historical necessity which in the constitution and disintegration of artistic models leads to an acquisition of space determined in time and always in turn susceptible, in its technical aspect, to coming apart in following the path of artistic intention. Panofsky was well aware of contemporary art's rejection of the rule of perspective and of the theory of proportions, and thus kept a prudent distance from Cassirer's optimistic belief in the fulfillment of the evolution of the symbol.

Here again at the base of historical becoming there is an antinomy: psycho-physiological space as opposed to rational space, that is, infinite, constant, and homogeneous space. Perspective, as the intuition of the rational space in the modern conception, is radically abstracted from qualitatively figured space and from fundamental facts of subjective vision, from the difference between the psychologically determined "visual image" and the "retinal image."[126] Classical antiquity was used to seeing with a perspective that was not measured. The plasticity of a figure was conceived without regard for the actual space that surrounded it; there was no integration between figure and residual space. The concept of the vanishing point, toward which the half-lines of Alberti's visual pyramid converged, was basically alien to the ancients, Panofsky says, because they had no concept of limit in infinity, no notion of the infinite. The space that ensues from the constructions of antiquity is not the systematic space required by modern times.[127] The result is that space is inadequate to figures in ancient works; the feeling of space was expressed in a systematic manner in the figurative arts, and none of the many theories of space of that time ever managed to define it as a system of mere relationships between height, width, and depth.[128]

We know in fact how difficult it was for Aristotle to define the essence of space and that he ended up rather delimiting the "place" as an extreme limit of the "container," thus rejecting Democritus's theory of void. If Panofsky had not been so strongly attracted by his inquiry into Renaissance perspective, he would have been able to dwell more upon the nature of space and the infinite in antiquity, especially the breadth of Plato's concept of *chora,* that space which, in surrounding things, delimits and determines them. In general, a literal interpretation of Aristotle's prohibition of the actuality of the infinite, which can exist only potentially, does not seem sufficient for an in-depth analysis of these concepts. Actually the ancients had a very complex notion of the infinite. One need only mention the theoretical difficulty Plato had in removing the concept of number or measure from infinite divisibility and from indeterminateness, or the formidable problems that spatial extension generated in the conception of the idea,[129] to realize that probably the simple opposition of the modern notion of the infinite to the infinite of the Greeks has become a platitude in the history of philosophy.

When Panofsky speaks of antiquity's "feeling of space" he intuits an enormous extension of his investigation and passes over this section rapidly so as to place himself again in the well-circumscribed terrain of the actuality of the work of art. "For, if Aristotle states there is no '*quantum continuum*' in which the determination of individual things is resolved, for him there does not exist even an *energeia apeiron* that transcends the existence of individual things . . . And precisely this reveals quite evidently how 'aesthetic space' and 'theoretical space' always translate perspective space into a sole, identical feeling, which in the first case is symbolized and in the second is logicized."[130] Is it perhaps a bit risky to affirm that the Greek figure, conceived without residues of spatiality—that is, without residues of unformed matter, matter not bound by limits—contained a power of determination and embraced and exhausted in itself that logical-metaphysical entity, that is, measure, and that for this reason expressed a supreme unity of the manifold that lies at the origin of every image and of every type upon which even today every cultural formation in the Western world depends?

Panofsky tackles a new phase of the thought concerning space: the medieval return to antiquity which, if it destroyed the classical age's model of perspective, still conserved its parts and assembled them in a different unity. "The road leading to this new unity passes first of all—paradoxical as this may seem—through the destruction of the existing unity, that is, the crystallization and isolation of the individual elements that were previously limited by mimetic-corporeal and perspective-spatial binds."[131] In the importance Panofsky attaches to this return to the past there are echoes of the theme of historical necessity, which once again appears as the need for polarity. Just as in the 1921 essay on Dürer Panofsky spoke of how it was necessary for an epoch of oblivion to be followed by an epoch of the rediscovery of antiquity in the Northern Renaissance, so here he theorizes the return to the past that is at once a breach with the formal unity proposed by the past and a new philosophical and artistic ideation. It is precisely the "primitivism" of the Middle Ages that paves the way for later rebirths. According to Panofsky there is a continuity in the history of art; it is not based on an ideal evolution but on a disintegration of unitary artistic models so as to constitute new models that are equally unitary as symbolic forms but are not understood as progressing toward the best model, since each model carries within itself the element of disintegration of the new unitary essence.

Therefore at the base of the definite structure of the symbolic form there remains an antinomical essence that is impossible to resolve definitively, just as it seems impossible to resolve philosophically the problem of historical becoming. Panofsky feels that in the understanding of the historical datum, there is superimposed upon the positive autonomy of cultural science theorized by Cassirer the pain-filled Warburgian belief that the image of all time reveals both the uncontrolled demon of fear and the sometimes melancholic, sometimes arrogant attempt to rationalize chaos, that is, to strive after absolute form.

Byzantine civilization conserved some forms from antiquity, and these were then transmitted to the Renaissance through successive elaborations. Other forms, though, gradually disintegrated, and thus the laws of spatial connection peculiar to antiquity were lost. As a result, space took on an ever more abstract value, sometimes homogeneous with figures (as in the Romanesque period), at other times independent of them (as in the Gothic age). Aristotle's infinite is again elaborated by Scholastic theological speculation, and this fascinating and precise picture of the Middle Ages as both revolutionary and conservative leads to the modern synthesis of spatial configuration in the art of Giotto and Duccio di Buoninsegna, where space is still heterogeneous with respect to the picture plane, but it has acquired greater unity. Finally, in the quattrocento there is posed, for the first time, the problem of a definition of space that is in a certain respect a priori, that is, before the objects that will be placed in this space. "Legitimate construction" is thus discovered (perhaps by Brunelleschi), and then the symbol of the vanishing point leads to an elaboration of theories on that concept of infinite space, which, though it had long been a part of artistic intention, had not yet been rationalized or rendered in mathematical form. "Thus the Renaissance had arrived at a total rationalization, on the mathematical plane as well, of that image of space that already for some time had been aesthetically unified by means of a progressive abstraction from its psycho-physiological structure and by rejecting the authority of antiquity."[132] In the history of art, this passage from psycho-physiological space to mathematical space reflects the results obtained in the same epoch by theoretical philosophy and by the philosophy of nature; it also helps to objectify the subjective.[133] Panofsky compares the Renaissance function of perspective to that of Kantian criticism, in that it rationalizes the subjective visual impression to the point of being able to construct an empirical world upon a solid and yet infinite foundation.

But in the final pages of the essay, which deal with perspective, the problem of polarity reappears. Perspective has rationalized and measured the distance between the observer's eye and the object, and yet one can also affirm that it has eliminated all distance by totally reabsorbing the object into the viewpoint of the subject. Perspective may be conceived "both as a consolidation and systematization of the outside world and as an extension of the sphere of the *I*."[134] In fact, from Plato to the Expressionists perspective was criticized on the basis of two opposing principles: as an introduction of the subject into the reality of the thing, and as an objectifying obstacle to the subject's free creation. This polarity is the twofold aspect of a single meaning: "Perspective mathematicizes this visual space, but it is precisely visual space that it mathematicizes—it builds an order, but precisely an order of the visual image."[135] Perspective lends form to what appears and is thus both a limitation set upon objectivity, which is reduced to a rule of the subject, and a limitation set upon subjectivity, which is bound to an objective law of the expression of its world view.

What fascinates Panofsky in following the course of humanity as it appropriates this science is exactly the character of limitation and at the same time of great power that perspective grants to pictorial figuration. The perspectival conception of space, in "transforming the *ousia* into *phainomenon,* seems to reduce the divine to a mere content of human consciousness, but at the same time it broadens human knowledge to the point of making it capable of taking in and containing within itself the divine."[136] Here we are witnessing a true apotheosis of Kantian criticism as well as the great Renaissance discovery that prefigures it, so that Kantian criticism is consolidated in Panofsky's historical inquiry as an essential interpretative tool. But far from admitting a "broadening of the Copernican revolution" that embraces the history of culture as in Cassirer, here there occurs instead a reduction of that otherwise unfathomable element that is the base of the artistic phenomenon: it is the question of the reproduction into sensibly perceptible symbols of a concept, of a rational order of the cosmos, and of an effort on the part of the creating subject to assimilate the irreducible evidence of the object.

The Ideality of the Artistic Problem and Historical Time

Panofsky's theoretical efforts in this period were aimed at determining the tools of historical research and of the interpretation of the artistic phenomenon. His 1925 essay "Über das Verhältnis der Kunstgeschichte zur Kunsttheorie" (On the Relationship between Art History and Art Theory) marked a new programmatic phase in this activity. Here he fully expounds the results of his reflection on the themes central to his thesis: the constitution of a priori concepts that regulate aesthetic reality, the definition of the nature of the basic artistic problem and hence of the fundamental antinomic nature of the artistic phenomenon itself, its relationship with historical becoming, and the limits of such becoming. At the same time Panofsky defends himself from the criticism made of the aprioristic nature of *Kunstwollen* and, more in general, of the formalism of his historiographic conception. In the same year and in the same journal that published his essay—the *Zeitschrift für Aesthetik und allgemeine Kunstwissenschaft,* where for some time there had been a debate concerning the problems attendant upon the construction of a new science of art history—Edgar Wind published a summary of his doctoral thesis (which he had written for Panofsky and Cassirer at Hamburg) on the systematics of artistic problems. (The original title of this 1922 thesis was "Aesthetischer und Kunstwissenschaftlicher Gegenstand"—The Object of Aesthetics and Art History.) Panofsky frequently refers to Wind's inquiry in his works, while Wind, as a confirmation of his thesis, in turn quotes Panofsky's contemporaneous essay, whose themes he had been acquainted with for some time through the scholarly community at the University of Hamburg. Like Panofsky, Wind poses the question of the nature of the artistic problem. Implicitly he already distinguishes between art history and art theory in noting the difference between the *artist's preliminary task,* which is connected to the realization of the artistic phenomenon and susceptible to the *reconstruction* of the motives that determined it, and the *artistic problem,* which is connected to the fundamental antinomic character of the artistic phenomenon and susceptible only to *speculation.*

The artistic problem is set by thought in relation to creation, not in such a way that the problem precedes the solution, but rather in such a way that the problem is sought in order to explain the solution. The problems are not reality, but ideal constructions (as Panofsky says, employing a Husserlian term, they have an eidetic nature).[137] Both Wind and Panofsky explicitly refer to Riegl, who had discovered the nature of the problem in the tension—hidden in artistic reproduction but constantly active in it, a preestablished motif of the unceasing development of art—which draws a new problem from every solution, precisely because the latter is intimately antinomical. The problem is thus configured as the need to transcend contradictions. In fact Riegl read in the latent contrasts a historical factor of artistic development, and Wind noted in that theory a dualism of a logical-immanent nature in the artistic phenomenon as its ideal content and a dynamic-psychological process of the energy inherent to artistic intention. The polarity is that between a *logos,* which is the constant posing anew of the artistic problem, and a *telos,* which animates the will to resolve that very problem.[138] Every artistic theory is open to thought only by way of the artistic sphere, the sphere in which sensible expression proves to be a solution. What divides the purely intuitive as an a priori form from the concretely intuitive as an empirical realization is sensory completeness. Completeness and form must therefore unite in order to constitute the artistic sphere, and the mode of such a connection is always an open problem and is the very root of the original problem of art theory.[139]

Panofsky too speaks of a meeting between the *plenum* of sensory data and the form that organizes them, and he methodologically reduces the former to time and the latter to space. "This meeting between two opposing principles can be effected only due to the fact that the *a priori* necessity of an antithesis is corresponded by the equally *a priori* possibility of a synthesis. . . . If the opposition between '*plenum*' and '*form*' is the *a priori* premise of the existence of artistic problems, the reciprocal action between 'time' and 'space' is the *a priori* condition of the possibility of their solution."[140] The relationship the a priori law has with experience is once again resolved in Kantian terms: artistic problems are recognizable only beginning with their solution, that is, the work of art. The a priori concepts that sustain art theory, however, operate in any case before, and over and above, any experience, even though they start from experience.[141] Therefore one must build a scientific conceptual system for the analysis of the artistic phenomenon because, as it is established along the lines of absolutely a priori principles, the system proves to be indestructible in its basic nucleus. Panofsky wages a battle against historic empiricism, which refuses to analyze the origin and legitimacy of artistic concepts—which all art historians use and without which the pure description of a work of art is even unimaginable.[142]

He therefore criticizes as being insufficient those concepts that limit themselves to ascertaining the "sensory qualities" of the work of art, since they take in only stylistic criteria without considering the problem of their inward connection, a relatedness that inevitably brings one back to the basic antinomy. The "transformation of art history into a transcendental science—or better, into an interpretative discipline—of art"[143] is the task Panofsky sets himself: to probe the very foundations, the criteria of legitimacy, of art theory and art history conceived as sciences. All disciplines must be understood as solutions to the problems and must proceed with the verification of their intimate coherence by comparing the solutions with the problems. This is the work of the historian of culture, since within a certain culture all the problems related to the spirit—artistic problems as well—can be solved in a sole and identical sense. In this part of the essay Panofsky passes from the specific aim of laying the ground of the study of art theory to a broader theme of speculation that looks into the possibilities of attributing to the "sciences of the spirit" (which Panofsky calls "humanistic disciplines") the same rules and criteria that before had been reserved for art history. The passage from this more general outlook concerning the historical disciplines to a definition of the question regarding historical time and to the very possibility of history is brief and coherent and is made in this same part of the essay, although in a still preliminary fashion.

Panofsky finds the nature of the work of art to be at once temporal and nontemporal. In the work the historical becoming of the various artistic choices converges in an indissoluble manner with the superhistorical validity of the solution and its root in the universal problem of the antinomy.[144] The unitary principle of an interpretation of the work of art can be established only upon the cognition of the structure of the artistic intention. And artistic intention is the junction between historical conditions (and thus temporal relativity) and individual strength in determining the problem of art, in reducing the ideal plane to the sensible, and in reproducing the unrepresentable antinomy in a perceptible result. In one respect the artistic phenomenon needs to be "understood in its being subject to conditioning, that is, being included in the historical link of cause and effect; and in another respect it must be understood in its absoluteness, that is, it must be taken from the historical link of cause and effect and be understood, over and above historical relativity, as a solution, extraneous to time and place, of a problem that is extraneous to time and place."[145] Panofsky takes care to specify that the necessity of the phenomenon understood through basic concepts "is not at all a necessity of the temporal process, but rather a necessity of the link of meaning."[146] In other words, side by side with the necessity of the theoretical principle, which Panofsky says is eternal, is the problem of historical development, to which the unitary meaning of cultural phenomena is also connected. This temporal process is not finalistic, but neither is it casual. In fact the phenomenon is intimately connected to other phenomena, and the general problem is expressed in the assembling and disintegrating of the phenomenon's different components. "The development of the individual artistic phenomena cannot be deduced in the sense of a causal or teleological series, but it can be understood in the sense of a convergence of general tendencies of development and of individual evolutive moments."[147]

Panofsky clearly senses the difficulty intrinsic to the historiographic reduction of a system of concepts, and often in his works, both the theoretical and the strictly historical ones, there will recur exhortations to prudence and extreme attention in the use of theoretical presuppositions. There remains, however, the need to face the problem and its nature, because it allows one to find the unitary sense without which the phenomenon is committed to its pure sensory appearance and disconnected from all first causes. Otherwise there is the risk of making the dialectical mistake of building an arbitrary causalistic system based on unverifiable laws.

In *Philosophy of Symbolic Forms* Cassirer also determines the various cultural spheres in their attempt at solving the a priori problems inherent to each sphere. But for Cassirer the problem is complicated in turn by the nature of symbol formation, which he tries to establish as that which allows for the explanation of the entire course of history. The determinations of time and space are different each time and even opposed, but the profound sense of their opposition lies in the progressive becoming of the symbolic form itself, which strives for its perfection and for complete identification with the concept of spiritual totality.

For Warburg, who never set forth the question in a specifically theoretical manner, there is a method of inquiry based on the parallelism intrinsic to certain cultural horizons. This method of inquiry corresponds to a constant experience of humanity, that is, to the impulse to express oneself in pathos formulas, and to set against a cosmos that is defined and as stable as possible the precariousness of the flux of phenomena and the impetus of uncontrolled emotivity. Warburg's most decisive influence on Panofsky lies in Panofsky's attempt to formulate a rigorous determination for individual spheres of culture, thus to broaden the field of investigation beyond the mere history of art to other disciplines, all of which concur in the definition of the "conformity to a meaning" of an artist's work and of a stylistic current or historic epoch.

In order to define the Warburgian characteristics in Panofsky's historiography—the theme of the complex course the image takes through successive superimpositions and transformations—the brief essay written together with Saxl (published in 1926) on the allegory of prudence in Titian is particularly significant. This essay grew out of a request made by Campbell Dodgson, then Keeper of the Print Room in the British Museum, who had sent the two young scholars the photographs of an engraving by Holbein on the allegory of time with three animal heads and a painting by Titian with the same motif (the *Allegory of Prudence*), this time with three human heads depicting the three ages of man. The same subject was again dealt with in Panofsky's "Herkules am Scheidewege" (Hercules at the Crossroads), published in 1930, which appeared in revised form in the collection of essays, *Meaning in the Visual Arts*. In their research Saxl and Panofsky dealt with the theme of time and prudence by following the long and tortuous course the three-headed monster took from the Egyptian cult of Serapis in Hellenistic Alexandria to Titian's Venice.

Tradition had erroneously reproduced not a triple-headed quadruped with a serpent wrapped round it, but a serpent with three heads. "It took the 'reintegration of classical form with classical subject matter,' achieved during the course of the Cinquecento, to break the spell of this persistent tradition."[148] Through antiquarian discoveries and the publication of emblem books and "iconologies" by Alciati and Ripa, the classical image of the triple-headed monster is reconstructed. In Titian it takes on a personal connotation because he paints, over the animal heads and with clearly intentional meaning, three human heads representing the three ages of man—heads that are highly expressive in their attitude, disposition, and in the play of light and shade, volumes and planes that at once mark the rhythm of this work. Concerning this motif of the revival of the theme of prudence in such a complicated superimposition of images, one can only make hypotheses connected to Titian's personal life and establish similarities with his self-portraits and other paintings of the period.

This essay ends with a succinct enunciation on the iconographic task Panofsky sets himself: "In a work of art, 'form' cannot be divorced from 'content': the distribution of color and lines, light and shade, volumes and planes, however delightful as a visual spectacle, must also be understood as carrying a more-than-visual meaning."[149] In order to determine this meaning as thoroughly as possible, it is necessary to consider the close connection between the image under observation and the problem of the passing of time. There is a convergence that is difficult to penetrate between the possibilities of the image's metamorphosis and its very meaning on the one hand, and the persistence of an unchanged representative and conceptual energy in the image's successive manifestations on the other. In tracking down the most ancient historical data, one can recover a history of the image itself only by bearing in mind this permanent structure of the image, its original sense, the artistic intention or, more generally speaking, the spiritual intention that lies at its base, its constant and expressive value. This history is a complicated and extreme struggle that the image's deep-seated form and immutable vigor wage against circumstances and against its own character of changeability in sensory expression. Asserting itself in and against the passing of time over the centuries, the image adapts itself to modifications that are not casual because they are closely connected to its original intimate law.

At this point Panofsky, so attentive to the theoretical premises of his work and to the themes being debated in his own epoch, has to face the problem of historical time, time that is ulterior to the time of knowledge, to the pure form of intuition in sensibility that had allowed him to determine the a priori basis of the symbolic form. It is now time, in which he places the meanings of artistic phenomena, that he investigates—the time that is the object of the "sciences of the spirit" and of the history of culture, as opposed to natural, astronomical time, which is the purely evident. In an appendix (published in 1927) to his essay on the overlapping of styles in Reims cathedral, Panofsky takes part in the contemporary debate on the difference between natural science and cultural science and on the legitimacy of this distinction. The problem of historical time thus arises in the context of art-historical research, where three successive generations of artists are distinguished in the construction and decoration of the Reims cathedral. The different stylistic currents are viewed in an evolutionary sequence, moving from one to another and at the same time as parallel developments, standing side by side but without influencing one another, each style taking part in the building plan with a motif connected to an experience of time.

In Panofsky's opinion there is a contradiction here: it consists of the representation of historical contemporaneity being flanked by the equally necessary appraisal of its correlative contrary, that is, the representation of variety in historical time. In this antinomical nature of opposed and meaningful times, the idea of the temporal historical relation proves to be impracticable as well as logically impossible.[150] Panofsky states that the historical time of culture is in no way the same as natural astronomic time, and his entire theory is based on the possible interference between cultural time and natural time. This observation leads his thought onto a new level with respect to the preceding inquiries.

We have seen how he upheld the importance of the determination of the historical contemporaneity in which a culture manifests itself in all realms of spiritual production. Delimiting a cultural sphere and seeking its different motifs—not only stylistic, but economic, religious, and literary as well—was the lesson Panofsky had learned from Warburg and, in certain respects, from Riegl before him. This corresponded to the concept of an artistic intention, a spiritual direction common to the epoch, that manifested itself in particular in artistic reproduction. In any case, Panofsky does not immediately accept the oft-rejected criterion of chronological succession. But once he extends this research to a broader period of time in which different styles succeeded one another, he modifies the concept of historical contemporaneity as a relationship among different stylistic and cultural motifs. In fact this relationship proves to be a contrast, a setting of the styles themselves in contradiction, and cultural unity is no longer a homogeneous result but is broken up into a variety of directions that, sometimes opposed, move in parallel without one being a limit for the other.

This complicated interaction of cultural products calls in question the concept of ordered relation and, from the logical point of view, makes the very coherence of artistic intentions and of historical time unthinkable. Panofsky points out that historical time always depends upon a certain historical space, which in turn is not geographically identifiable and is not the natural space in which cultural phenomena are placed. In general one can assert that the concepts of time and space primarily mean nothing else for the historian than a sensory unity that dominates a certain group of individual phenomena; and yet this sensory unity is viewed in one case as a succession, and in another as contemporaneity.[151] This occurs because historical time is interpreted, quite independently of natural time, as a unity of meaning that each time takes on a different temporal dimension according to the system of reference the historian chooses. The historian does not consider homogeneous time and space, but qualitative, hence infinitely varied and changeable, time and space. In fact the systems of reference are infinite and one must forgo setting them in an absolute temporal order. By this Panofsky does not intend to deny there is a lack of order in the totality of the historical world; he wants to point out that this order is only of secondary importance and that it acquires reality only in a later moment, through the process of the historically qualified system of reference being anchored to the course of natural homogeneous time and to the extension of natural homogeneous space.[152] Natural time and space are thus the constants to which the innumerable variations offered by the cultural datum can and must refer.

Therefore the historian is offered an infinite givenness, which has an apparent order only in the meaning according to which he delimits and defines this givenness. It is pure evidence. But the notion of time is also evidence. The choice of the sphere of meaning in which phenomena are ordered is independent of chronological evidence, even though the historical value of that order consists in its leading back, necessarily, to chronological order. There is therefore an ideal time that takes shape in the mind of the historian and that is connected to the meaning of cultural phenomena, and there is a cosmic order which the ideal system must reckon with in order to be a real order as well. The historical system of reference must be delimited in view of the work of art that is to be dated, and only secondarily will it be anchored to natural time.[153]

At this point Panofsky quotes from Georg Simmel's essay, "Das Problem der historischen Zeit" (The Problem of Historical Time), written in 1916, declaring he almost wholly agrees with the thesis of this work. Simmel in fact dealt with the ideal content's independence from historical time. The decisive component of the concept of the object of history, which manifests itself as the occurrence of a theoretical creation, lies in time.[154] Time, as a form of reality, sets us face to face with phenomena that follow one another necessarily in order and duration and that constitute a content that must be understood in order to give rise to historical knowledge. Interpreting and understanding phenomena does not reveal their place in historical time. The ideal content of research must therefore find a place in time so that comprehension can take on a historical character. "Time is only a relationship between the contents of the event, while the whole of history is timeless."[155] Defining time as history is a paradoxical yet inevitable task if one wants to obtain a historical result—that is to say, taking the result of the analysis univocally, for reasons intrinsic to the phenomenon and totally indifferent to their place in time, and setting them vice versa in a precise point in time. Only when a content is temporalized on the basis of nontemporal understanding is it truly historical.[156] This process of determining time is viewed by Simmel as making the phenomenon individual and is set against the procedure of natural science in which the historical relationship and the relationship of content between the "before" and "after" of a certain scientific experiment, are totally lacking.[157]

Panofsky distinguishes between historical time, as the time of contents given through understanding the phenomena, and natural time which is immanent to the phenomena themselves in their nature as data. Simmel offers a more confused picture of the peculiarity of historical research: he distinguishes between time immanent to phenomena and unrelated to history, and time in which one must introduce the ideal contents in conformity with a significative "before" and "after." Only in this way can one obtain historical time; yet it is not clear what the other two types of time are, above all, a relationship between the "before" and "after" is not adequately established and seems not to depend at all on the contents.

Simmel's analysis is carried out in the domain of the opposition between history and life. Life is the expression of the event, of a continuity that occupies a duration. The history of this event is not a continuity: "The historical picture, which we have really drawn from research and a construction of fantasy, consists of partial discontinuous images that flow contemporaneously all around a central concept."[158] History is an atomization and crystallization of every detail, and only by placing the content into a concept does the historian lend it a relative unity, which is lived reality and has the character of continuity. "Historical knowledge moves in a permanent compromise between the placement of extended unitary formations whose continuity reproduces the form of the event—but this continuity cannot be filled with the single real intuitions—and these latter, which mark only a chronological point in the scientific ideal and precisely for this reason remove this ideal from the continuity of the real event."[159] An antinomy is thus to be found in Simmel as well. This is not an antinomy between historical time and natural time—a problem which in Panofsky is inherent to the very inquiry into history—but rather between the annulment of time, in the search for contents and the relationships between phenomena, and the time of the event, which is continuous and "vital."

This antinomy is resolved somewhat precipitously by Simmel with the affirmation that history belongs to the manifestations and actions of life. "For even the opposite of life is a form of life."[160] In this position regarding life as an inevitable being other than life, history must yet arise from the same force and rules of life. It is evident that something generated by its opposite will not last long in the sphere of opposition and will thus be understood precisely in its character of identity with what it derives from. But if Simmel seems to take consolation in the thought that history in the end is not something completely different from life, because on the contrary it shares its primal energy and constitutive laws, once again one fails to understand how different times are distinguished and how history, in a certain sense by conceptualizing the event and the continuity, can in reality be a moment of understanding subsequent to the phenomenal datum, if basically it is intimately similar to it.

It is strange how Panofsky says he agrees, albeit partially, with Simmel's essay, for Simmel's romantic vitalism, which does not even have Bergson's coherent distinction between time and concept, cannot coincide with Panofsky's continuously confirmed dualism. In Panofsky's view time is a constant, sensible reference to matter, what Kant in *Confutation of Idealism* said was the reality outside us. The scholar must bring his understanding and intuition to bear on the possibility of leading the artistic phenomenon back to natural time, and the two times are part of the same categorical system, as is space, which is essential to the identification of historical meaning.

In fact, one must not think that natural time is an absolute in itself extraneous to the categorial system, or that it is pure evidence given as presupposed, for otherwise Panofsky's entire historiographic scheme would collapse precisely in its aprioristic foundation, which he went to such pains to deduce. Natural time also is based on laws which are constitutive of our knowledge and without which one could not even state that it is chronological, that is, linear and successive. The very attribute of "natural" that determines this time belongs to those disciplines that investigate the datum in accordance with the law of cause and effect and that, in this respect, differ from the historical disciplines only in their object, which is not a cultural phenomenon in the strict sense of the word. If history too must refer to natural time, this is because it has in common with natural science that evidence that is given in the pure intuition of time and in the regulative principles of its relationship with a possible experience. Both times, historical and natural, have something to do with phenomena whose law of occurrence must be found in order to understand fully these phenomena. Furthermore, both times reveal the existence of things outside us, and our consciousness of things is simultaneous to their taking on form as objects for us and whose relationship to these objects guarantees the permanence of the object of the senses and its conformity to the rules of the intellect.

When Panofsky speaks of the evidence of natural time we must therefore hold that such evidence is not undemonstrated, but that it is in relation to it—in that it is given in an experience and according to the regulative laws of experience—that the historical phenomenon is temporalized and only now becomes an element of history, that is, an element of a temporal connection. For Simmel and Panofsky historical understanding is made up of successive elements, among which the inclusion in a chronology comes last. Yet for Simmel it is an alteration of life and the event which incoherently justifies itself only in virtue of being derived from the common foundation of life and of the event, whereas for Panofsky, the sober reader of Kant and disciple of Riegl, one understands historically when the various categories at the disposal of those carrying out the investigation are made to converge in the same meaning.

What stands out here is the different conception of the relationship between "sciences of the spirit" and physical sciences. While Panofsky attributes to natural time, the object of the physical sciences, the same nature of a system of reference as historical time, ideally built on possible meanings, Simmel sets the two times against each other and holds that history is built upon temporal foundations utterly different from those proper to natural science. Let me mention at this point that Cassirer refused to admit of such a need for distinction, for in his view history and science utilize the same categories of thought and are born in the same terrain of symbolization and it is therefore superfluous to establish their opposition.[161]

The question of the two times that help explain the artistic phenomenon returns in a paper by Panofsky on an art-historical problem. The essay sets out to establish why Giorgio Vasari, who was opposed to the Gothic style, which was considered a symbol of barbarism that impeded the total realization of classicizing art, could have drawn a Gothic decoration for the frame of the first page of a book of drawings that were formerly attributed to Cimabue.[162] First there is a general consideration typical of Panofsky's historiographic method: this episode of late Renaissance art belongs to the manifestation of that law of contrasts on which the rise of a particular artistic vision is based. In fact it was the typical Southern opposition to the Gothic style that created the basis for its historical recognition in Italy, and in such hostility, made quite explicit in Vasari's judgment, there lie many different factors. There is, for example, the acknowledgment on the part of Renaissance artists that the foundation of their research and achievements lay in the works of the early trecento and that they approached this period with a "specifically 'artistic' interest."[163] There is also the acquisition of a sense of historical distance caused by the Renaissance setting itself in a particular relation or opposition to the Middle Ages and antiquity. Precisely this judgment of the Gothic and the problem of restoring art works of the past reveals the emergence of a historical point of view, "in the sense that the phenomena are not only connected in time but are also evaluated according to '*their* time.'"[164]

For the first time the history of art is divided into single, self-contained epochs, each with its own autonomous value. In Vasari, Panofsky sees a concept of history "dominated by two essentially heterogeneous principles which were to be separated only in the course of a long and laborious development."[165] The theme of the two times that differ qualitatively in the analysis of the datum is here radicalized in an accentuation of the extratemporality of artistic problems (as was theorized also in Panofsky's 1927 essay), while he also tries to identify historical time with natural time. The former in fact is considered a very restricted portion of time, almost to the point of coinciding with the latter, so that the placement of the content in time is utterly coherent. The distinction is between art history as an understanding of the relationships between individual creations, and art theory as the critical or phenomenological approach to the general problems posed or solved by the works of art. "And just because we are conscious of this distinction we are able to envisage a synthesis which may ultimately succeed in interpreting the historical process with due regard to 'artistic problems' and, conversely, to appraise the 'artistic problems' from a historical point of view."[166]

Vasari's notion rests upon an antinomical character which the Renaissance historian was not yet aware of and which thus proved to be a contradiction in his theory. Precisely with regard to the Gothic style there is this ambivalent judgment that combines pragmatism—which led to attributing to the Gothic an aesthetic value proper to the epoch this style grew up in and was conditioned by—with a dogmatism expressed in the search for an absolute value of form as perfection in itself. From this dogmatic point of view there was in Vasari a teleological conception of art history that in every moment tended to comply with the "perfect rule of art." This aim, which represents the individual phenomenon's destiny to achieve the perfection intrinsic in it, clashes with the view of a cyclical alternation of barbarism and civilization in history which is not even dominated by Vasari's thesis of the art-historical process as corresponding to the three ages of man, since natural aging and decline are impossible to reconcile with the dogma of the glorious rebirth of the classical age which had been destroyed by catastrophic barbarism.[167] The classical age thus influences the Renaissance conception of history through the domination of an ideal that must assert itself independently of the changes wrought by historical evolution. This is a confirmation of the nontemporal nature of the classical ideal, which is liberated from the progressive, linear historical design and establishes itself upon a history whose only meaning consists in continuously leading back to the absolute beauty of classical forms over and above the various epochs of "barbaric obscurity."

The distinction Panofsky makes between pragmatism and dogmatism in Vasari is quite complex: the pragmatic method is the process that moves from cause to effect; the dogmatic method admits of an absolute rule of beauty. But the appraisal of the Gothic style as having its own peculiar type of beauty is to be considered both pragmatic (in its being historicized) and dogmatic (in that every work of art pursues perfection since this is the teleology of the artistic phenomenon). Both types are necessary for historical consideration, and distinguishing them or setting them one against the other is merely a means for using them with more ability and legitimacy in historical research.

We can look at Panofsky's reconstruction to note how the two methods, which only obscurely and contradictorily operated in Vasari, are consciously blended in the modern art historian. In observing historical change and becoming and in laying down an order that can make them rationally comprehensible, we direct our attention to an immutable model which is our point of reference and which is taken both as the origin of the change and its end—the goal it is striving for. The evident, immediate so to speak, datum is often characterized in Panofsky by infinity, infinite multiplicity, incommensurability in itself—so that the only possible way to make data accessible to an interpretation and even to their very perception and assumption as such, is to distinguish a priori principles, principles with the greatest possible verifiable validity and of a universal nature. By means of these principles one can note a homogeneity between the natural course of events, albeit in its irrevocable necessity, and the direction that an individual event, or group of contiguous and somewhat related events, has taken either for and within itself or in the context in which it has been decided to examine it.

Historicism and the Violence of Interpretation

The intertwining of the historicist and dogmatic planes must become for the modern interpreter more and more fluid and at the same must be kept more and more under control. The historian's tool has two faces: one is the absoluteness of the criteria that govern artistic formation, and the other is the patient reconstruction of a possible system of historical reference through the ascertainment of facts which acts as a natural and necessary restraint upon the audacity of the interpretation. Panofsky incessantly sharpened and refined this tool, always questioned its validity, experimented with it in historiographic research, and compared it with the results of that research.

In a lecture given at the Kiel Kant Society in 1931, he again tackled the problem of describing the work of art that had been posed by Lessing and proved to be so fecund for Warburg. Pure formal description is considered impossible here, because in any case the domain of the meaning of form opens itself to such description, and this domain is in turn bound by numerous interactions to subjective and objective motifs that govern even the most elementary interpretation.

Panofsky therefore proceeds to take apart both the artistic phenomenon and the interpretative process in order to find their points of contact and of greatest separation. Already in the foreword to "Hercules at the Crossroads,"[168] the importance attached to iconographic research carried out on the complicated relationship of exchange between the literary tradition and the iconographic one had been forcefully declared in the name of a necessary unity of form and content in the meaning of the image. The breaking up of this actually given unity brings about a rupture that leads the interpreter astray from the correct meaning to be attributed to the symbol or work of art. This separation is an arbitrary (Panofsky, in a Kantian sense, says "dialectic") claim on the part of reason that operates without referring to the nature of the thing.[169] Despite the doubt that pervades this part of the essay concerning the iconographic method in its greatest risk—the risk of freeing the artistic from the nonartistic and thus of breaking up in turn an inseparable connection—the criticism of formalism, which does not pose for itself the problems of an analysis and exegesis of the content, and the ambiguity of historical distance lead Panofsky to defend his interpretative school.

Tradition hands down sources that are still alive, as well as sources that have been dried up by time. It is indispensable for the historian to concentrate his efforts exactly on the latter to discover what modern consciousness cannot grasp in works of the past because they were created with a different mentality, in a different cultural milieu, and in contact with traditions that have become empty and meaningless. The meeting between the new subjectivity and a content belonging to the past must be effected with extreme caution and with the greatest possible awareness. In that foreword written in 1930, which was also a sort of work program and a critical warning aimed above all at himself, Panofsky distinguished between a primary phenomenal plane and a secondary phenomenal plane. Inner experience (*Erlebnis*), the conditioning of immediate and historical life, belong to the former, while the latter takes in something known that is ulterior to inner experience and that concerns the image, the way it has been handed down, understood, and absorbed. Formal analyses limit themselves to the primary level, while iconological analyses, though taking the primary level into account, approach the secondary level. The plane of the inner experience of the *I* and of its expression in linear or coloristic forms is the just limit for the secondary, since there are epochs or cases in art history in which the artistic manifestation has no meaningful content regarding the image or the history of images. But most times this history presses upon inner experience and upon the purely formal plane, it interacts with them in an indissoluble manner—and it is up to the historian to point this out.

The distinction between primary and secondary strata, between phenomenal sense and the intrinsic, or deeper, meaning of the literary and iconographic tradition, is taken up in the 1931 lecture together with the theme of the sources still open, and those that are occluded, to contemporary consciousness. Even the simple reading of a work is an interpretation, a glance thrown at a world that partly corresponds with our world and partly eludes it. The pure pleasure of vision itself is linked to our actual experience, to the meaning of things and of expression which in turn submits to the meaning our culture attributes, more or less rightly and obviously, to the images. No one educated in the Western cultural sphere can contemplate Leonardo's *Last Supper* without referring to the story in the Gospels. In Panofsky's antiformalistic polemic there is always the veiled certainty that the image's acquisition of historical meaning increases the pure aesthetic enjoyment of it, since this pleasure ends up drawing from a higher sphere of the beautiful.

To the two strata of meaning into which the work of art is separated when interpreted, Panofsky now adds the intervention of a "superior instance" represented by the theory of types, that is to say, by that alliance between phenomenal sense and intrinsic meaning that gave rise to a certain image that established itself in tradition. Only through the *type*, in which creative energy is impressed, and its history does expression become a vehicle of meaning,[170] and therefore aesthetic judgment cannot detach itself from that totality of literary reconstructions and inquiries into style that goes to make up the history of types.[171]

But Panofsky's interest, which engenders his careful analysis and constant reflection in that period, is certainly not limited to an increase in aesthetic taste or to the historian's mere curiosity, his pleasure in discovering ancient links and in going back over little known paths canceled by time to find their lost destination. Since the formalistic description is considered absolutely inconsistent and conceals the "guilty conscience" of the viewer who hides from himself the true cultural origin of his viewpoint, one must intensify the necessity and true essence of the interpretation. In this movement of the subject who looks, both in his simple attitude as a viewer and in the complex reconstruction of thoughts and facts in his role as conscious historian, past and present meet and together impress a direction upon this look and upon reflection. Just as the artist was not only the bearer of the experiences of his epoch and of the types consolidated in that epoch by tradition, but also the creator of his own interior intellectual and emotional order, so his interpreter superimposes upon the notions consciously taken from the past the inner experience of the past, which his civilization communicates to him, and of the present, in which he continuously transforms his heritage of images into a world view. Like the artist, his mediator and judge is also a subject who acts and suffers in a history that may be quite different from, or quite similar to, the preceding ones, but is in any case a history that leads to situations and solutions that are undoubtedly different. Whatever the direction the interpreter has impressed on his historical choice, he cannot deceive himself about the affinities and differences that may ensue from past history, and he must patiently face the task of following the most objective research criterion possible. One must therefore look into the nature of the subject and its relationship with the surrounding world in order that the subject's irruption into the past may conform to the laws of time and of historical understanding and so that that violent irruption can be moderated by the consciousness of its intimate meaning.

In regard to the violence of interpretation, Panofsky quotes from Heidegger's *Kant and the Problem of Metaphysics,* in which the philosopher tries to justify his remarkable aptitude for forcing Kant's writing so as to make the words say what they per se simply do not say.[172] Only in this way can one gain an explication of Kant's thought and of all philosophy, says Heidegger; repeating a philosopher's propositions is a useless tautology if they are not interpreted, that is, taken from their apparent order and led to reveal an order they mention and refer to only through the reader's active intervention. Panofsky holds that this operation, which is necessarily violent, must be carried out also with works of art, whose formal aspect, or what immediately appears in them (which strictly speaking does not even exist), must be violated in order to lead it back to the complex network of meanings that are its vital tissue. But this violence is worked by a subject who promotes it "on the basis of an idea that is intuited beforehand," as Heidegger asserts, and it is legitimate to ask what proportions the risk of this arbitrary act will take on, and whether it is avoidable or can be controlled.[173] Interpretation does violence to pure expression or to apparent meaning because it forces both to reveal what they simply do not say; its limit is imposed by the tradition of the ascertained facts, what Panofsky calls the "history of types."

Both arbitrary violence and rigorous factual determination are conditioning factors. They limit and watch each other in the historian's oeuvre; they refer to each other in what Panofsky, quoting Wind, calls not a vicious circle, but a methodical circle. Taking his cue from an example naturalists are well aware of, he affirms that the reciprocal influence of the tool of knowledge and of its object, far from exhausting the possibilities of interpretation, establish the possibility of knowledge and of the object itself.[174]

The audacity of this authentic proposition of critical idealism is restrained, as in the preceding essays by Panofsky, by reference to the evidence of the datum. But once one has entered the sphere of interpretation and thus of its dependence upon a subject (which is in turn a historical element and exists in virtue of its complex relationship with the past and with the present, with its own having become and still becoming) the slightly ambiguous and opaque term *evidence,* which expresses something beyond which it does not seem possible to go—the impossibility for the datum to be transparent—takes on a new meaning that is more pliant and is similar both to the subject who investigates and to the nature of the change he bears with him. Panofsky here notes an ultimate and essential content of the work of art—the "domain of the meaning of the document."[175] The iconographical and formal elements must be united in the interpretation of the unitary meaning expressed by the world view contained in the work of art. "In order to realize such an enterprise—through which the interpretation of a work of art truly rises to the same level as the interpretation of a philosophical system or a religious conception—not even our knowledge of literary sources serves any purpose, unless they are sources that can immediately be placed in relation to the given art work."[176]

If we make use of literary texts to understand what Dürer's *Melencolia* represents in terms of intrinsic meaning, we have no direct information concerning what is expressed in this work as the "meaning of the document." Even an explanation furnished by Dürer himself could not express the intimate essence of this engraving, and here too we would have to submit both to the course of our interpretative violence and to the sources that tell us something about Dürer's world view and epoch.

"The source of that explanation, which aims at unveiling the essential meaning, is rather the interpreter's original behavior vis-à-vis his world view."[177] Such a source is thus absolutely subjective and personal and its corrective consists in the factuality of the historical datum, which now is not understood exclusively as a mere document but as belonging to the world view which can be determined by means of the general history of the mind. Factuality presents itself to us through categories (which Panofsky, along with Cassirer, calls *modalities*) that allow us to establish certain relationships and connections that engender that unitary essence which we in our interpretative violence must meet with as a limit and verification. "It is the general history of the mind that shows us what, in the sphere of the world view, was possible in a certain epoch and in a certain cultural milieu—just as the history of representations showed us the sphere of what could be depicted and the history of types showed us the territory of what could be represented."[178] The "history of the mind" here is the study of the various conceptions of the world that reveal a historically different manner in which the intrinsic meanings are filled with content related to the essential tendencies of the life of that time. The concept of development or evolution that the phrase "history of the mind" takes on in Panofsky's work does not mean progress, but rather a nature of becoming intrinsic to the historical course, which precisely in the reproduction of certain of its manifestations and modalities offers us the possibility to speak of factuality and objectivity, that is, something which, with respect to our interpretation—and also through it—is consolidated in the datum. The historian is conscious of the fact that the interpretation, effected in conformity with the superhistoric model of a unity intrinsic to the real, is called into question by the needs of historiography and by the historian's familiarity with the other and the changeable in history—the sudden deviations, ruptures, and discontinuity.[179]

One of the recurring criticisms made of Panofsky is that he is too theoretical and attaches little importance to such a pivotal element in aesthetic thought as sensibility.[180] It is exactly in the light of his most essentially theoretical writings that this criticism betrays all its weakness. In fact, what is defined as extreme conceptualization is nothing but the intellectual reproduction of the manifold meanings sensible expression can take on. Panofsky tries to make conceptual, that is, expressible according to an order, the totality of historical factors that lie at the base of the work of art, including the perceptive ones. Since it is clear by now that Panofsky's theoretical point of departure is Kantian philosophy,[181] we can consider his position regarding sensory perception critical of the objective limits of perception itself. One can account for it only by interpreting it in the light of conceptual schemes and modalities in its historical becoming.

Panofsky puts to the test the theory of the unifying principle of the cognitive process in the practibility of the historical task, which in turn searches for that unifying principle as it is manifested in the sphere of figurative creations. He notes the limit of the interpretation of givenness in its imperviousness to history, because the facts have become immutable once and for all by their very belonging to a past and to a self-contained sphere of existence. In order to unveil givenness to interpretation and make it historically comprehensible—which is like making the very structure of historical time comprehensible—one must find in it expressions that go beyond its appearance and that involve an entire epoch.

One must discover in historical data that energy which sets them in relation to one another, which constitutes areas of validity, and which removes representation from the level of a mere inventory of fragments of images and makes it an autonomous and significant creation per se. As Panofsky noted in "Hercules at the Crossroads," Warburg had captured that essential moment of the Renaissance that consisted in the "dynamic re-awakening of an ancient totality of images."[182] In the modality by which a work of art comes to light, past and by now inert objects are set in motion, and they are viewed in a connective force by means of the categories of judgment. This basic unity, which is elusive at first glance, becomes a constant once it is found again, and it confirms the validity of the categories and conceptual schemes, revealing their genesis in history itself and at the same time showing how history, through such an inquiry, takes on form beginning with those schemes. At this point the vicious circle becomes a methodical circle, since the violence worked by the interpreter is opposed by a no less efficacious violence—that of the dynamic energy of the data.

Reproaching a Kantian like Panofsky for making sensibility a simple presupposition means not having understood the core of the exegetic and theoretical effort he made in order to gain the historiographic objectivity that lies in the subjective sphere of the weltanschauung.[183] In this sense Panofsky (as we have already seen with regard to historical time) is very close to the Kantian confutation of idealism, especially in his coherent refusal to set historiographic categories on an empirical plane.[184] If in the field of iconology one notes in Panofsky's writings an increase, over time, of pure historical investigation, this does not mean that he reevaluates the role of givenness in interpretation. In fact Panofsky certainly bore this role in mind as early as his 1915 essay on Dürer, where his method is already defined. Rather one must consider that, precisely in his continuous contact with historical reality and its problems, he manifested the need to determine the foundation of his research as he went along by dedicating some essentially theoretical pages to their deduction and clarification.

The most important moment in this process of clarification lies in the 1931 lecture and is marked by the connection between subject, world view, and history of the mind as a history of the different world views. Here Panofsky not only makes himself part of the classical interpretative model that he recognizes in Lessing, Burckhardt, Warburg, and Heidegger, but he also shows he is conscious of belonging to what Heidegger twenty years later called "the epoch of the world-image."[185]

Panofsky had seen to begin with Vasari a distinction between a historicist and dogmatic level of interpretation, that is, between epochal relativity and the absoluteness of intrinsic value or the substantiality of the artistic phenomenon. This distinction was proving to be the modern historian's most refined tool.

The question lying at the heart of a historiographic inquiry, understood in Panofsky's sense, is the same one that, in different meanings and manners, was debated in Burckhardt's historical views, in Warburg's iconology, and in Cassirer's historical-philosophical analysis, and it is a strictly philosophical question. It concerns the subject-object relationship as it was being transformed in the history of Western culture through the Renaissance, a relationship whose consequences are reflected on the one hand in the philosophical and scientific thought of the modern age, and on the other in the modern way of understanding history and in the slow progression toward the shaping of a historical mentality.[186]

The quotation from Heidegger in the 1931 lecture is certainly not casual, nor is it a polemical allusion.[187] Taking this essay as a whole, it does not seem possible to note a polemic on Panofsky's part against interpretative arbitrariness and in favor of total historicism. On the contrary, the historicist formulation that reappraises the factuality and spirit of an epoch cannot avoid seeking a corrective in the awareness of the world view necessary for an interpreter and of the a priori categories that govern the historiographic task and the very essence of the historical phenomenon's formation. One must then surmise that Panofsky had read Heidegger's 1929 book on Kant with deep interest, and in this regard it is interesting to note that an analysis of those readings would be useful for an understanding of the meaning Kant's philosophy and Heidegger's interpretation of it had in that period.[188] The specific reference to Heidegger has a broader significance both for an appraisal of the general problem of historicism and, above and beyond this, for the philosophical and cultural situation in which the subject of historical time and the nature of historical living was being debated. What is called an "irrationalistic instance" in Panofsky is perhaps what he calls a "superior instance" and is what counts both for the historical period under consideration—and it thus takes on a historicist connotation—and for the interpreter—and in this case it expresses an "irrationalistic" note because it is connected to individual arbitrariness.

Yet Panofsky says that interpretation is not only an imperative claim, but has inherent duties that he attempts to determine.[189] Twice in his essay on interpretation he turns back to the subject of Dürer's *Melencolia,* perhaps because he realizes that he had given that engraving a meaning that was different from, and in certain respects contradictory to, the meaning given by Warburg,[190] and thus takes up this subject almost as if to put it to the test once again and to justify his own viewpoint. This theme thus becomes central to an understanding of the doubt that animated his historiographic research. At the same time it demonstrates his coherence in maintaining a difficult equilibrium between the critic's rationality and "irrationality," which consists precisely in the delicate meeting between actuality and the past, in the ambiguity with which historical time is not only the time of the past but is essentially the time of the past's moving forward into a present that is not innocuous, not simply passive and receptive, but active and endowed with an energy of its own. This energy must express itself in the interpretation in order to offer in turn a world-image and to create the symbol that determines it and binds it forcefully to its reality, thus preventing incessant becoming from denying it its sole positive faculty of revealing its own essence in an image.

Without the violence of interpretation our current becoming proves to be "too dead," as Eugenio Montale said,[191] with respect to the vitality of the images or the thought of the past and with respect to the impetus of the energy that is expressed therein and that can come to our aid only by our facing it with equal vitality and effort on the part of our imagination.[192] "The testimony of the Renaissance . . . tells us art historians what premises allowed him to unify, in his *Melencolia,* a *'Typus Acediae'* with a *'Typus Geometriae'* and thus to lend for the first time a spiritual content to the pain of a creature and, at the same time, to render pathetic for the first time a moment of the spirit that is only personal."[193] The premises taken from Renaissance documents lead the interpreter to circumscribe his impetus prudently. "But in thus doing they delimit Dürer's 'melencolia' with respect to what we would be led to interpret as modern 'cosmic sorrow.' "[194]

Only here does there ring a note of renunciation of the subjective interpretation and Panofsky's propensity for the historicist approach. His allusion to a knowledge of the context of eighteenth-century thought needed for an ontological interpretation of Kant that sets out at being just that, is a defense of the Cassirerian criteria of philosophical inquiry. But far from being a polemic against Heidegger, this passage can be seen as being in contradiction with the line of thought of the entire Kiel lecture and at the same time consistent with the historiographic and theoretical style of its author. In fact it appears to be a correction of the very tendency to force the meaning of the sixteenth-century image so as to capture Dürer's tremendous solitude when he finds himself before a terrible creative limitation: "Was aber die Schönheit sei, dass weiss ich nit" (But what beauty is, I know not).[195] This expression of a Faustian impossibility of knowing is not only a motif of the old myth of Saturn, but is an intellectual condition of the modern world, one of whose greatest manifestations was the personality and individuality of Dürer.

If Panofsky feels the need to corroborate and at the same time to correct his own interpretation, this means he fully understands the weight the historian's cultural world brings to bear on him and how much effort is needed to dominate and acknowledge it. He implicitly rejects Warburg's humanistic interpretation and, after much perplexity, prudently withdraws from the "Faustian meaning" and with the modesty of rationality adheres to the totality of motifs suggested by iconological research. Warburg tried to see the demon of superstition defeated in the "type" of spirituality and philosophical meditation, offering at once an insuperable example of equilibrium between historicism and the reemergence of the perpetual and essential nature of civilization; Panofsky also tries to control the irrationality of "life" and immediate inner experience through iconology, even though that experience, by means of various mediations, is the first design that lends form to the "superior instance," the world-image, the unitary principle of the work of art.

Panofsky had understood the limits of Dilthey's *Erlebnis* in its immediacy and indefinite relationship with the object and with givenness. Dilthey made a considerable intellectual endeavor to establish the humanistic disciplines and to define the characters of historicity.[196] His conclusions are still to be found in the section of Heidegger's *Being and Time* dedicated to the historicity of *Dasein*[197] and appear in the discussions that were at their furious height in the first decades of this century, debates concerning the essence of historical time, the distinction between the physical sciences and the "sciences of the spirit" and the meaning of weltanschauung. And yet Panofsky's rigorous sense of objectivity could not agree, not even in taking in certain results of that experience, with a doctrine that laid an immediate foundation to the logical process—whether it was verified in givenness or in man's psychic structure. In his greater coherence he rather tends to modify those concepts of Dilthey's that had become the common heritage of all reflection on the nature of the "sciences of the spirit." For example, the undemonstrated relationship Dilthey set between the conceptual process and consciousness of evidence must have supplied the art historian with a cue around which he could develop his complex theory of historical evidence.[198] This was also the case with the consolidation of the inquiry into the link between the idea of history and the theory of perception and learning that take place on the basis of a general life experience and lead to those creations of collective life, language and myth,[199] and above all to the historical essence of the individual in being determined by his position in time and by his place in space.[200]

In Dilthey historical knowledge developed by means of categories that partly had to remain indefinable, since temporality, which is the substratum of historical living, cannot be reduced to knowledge. History proved to be, in part, a conceptual reduction of the understanding on the part of *Erlebnis*. But in part, in being the depository of the reality of life, history was involved in *Erlebnis,* though *Erlebnis* was made as abstract and objective as possible. History is the object in which the subject, as the author of his own emotions, becomes the spectator of those emotions in accordance with a meaning they have taken on in time: it is the history of interrupted processes of inner experiences. "*Erleben* [that is, the function of inner experience] is a passing of time in which each state, before becoming a distinct object, changes, so that the successive change is always built upon the preceding one, and in which each element—not yet grasped—becomes the past."[201] "Of life we perceive only the memory, which becomes form and is no longer life."

"Wherever life is past and enters understanding, there is history; and where history is, there is meaning in its multiplicity."[202] From Dilthey's often contradictory, and at times totally incoherent, analysis there yet emerge motifs such as collective memory, meaning, the symbol as the bearer of the rule of time and at the same time of its flow, the historical type as the consolidation of inner experiences of the community—motifs we often find again in Panofsky. But Panofsky keeps himself cautiously detached from Dilthey's conceptuality, which continuously shifts—and not always consciously—from the real to the ideal plane, which Dilthey believes he has kept distinct. Above all Panofsky does not take in the motif of a history of the mind as progress toward historical knowledge because it renders spiritual totality explicit. When he uses the expression "history of the mind," he means only the abode of the different world views, those that emerge from historical documents, and not progress with an aim, or an increase of knowledge in time. The very notion of "different" world views, that is to say, a difference in cultural spheres and hence a change produced by becoming, leads the historian to a relativism of epochs that excludes their developing from one to the other. If history is conceivable as a totality, this is possible not in virtue of what changes and becomes and what some people take to be progress, but by virtue of the immutable categories of the object's occurrence in accordance with which the historian must seek the most suitable criteria for the interpretation of the past.

In 1936 a famous essay of Panofsky's was published in *Philosophy and History*, a book of essays collected by Raymond Klibansky and presented to Ernst Cassirer on his sixtieth birthday (he had already abandoned Nazi Germany by then). In its homage to the philosopher of symbolic forms, the book sets out to gather together in a testimony of solidarity all those whom historical events had scattered here and there and to make felt the presence and unity of a civilization which in those years appeared to be dramatically called into question and undermined.

The subject was a discussion of the bases of history and its study, the possibility of its becoming a science, and its relationship with those disciplines that in preceding centuries had asserted themselves as exact sciences—the sole, irrefutable exponents of incontrovertible knowledge. The discussion took place on a quite profound theoretical and historical level and included the question of the nature of time, its transcendence or immanence in the field of experience, and the rupture Descartes's thought had established between antiquity and the modern subjective consciousness. The contributions include the following: Huizinga's analysis of the teleological nature of the concept of civilization and the finalistic knowledge of historical learning;[203] Alexander's treatment of the subject of the changes that take their place in the growth of events and of the meaning of the eternal in historical thought;[204] the transcending of time in history as viewed by Gentile;[205] Ortega y Gasset's fine and long essay with its critique of the concept of spirit and its careful inquiry into the concept of variation;[206] and last, Klibansky's theoretical consideration of the possibility to establish correctly a critique of historical reason. All show how this book seems to have replaced the idea of our epoch as an "age of exact sciences" with that of the "age of historical science."

What Gentile had considered in Giordano Bruno a faith in historical knowledge, a faith that was isolated and that contrasted with all of Renaissance and European culture at least up to Vico,[207] is confirmed by several authors in the sense of the subject's new relationship with the object which characterizes the modern world, in which the subject makes the past, as it belongs to his own experience and his own becoming, the image of himself projected in time.[208] Therefore these thinkers bear in mind that conception of their own world as a representation, a totality of images that reveals the essence of the mode of cognition and of their own living structure, which Heidegger later calls "the epoch of the world-image," radicalizing Nietzsche's critique of history and also Bergson's thesis of time as the pure flow of sensations which in crystallizing into concepts lose their nature of reality. Heidegger will grasp the essence of the subject-object relationship in modern representation, in the humanistic notion of weltanschauung, in man having become a subject and the world an image.[209]

Among the essays in that 1936 collection which, within the overall context of the present volume, can also be considered the point of arrival of the Warburg Institute experience and its protagonists in the Hamburg period, there is the erudite joke played by Fritz Saxl, a master of variation in history, on the use of the motto *Veritas filia temporis* in different contexts,[210] and Panofsky's research into the phrase *Et in Arcadia Ego* and its iconographic reproduction.[211] While Saxl demonstrates how images are handed down in historical memory in such a bizarre way and how they are made to comply with the spiritual or material need, the worldly or otherworldly faith, of the subject using these images, Panofsky finds variation in two works by Poussin that represent the same subject, but in such different guises that they make it necessary to inquire into the meanings of the Latin phrase so as to bring the reason for that variation to light.

Just as Virgil had suddenly changed the most ancient sense of Arcadia, which was a bleak and bare world—and even the idyllic realism of Theocritus, which set the scene in a flowery and pleasant Sicily but still described the unhappiness of abandonment and the violence of death—by building a utopian domain of melancholic pleasure and the refined elegy as an end in itself, so Poussin passes from the representation of death, which even in Arcadia is ever present and frightful, to the representation of a "judicious" pastoral scene where the memory of the person lying in the tomb communicates to the living the tone of a placid, elegant joie de vivre. From the accent put on the transitoriness of earthly things, which even in Arcadia makes the lighthearted song of the revellers die out, one has passed to the memory of the person who was once happy—a warning and incitement to those who, cheerfully thoughtful, discover his tomb. From the grammatically correct "Even in Arcadia there am I [Death]," the phrase has taken on the literally inexact meaning, which however is a correct interpretation of the image of the world view expressed in it, of "I, too, was in Arcadia."

The event Panofsky makes alive for us does not consist only in an increase in beauty and in its evocative powers, and it is not only a contribution to the art-historical interpretation of Poussin's work, which is illuminated by this delicate violence and, in the greatness of its moment, takes on an agelong profundity. It also teaches us that it is possible to reconstruct the configuration of a memory whose parts are connected in a totality of meanings toward which they converge from the obscure areas and interrupted episodes of history. In the solid structure of the image's meaning, the world view itself—the "superior instance" of historicism that controls and at the same time vitiates the viewer-interpreter's arbitrariness, the insufficiency of which still tormented Heidegger's thought—becomes an element, and only one element, in the free play that the acts of meaning work in time. The variation Poussin imposed upon the vision of the subject of his painting, thus reconstructed by Panofsky, clearly reveals the aptitude, which one can note in every moment of history, to dominate with words and images the risk the transitory and contingent oppose in time to the intelligence of reality and the certainty of one's own being. Death lies in wait even in the sweet utopian realm of beauty. But others have lived in that world, and what remains of them testifies that that world has a reality all its own.

NOTES

TRANSLATOR'S NOTE

Wherever possible, English editions have been cited for the quotations in this book. The only exception is Tito Vignoli's *Myth and Science,* an English translation of which was published in 1882 (see chap. one, nn. 13–22); in this case I have chosen to use my own translation. All the other quotations have been translated from their original sources in Italian and German.

Since the titles of Aby Warburg's papers on the Renaissance are indicative of his historiographic method, they have been translated into English in the notes for the reader's convenience.

In *Aby Warburg: An Intellectual Biography,* Sir Ernst Gombrich discusses the difficulties Warburg's thought and writing style entail for the translator (see pp. 14–18). His discussion of the words *pathos* and *pathetic,* key words in Warburg's art-historical vocabulary, is of particular interest to the reader of *Cassirer, Panofsky, and Warburg.* He points out that these terms "derived from Greek concepts" have different meanings in German and English; for *pathos* "the English tradition has continued to stress the aspects of misfortune, while German usage concentrated on its overtones of grandeur and sublimity." This term is later described as violent movement and gesture in the "grand manner." The reader should bear these distinctions in mind.

I would like to take this occasion to thank Judith Calvert and the anonymous readers for Yale University Press for their critical reading of this translation and their helpful comments and suggestions.

INTRODUCTION

1. Saxl's letter, together with others written by Warburg, Cassirer, Panofsky, and many more by Saxl himself, is kept in the archives of the Hamburg Staatsbiliothek. I was able to consult all of these letters in 1978, thanks to the kind assistance offered by the director of the library's manuscript department.

2. Arthur Lovejoy, *The Great Chain of Being* (Cambridge, Mass.: Harvard University Press, 1953), 12–14.

3. Ernst Gombrich, *In Search of Cultural History* (Oxford: Clarendon Press, 1969), 6–14.

4. Lovejoy, *Great Chain of Being,* 13: "What is there more beautiful or more venerable about the numeral one than about any other number?"

5. For information concerning the Warburg Institute's activities in the 1920s, see Peter Gay, *Weimar Culture: The Outsider as Insider* (New York: Harper & Row, 1970). Gay does not seem to have noted any difference between Cassirer's and Warburg's philosophical conceptions.

6. These letters belong to the Von Melle Nachlass and are kept in the Hamburg Staatsbibliothek.

7. Ernst Gombrich, *Aby Warburg: An Intellectual Biography* (London: The Warburg Institute, University of London, 1970).

I: ABY WARBURG

1. Ernst Cassirer, *A. Warburg zum Gedächtnis. Worte zur Beisetzung von Professor Dr. Aby Warburg* (Darmstadt, 1929), 9–20; republished in *Mnemosyne, Beiträge zum 50. Todestage von Aby Warburg* (Göttingen: Gratia-Verlag, 1979), 15–22.

2. Aby Warburg, "A Lecture on Serpent Ritual," *Journal of the Warburg and Courtauld Institutes* 2 (1939), 277–92. Regarding this essay by Warburg and its relationship to Cassirer's thought, see Fritz Saxl, "Warburg's Visit to New Mexico," *Lectures,* vol. 1 (London: The Warburg Institute, University of London, 1957), 330 (now in Aby Warburg, *Ausgewählte Schriften und Würdigungen,* hrsg. v. Dieter Wüttke and Carl Georg Heise [Baden-Baden: G. B. Teubner, 1979]), 317–47. For the relationship between Cassirer and Warburg, see also Erwin Panofsky, "Nachrufe für Aby Warburg," *Mnemosyne,* 29–33.

3. For Cassirer's conception of time, see chap. two, above.

4. For the influence of Usener's teaching on Warburg, see Gombrich, *Aby Warburg,* 29–30. Gombrich's monograph is quite useful for its reconstruction of the course of Warburg's studies and of his sources and inspirations. The sources and biographical-bibliographical information found in Gombrich's volume are implicit in references hereafter and will not be cited specifically.

For a balanced critique of Gombrich's book written upon its publication in the United States, see Willibald Sauerländer, "Rescuing the Past," *New York Review of Books,* March 3, 1988, 19–22. There is also a very interesting and indicative critical review by Edgar Wind, "Unfinished Business. Aby Warburg and his Work," *Times Literary Supplement,* June 25, 1971, 735ff., republished in the first volume of Wind's selected essays, *The Eloquence of Symbols. Studies in Humanist Art*, ed. J. Anderson (Oxford: Clarendon Press, 1983), 106–13. In this connection, see also Kurt W. Foster, "Aby Warburg's History of Art: Collective Memory and the Social Mediation of Images," *Dedalus, Journal of the American Academy of Arts and Sciences* (1976), 169–76. "[Warburg's] scholarly achievement remains rather obscure despite a recent 'intellectual biography' by Sir Ernst Gombrich" (ibid., 169). For a commentary on Gombrich's "biography" of Warburg and the subjects it dealt with, see Martin Jesinghausen-Lauster, *Die Suche nach der symbolischen Form* (Baden-Baden: Verlag V. Koerner, 1985).

For Warburg's relationship with Usener, see Arnaldo Momigliano, "History and Theory. Studies in the Philosophy of History," *New Path of Classicism in the Nineteenth Century* (1982), 33–48, and Eugenio Garin's preface to Fritz Saxl, *La storia delle immagini* (Bari: Laterza, 1965), xii. See also the recent essay by Maria Micaela Sassi, "Dalla scienza delle religioni di Usener ad Aby Warburg," *Aspetti di Hermann Usener, filologo della religione* (Pisa: Giardini, 1982), 65–91; here the author, by using a well-structured bibliography, underscores the path that leads from Usener to Warburg (also through Dilthey's mediation) and attempts to find the source of Warburg's famous motto "The Good Lord hides in details" precisely in an expression of Dilthey's regarding Usener's "momentary gods" (ibid., 86–91). This endeavor is rather puzzling, however, especially in regard to the conceptual similarity established between the *Einzelding* (detail) that Dilthey speaks of, and in which the "momentary god" lies, and Warburg's details, which are rather the ones whose structural rule is totally consonant with the structural rule of the whole. A hypothetical relationship between the theories of Dilthey and Warburg is proposed in Felix Gilbert, "From Art History to the History of Civilization: Gombrich's Biography of Aby Warburg," in *The Journal of Modern History* 44 (1972), 387f.

5. Hermann Usener, *Götternamen, Versuch einer Lehre von der religiösen Begriffsbildung* (1896; Frankfurt am Main: Bulmke, 1948), 3.

6. Ibid., 57. In this connection, see Ernst Cassirer, *Language and Myth* (1925; New York: Harper & Brothers, 1946), 17–23. For Cassirer's relationship with Usener, see the essay by Remo Bodei, "Hermann Usener nella filosofia moderna: tra Dilthey e Cassirer," *Aspetti di Hermann Usener*, 38–42.

7. Charles Darwin, *The Expression of the Emotions in Man and Animals* (London: John Murray, 1872), 17.

8. Usener, *Götternamen*, 273.

9. Ibid., 274.

10. Darwin, *The Expression of the Emotions*, 361.

11. Ibid., 28, 29.

12. A brief mention of the relationship between Warburg and Vignoli is also to be found in Sassi, "Dalla scienza delle religioni," 83–85.

13. Tito Vignoli, *Mito e Scienza* (Milan, 1879), 32.
14. Ibid., 1.
15. Ibid., 2.
16. Ibid., 7.
17. Ibid., 18f.
18. Ibid., 68.
19. Ibid., 70.
20. Ibid., 72.
21. Ibid., 20.
22. Ibid., 22f.
23. Darwin, *Expression of the Emotions*, 367.
24. Erwin Rohde, *Psyche, The Cult of Souls and Belief in Immortality among the Ancient Greeks* (Chicago: Ares Publishers, 1987), 16, 266. The first German edition of this work was published in 1894.
25. Darwin, *Expression of the Emotions*, 367.
26. Giorgio Pasquali, *Pagine stravaganti di un filologo* (Lanciano, 1933), 73: "Aby Warburg became part of a current of thought that expressed a new conception of antiquity as the synthesis of opposites, as formulated by Nietzsche, Rohde and Wilamowitz, as opposed to the traditional Enlightenment tradition."
27. Friedrich Nietzsche, *The Birth of Tragedy from the Spirit of Music, The Philosophy of Nietzsche* (New York: The Modern Library, 1927), 1028. *The Birth of Tragedy* was first published in Leipzig in 1872.
28. Ernst Cassirer, "Die Antike und die Entstehung der exakten Wissenschaften," *Die Antike* 8 (Berlin, 1932), 276ff.
29. Ibid., 291.
30. Ibid., 299.
31. The relationship Cassirer's philosophy of symbolic forms had with the author of "Das Symbol" will be dealt with in chap. two (see also chap. two, n. 94).
32. Aby Warburg, "Sandro Botticellis 'Geburt der Venus' und 'Frühling'" (Botticelli's 'Birth of Venus' and 'Spring,' Research on the Image of Antiquity in the Early Italian Renaissance; 1893), *Gesammelte Schriften*, vol. 1 (Leipzig-Berlin: G. Teubner, 1932), 5 (hereafter, the *Gesammelte Schriften* will be cited as *G.S.*).
33. Usener, *Götternamen*, vii.
34. Ibid., 74.
35. Aby Warburg, "I costumi teatrali per gli intermezzi del 1589. I disegni di Bernardo Buontalenti e il 'Libro di conti' di Emilio de' Cavalieri, Saggio storico-artistico" (Theater Costumes for the 1598 'Intermezzi.' Bernardo Buontalenti's Drawings and Emilio de' Cavalieri's 'Accounts Book,' An Art-Historical Essay; 1895), *G.S.*, 1:280f.

In this regard one must bear in mind a consideration made by Karl Lamprecht, who was one of Warburg's teachers, concerning our capability of judging the individualism of the primitive Germans. Lamprecht affirms that if we observe the life of that time with our modern-day eyes, the individual will appear to be part of a uniform, leveled pattern. But if we observe this life with the eyes of *that* time, we will discover that the individual qualities are cultivated above all in view of being used for the conservation of the state (*Einführung in das historische Denken* [1912; Leipzig, 1913]), 9. For the modalities of the process of culture and the notion of the development of national individual characteristics in Lamprecht, see Alfred Doren, "Karl Lamprechts Geschichtstheorie und die Kunstgeschichte," *Zeitschrift für Aesthetik* 11 (1916), 353–89. And for Lamprecht's historical methodology, see Ernst Cassirer, "The Theory of Psychological Types in History: Lamprecht," *The Problem of Knowledge: Philosophy, Science, and History since Hegel*, trans. William H. Woglom and Charles W. Hendel (1950; New Haven and London: Yale University Press, 1969), 281–93.

36. Momigliano, *New Path of Classicism*, 33ff.

37. Benedetto Croce, "L'estetica della Einfühlung," *Storia dell'estetica per saggi* (Bari: Laterza, 1942), 203ff. See also ibid., "R. Vischer e la contemplazione della natura" (1934), 210ff. For an account of the relationship between Warburg and Robert Vischer see Gianni Carchia, "Aby Warburg: simbolo e tragedia," *Aut-Aut* 199–200 (1984), 92–108.

38. Robert Vischer, "Über das optische Formgefühl. Ein Beitrag zur Aesthetik" (1873), *Drei Schriften zum ästhetischen Formproblem* (Halle-Salle: M. Niemeyer, 1927), 15. An analysis of the connection between philosophy and art theory (or aesthetics) and of the concept of empathy is found in Hans Glocker, "Robert Vischer und die Krisis der Geisteswissenschaften im letzten Drittel des neunzehnten Jahrhunderts," *Logos* 14 (1925), 297–343, and 15 (1926), 47–102.

39. Vischer, "Über das optische Formgefühl," 18.

40. Ibid., 18.

41. Ibid., 20ff.

42. Robert Vischer, "Der ästhetische Akt und die reine Form," *Drei Schriften*, 52.

43. Vischer, "Über der optische Formgefühl," 21.

44. Ibid., 21.

45. Ibid., 28.

46. Ibid., 18.

47. Ibid., 22.

48. Ibid., 35.

49. Ibid.

50. Ibid., 37.

51. Ibid., 43.

52. Jacob Burckhardt, *The Civilization of the Renaissance in Italy* (New York:

The New American Library, 1961), Pt. 3: "The Revival of Antiquity," 145. Aby Warburg, *Italienische Kunst und internationale Astrologie im Palazzo Schifanoja zu Ferrara* (Italian Art and International Astrology in the Schifanoia Palace in Ferrara; 1912), *G.S.,* 2:479.

53. Burckhardt, *Civilization of the Renaissance,* 301.

54. Fritz Saxl, "Three 'Florentines': Herbert Horne, Aby Warburg, Jacques Mesnil," *Lectures,* 1:336.

55. Warburg, "Sandro Botticellis 'Geburt,'" 45, 46.

56. Gotthold Ephriam Lessing, *Lessing's "Laocoön,"* trans. E. C. Beasley (London: George Bell & Sons, 1888), 33–43.

57. Arthur Schopenhauer, *The World as Will and Representation,* trans. E. F. J. Payne, 2 vols. (New York: Dover Publications, 1969), 1:178.

58. Nietzsche, *Birth of Tragedy,* 954.

59. Johann Joachim Winckelmann, *History of Ancient Art,* trans. G. Henry Lodge (1764; New York: Ungar, 1968), 1:122.

60. Warburg, "Sandro Botticellis 'Geburt,'" 54–55.

61. Jacob Burckhardt, "Über die niederländische Genremalerei," *Gesamtausgabe,* vol. 14: *Vorträge* (Stuttgart-Berlin-Leipzig: Deutsche Verlags-Anstalt, 1933), 110–50.

62. Usener, *Götternamen,* 74f.

63. Ernst Cassirer, *Freiheit und Form. Studien zur deutschen Geistesgeschichte* (1916; Darmstadt: Wissenschaftliche Buchgesellschaft, 1975), 91–107. This work is interesting above all for its treatment of the relationship between genius and rule in Lessing. On the same subject, see Pierre Grappin, *La théorie du génie dans le préclassicisme allemand* (Paris: Presses Universitaires de France, 1952) as well as Herman Wolf, *Versuch einer Geschichte des Geniebegriffs in der deutschen Aesthetik des 18. Jahrhunderts* (Heidelberg: C. Winter, 1923). The latter work demonstrates that the origin of the theory of genius lies with Leibniz.

64. Karl Justi, *Velazquez und sein Jahrhundert* (1888), (Bonn: F. Cohen, 1903), 2.

65. Schopenhauer, *The World as Will,* sect. 36: 184, 185.

66. Immanuel Kant, *Critique of Judgement,* trans. J. H. Bernard, 2d ed. (New York and London: Hafner Publishing, 1966), 150.

67. Ibid., 152.

68. Ibid., 153.

69. Ibid., 163.

70. As regards the theme of the irrationality of genius in Lessing and Kant, see Armand Nivelle, *Kunst- und Dichtungstheorien zwischen Aufklärung und Klassik* (Berlin: De Gruyter, 1960).

71. Schopenhauer, *The World as Will,* 185.

72. Nietzsche, *Birth of Tragedy*, 975.

73. Vischer, "Der ästhetische Akt," 51.

74. Fritz Saxl, "Continuity and Variation in the Meaning of Images," *Lectures*, 1:9–12.

75. Erwin Panofsky and Fritz Saxl, "Dürers 'Melencolia I,'" Eine Quellen- und Typengeschichtliche Untersuchung," *Studien der Bibliothek Warburg* (Leipzig-Berlin, 1923). For a discussion of this work, see chap. three.

76. Aby Warburg, "Heidnisch-antike Weissagung in Wort und Bild zu Luthers Zeiten" (Ancient Pagan Divination in Texts and Images of Luther's Age; 1920), *G.S.*, 2:528. Warburg's interpretation of Dürer's engraving will be discussed later in this chapter.

77. Jacob Burckhardt, *Force and Freedom. Reflections on History*, ed. James Hastings Nichols (New York: Pantheon, 1943), 144.

78. Ibid., 322.

79. Burckhardt, *Civilization of the Renaissance*, 145.

80. Ibid., 148.

81. Warburg, "Sandro Botticellis 'Geburt,'" 22.

82. Warburg, "I costumi teatrali," 289.

83. Ibid., 296.

84. For a critique of the idea of progress in Burckhardt, see Gennaro Sasso's article "Progresso," *Enciclopedia del Novecento* (1981), 5:627ff.

85. Gertrud Bing, "Aby Warburg," *Journal of the Warburg Institute* 28 (1965), 310.

86. Aby Warburg, "L'ingresso dello stile anticheggiante nella pittura del primo Rinascimento" (The Entry of the Idealizing Classical Style in Early Renaissance Painting; 1914), *La rinascita del paganesimo antico: Contributi alla storia della cultura raccolti da Gertrud Bing* (Florence: La Nuova Italia, 1966), 307.

87. Aby Warburg, "Bildniskunst und florentinisches Bürgertum" (The Art of Portraiture and the Florentine Bourgeoisie; 1902), *G.S.*, 1:94.

88. Jacob Burckhardt, "Die Anfänge der neuern Porträtmalerei," *Vorträge*, 321.

89. Ibid., 323.

90. Warburg, "Bildniskunst und florentinisches Bürgertum," *G.S.* 1:95.

91. Ibid., 1:96.

92. For the relationship between Warburg and Burckhardt, see Werner Kaegi, "Das Werk Aby Warburgs," *Neue Schweizer Rundschau*, n.s., 1 (1933), 282–93. "One could define a considerable part of Warburg's early writings as 'works of Jacob Burckhardt's school,'" ibid., 286. See also Hans Liebeschütz, "Aby Warburg as Interpreter of Civilisation," *Year Book XVI of the Leo Baeck Institute* (London, 1971). Liebeschütz speaks of the 1926–27 seminar in Hamburg on

Burckhardt and Nietzsche (some notes of which have been published in *Adelphiana 1971* [Milan, 1971], 9–13, entitled "Burckhardt e Nietzsche"). On the same subject, see also Gombrich, *In Search of Cultural History*, 19 and 40.

93. Nietzsche, *Birth of Tragedy*, 1042.

94. Ibid., 1043.

95. Aby Warburg, "Austausch künstlerischer Kultur zwischen Norden und Süden im 15. Jahrhundert" (Cultural Exchanges between North and South in the 15th Century; 1905), *G.S.*, 1:184. For a clear exposition and analysis of polarity in Warburg's oeuvre, see Fritz Saxl, "Rinascimento dell'antichità. Studien zu den Arbeiten A. Warburgs," *Repertorium für Kunstwissenschaft* 43 (1922), 220–73, now also in Warburg, *Ausgewählte Schriften*, 347–400.

96. Warburg, "Delle 'imprese amorose' nelle più antiche incisioni fiorentine" (On the 'Imprese Amorose' in the Most Ancient Florentine Engravings; 1905), *G.S.*, 1:80.

97. Winckelmann, *History of Ancient Art*, 200.

98. Ibid., 201. In connection with the problem of Winckelmann's idealism, see the erudite volume by Rosario Assunto, *L'antichità come futuro. Studio sull'estetica del neoclassicismo europeo* (Milan: Mursia, 1973).

99. Thomas Mann, "Zu Goethes 'Wahlverwandtschaften,'" *Gesammelte Werke* (Frankfurt am Main: Samuel Fischer Verlag, 1974), 9:177.

100. Friedrich Schiller, *On the Naive and Sentimental in Literature*, trans. Helen Watanabe-O'Kelly (Manchester: Carcanet New Press, 1981), 39.

101. Ibid., 40.

102. Ibid., 41–42.

103. Georg Wilhelm Friedrich Hegel, *Hegel's Science of Logic*, trans. Arnold V. Miller (London: George Allen & Unwin, 1969; rpt. New York: Humanities Press, 1976), 149.

104. See also the section concerning affirmative infinity, ibid., 154ff.

105. Ibid., 150.

106. Kaegi, "Das Werk Aby Warburgs," 287.

107. Aby Warburg, "Arbeitende Bauern auf burgundischen Teppichen" (Peasants at Work in the Burgundian Tapestries; 1907), *G.S.*, 1:229.

108. Warburg, "Delle 'imprese amorose,'" 87.

109. Aby Warburg, "Francesco Sassettis letztwillige Verfügung" (Francesco Sassetti's Last Will and Testament; 1907), *G.S.*, 1:129–58.

110. Ibid., 145, 146.

111. For the incompatibility between the tendency to rationalize human events in order to dominate them fully, and the consciousness of Fortune's mad inconstancy, see the famous essay by Alfred Doren, "Fortuna im Mittelalter und in der Renaissance," *Vorträge der Bibliothek Warburg* (1922–23), Part 1, 71–140; above all see the parts regarding Machiavelli and Warburg's interpretation of Sassetti's

and Rucellai's behavior (122ff.). Doren's research has totally penetrated the sphere of Warburg's thought and thus precisely determines its outlines, if that were necessary. Cassirer, in *Individual and Cosmos in Renaissance Philosophy* (trans. Mario Domandi [Oxford: Basil Blackwell, 1963]), 73ff., also perfectly agrees with Warburg's and Doren's research, though the meaning he attributes to the pathos formulas, of which Fortuna is a typical example, accentuates more their nature of continuity with tradition, while taking in the novelty of images, rather than their strong contrast and contradiction. For a criticism of Cassirer's lack of understanding of the problem of Fortune in the last chapter of Machiavelli's *Prince*, see Gennaro Sasso, *Niccolò Machiavelli* (Bologna: Il Mulino, 1980), 363f., nn. 76 and 77, where Cassirer's *Myth of the State* is quoted. For the context in which the subject of Fortune was discussed in the early Florentine Renaissance, see Edgar Wind, "Platonic Tyranny and the Renaissance of Fortuna," *Lectures*, 86–93.

112. Warburg, "Francesco Sassettis letztwillige Verfügung," 146.

113. Ibid., 149.

114. Ibid., 149.

115. Burckhardt's commentary on the triumph of Fortune in the part of the procession reserved for the Florentines during the celebration of Alfonso the Great's entrance into Naples in 1443 betrays a singular tone of annoyance and reproof: "The goddess herself, in accordance with the inexorable logic of allegory to which even the painters of that time conformed, had hair only on the front part of her head, while the back part was bald . . . And the genius who sat on the lower steps of the car and who symbolized the fugitive character of Fortune, had his feet immersed in a basin of water" (Jacob Burckhardt, *Civilization of the Renaissance*, 296). And in a note [which is not in the English translation] he adds: "One of the true acts of ingenuousness on the part of the Renaissance was to have assigned such a place to Fortune." And by "place" he means a dominating position over the other symbolic personifications of the virtues. Evidently in Burckhardt's conception of the Renaissance, which considered individual virtue to be essentially heroic and highly innovative, there was no place for that wild goddess who instilled uncertainty and oscillation in the soul, whereas Warburg considered this figure an intrinsic necessity for the very meaning of the epoch. In his essay on Fortuna, Doren noted this different conception of the polarities of the epoch in the two historians: "Today we know that J. Burckhardt's interpretation of Renaissance man was the ideal construction of a conscious stylization" (*Fortuna*, 100).

116. Warburg, "Francesco Sassetis letztwillige Verfügung," 151.

117. Ibid., 153.

118. Ibid., 154.

119. Ibid., 157.

120. "Epistola di Marsiglio Ficino a Giovanni Rucellai," in Warburg, "Francesco Sassettis letztwillige Verfügung," 147–48.

121. Warburg, *Italienische Kunst*, 479.
122. Ibid., 461–62.
123. Ibid., 464.
124. For the origin of these astrological figures and their "migration" in the ancient and medieval East, see the fundamental work by Franz Boll, *Sternglauben und Sterndeutung. Die Geschichte und das Wesen der Astrologie* (Leipzig-Berlin: G. Teubner, 1918). For Warburg's and Cassirer's relationship with Boll, see Eugeni Garin's preface to Franz Boll, Carl Bezold, and Wilhelm Gundel, *Storia dell'astrologia* (Bari: Laterza, 1979), vii–xxiii.
125. Warburg, *Italienische Kunst*, 479.
126. Ibid., 478.
127. Aby Warburg, "Dürer und die italienische Antike" (Dürer and Italian Antiquity; 1905), *G.S.*, 2:446.
128. Ibid., 2:448.
129. Nietzsche, "The Birth of Tragedy," *Ecce Homo*, in *Philosophy of Nietzsche*, 939.
130. Ibid., 940–41.
131. Nietzsche, *Birth of Tragedy*, 954.
132. Ibid., 959–60.
133. Ibid., 1033.
134. Warburg, "L'ingresso dello stile anticheggiante," 296.
135. Ibid., 297.
136. Ibid., 298.
137. Ibid., 298.
138. Ibid., 302.
139. Nietzsche, *Birth of Tragedy*, 963–64.
140. Ibid., 966.
141. Ibid., 940.
142. Warburg, "L'ingresso dello stile anticheggiante," 304.
143. Ibid., 338.
144. Ibid., 306.
145. Ibid., 306.
146. Ibid., 307.
147. Nietzsche, *Birth of Tragedy*, 1071.
148. Rohde, *Psyche*, 25. See also Rohde's reviews of Nietzsche: "Comunicazione per il 'Litterarisches Centralblatt'" (1872) and "Comunicazione nella 'Norddeutsche allgemeine Zeitung'" (May 6, 1872), Friedrich Nietzsche, Erwin Rodhe, Ulrich von Wilamowitz, and Richard Wagner, *La polemica sull'arte tragica*, ed. F. Serpa (Florence: Sansoni, 1972).
149. Rohde, *Psyche*, 25.
150. Ibid., 88.

151. Erwin Rohde, "Filologia deretana, per chiarificazione del pamphlet 'Filologia dell'avvenire!' del Dr. phil. Ulrich von Wilamowitz-Möllendorff, 'Lettera di un filologo a R. Wagner,'" *La polemica sull'arte tragica*, 251–95.

152. Nietzsche, "An Attempt at Self-criticism," *Ecce Homo*, 934–46.

153. Warburg, *Heidnisch-antike Weissagung*, 528.

154. Winckelmann, *History of Ancient Art*, 37–38.

155. See chap. three.

156. See Carlo Antoni, "Momenti della storia della storiografia, Johann Joachim Winckelmann," *Studi Germanici* 4 (1940), 111–35, and Carlo Antoni, *La lotta contro la ragione* (Florence: Sansoni, 1942), 37–52. See also, above all for the Apollonian and Dionysian in Winckelmann, the recent study by Max L. Baeumer, "Winckelmanns Formulierung der klassischen Schönheit," *Monatshefte* 65 (1973), 61–75: "It is Winckelmann who laid down the premises and true starting point for the so-called Dionysian phenomenon in German spiritual life" (72). Furthermore, see the critical essay by Eliza-Marian Butler, *The Tyranny of Greece over Germany* (Cambridge, Mass.: Harvard University Press, 1935).

157. Warburg, *Italienische Kunst*, 478.

158. Carl Georg Heise, *Persönliche Erinnerungen an Aby Warburg* (New York: Erich Warburg, 1947), 42ff. (republished in Germany [Hamburg: Gesellschaft der Bücherfreunde zu Hamburg, 1959]).

159. Warburg, *Heidnisch-antike Weissagung*, 491.

160. Jacob Burckhardt, *The Age of Constantine the Great*, trans. Moses Hadas (London: Routledge & Kegan Paul, 1949), 163.

161. Ibid., 164.

162. Ibid., 185.

163. Ibid., 188. For a harsh criticism of this attitude of Burckhardt's with respect to history, see Benedetto Croce, *La storia come pensiero e come azione* (1938; Bari: Laterza, 1965), 90–102.

164. Burckhardt, *Age of Constantine*, 190.

165. Ibid., 193.

166. Ibid., 201.

167. Kaegi, "Das Werk Aby Warburgs," 286.

168. See chap. two.

169. Burckhardt, *Age of Constantine*, 201.

170. Warburg, "Heidnisch-antike Weissagung," 492.

171. Ibid., 496.

172. Ibid., 504.

173. See Saxl, "La Villa Farnesina," *Lectures*, 1:189–99.

174. Warburg, "Heidnisch-antike Weissagung," 511–12.

175. Ibid., 529.

176. For an interpretation of the function of magic in the Renaissance, see

Cassirer, *Individual and Cosmos*, 98ff., and Eugenio Garin, *Medioevo e Rinascimento* (Bari: Laterza, 1954), 150–69. Whereas Warburg opposes the obscurantist spirit of magic to the "enlightened" spirit of those who through scientific speculation went beyond this, both Cassirer and Garin proceed to integrate magic and science, finding a continuity between them. Kaegi has the following to say about Warburg's observations concerning astrology: "Only he who has understood that Olympus existed for the Middle Ages in a demoniac form, can understand what sort of liberation the Renaissance represented" ("Das Werk Aby Warburgs," 289). In this regard, see chap. two. For the survival of astrology and magic and humanism's strength to resist these remnants of the past, see Delio Cantimori, "Valore dell'Umanesimo," *Studi di Storia* (Turin: Einaudi, 1959), 2:385.

177. Warburg, "Heidnisch-antike Weissagung," 531.

178. In his *Symbolik und Mythologie* (Leipzig-Darmstadt, 1822), Frederick Creuzer had made a philological and philosophical analysis of the origins and meaning of the term *symbol* and of its relationship with sensibility, on the one hand, and with the purely intelligible, the idea, on the other. His distinction between the obscure, mystical symbol and the "plastic symbol" is especially noteworthy for the subsequent meditations on the symbol and on the history of ancient mythology: "Due to the need to use the symbol in the sensible expression of artistic or religious ideas, it is placed vis-à-vis the infinite and the boundless. But since the conditioned cannot replace the unconditioned, the symbol has two possible paths to follow: either it embraces *mysticism,* the obscurity and incomprehensibility of expression, or it stops to dwell at the subtle discriminating line between spirit and nature. This is the *symbol of the gods,* or *plastic symbol*" (*Symbolik und Mythologie* 25). The plastic symbol is the one that is expressed in Greek sculpture. Its properties are clarity, brevity, delightfulness, and beauty.

179. Warburg, "Heidnisch-antike Weissagung," 497.

180. For an interpretation of the concept of progress in Warburg, see Forster, "Aby Warburg's History of Art," 171 and 173: "As a student of Darwin, Warburg considered the acquisition of culture a very gradual process, but doubted that the territory of freedom and mental control was a permanent gain."

181. Warburg, "Heidnisch-antike Weissagung," 491–92.

182. For a critique of the concept of the age of transition, see Delio Cantimori, "La periodizzazione del Rinascimento," *Studi di storia,* 2:350.

183. Warburg, "A Lecture on Serpent Ritual," 282.

184. Ibid., 277.

185. Ibid., 288.

186. See chap. two.

187. Edgar Wind, "Warburgs Begriff der Kulturwissenschaft und seine Bedeutung für die Aesthetik," *Vierter Kongress für Aesthetik und allgemeine Kunst-*

wissenschaft, October 1930 (Bericht, 1931), 171f. Now in Wind, *The Eloquence of Symbols,* 28–29.

188. Ernesto De Martino, *Il mondo magico. Prolegomeni a una storia del magismo* (1948; Turin: Boringhieri, 1973), 95f., n. 3.

189. Ibid., 95.

190. Ibid., 95.

191. Ibid., 136.

192. Ibid., 190f.

193. Ibid., 193.

194. Ibid., 188.

195. Ibid., 189, 191.

196. Warburg "A Lecture on Serpent Ritual," 289.

197. Ibid., 291.

198. Ibid., 291.

199. Ibid., 291.

200. Ibid., 292. This problem is discussed in Götz Pochat, *Der Symbolbegriff in der Aesthetik und Kunstwissenschaft* (Cologne: Du Mont, 1983; 1st Swedish ed., 1982), 86: "Warburg, like his contemporary Cassirer, also seems to conceive of discursive thought as a sort of 'symbolic form.'"

201. Thomas Mann, *Joseph and His Brothers,* trans. H. T. Lowe-Porter (Harmondsworth, Middlesex: Penguin Books, 1978), 427.

202. Ibid., 431–32.

203. Ibid., 443–44.

204. Ibid., 444.

205. For Mann's conception of history, see Gennaro Sasso, *Tramonto di un mito* (Bologna: Il Mulino, 1984), 9–14. For a clarification of the relationship between mythical scheme and history in Mann, see Silvia Ferretti, *Thomas Mann e il tempo* (Rome: Jouvence, 1980), 77–148.

206. Regarding Warburg's *Bilderatlas* (picture atlas), see the recent study by Martin Warnke, "Der Leidschatz der Menschheit wird humaner Besitz," in Werner Hoffmann, Georg Syamken, and Martin Warnke, *Die Menschenrechte des Auges: Über Aby Warburg* (Frankfurt am Main: Europäische Verlagsanstalt, 1980), 115–64.

2: ERNST CASSIRER

1. Johan Huizinga, *Wege der Kulturgeschichte,* German trans. by Werner Kaegi (Munich: Drei Masken Verlag, 1930), 104ff.: "Burckhardt was the first to free the Renaissance from its relation to the Enlightenment and to progress and to view it as his ideal of *sui generis* culture." Huizinga points out that Burckhardt

lacks knowledge of the Middle Ages outside of Italy and therefore criticizes him for having too narrow a temporal range, and above all for having set an unjustified spatial limit upon historical reality (ibid., 107). Regarding Burckhardt's knowledge of the Middle Ages, see Werner Kaegi, *Jacob Burckhardt. Eine Biographie* (Basel: B. Schwabe, 1956), 3:650ff., quoted by Liebeschütz in "Aby Warburg as Interpreter of Civilisation," 234. Huizinga emphasized the nature of isolation of the Burckhardtian Renaissance vis-à-vis the course of history, not in order to replace it with a concept of evolution from the Middle Ages, but on the contrary in order to claim precisely for the Middle Ages all the features that Burckhardt had attributed to the Renaissance; and he interpreted the latter as a period of decadence and mummification, when the fundamental unity of medieval culture disintegrated. Yet such is Huizinga's admiration for the Swiss historian ("The structure of this inimitable model of historical-cultural synthesis is as sure and harmonious as a work of the Renaissance itself," ibid., 104f.) that he rather tends to criticize those followers of Burckhardt who made a "Nietzschian" myth, so to speak, of the results of that research (ibid., 108).

2. Delio Cantimori also noted that Warburg went beyond the teachings of Burckhardt: "From Burckhardt to Warburg to Saxl to Frankfort to Bing . . . there is an uninterrupted line . . . Naturally the studies, research and historiographic invention progressed, and the image of the Renaissance marked out by Warburg is different and richer, more profound and complete than the image created by Burckhardt" ("Avventure di un devoto di Clio," *Itinerari* 79–80 [1964], 92). See also Fritz Saxl, "Die Bibliothek Warburg und ihr Ziel," *Vorträge der Bibliothek Warburg* (1921–22), 1, where the author points out that Burckhardt was Warburg's model as far as art history—understood as the history of culture—was concerned: "And yet Warburg was not a follower of Burckhardt, but rather a continuator of his." As regards the difference between Warburg and Burckhardt, see Michael Podro, *The Critical Historians of Art* (New Haven and London: Yale University Press, 1982), 172–74.

3. See chap. one.

4. See Donald Phillip Verene's introduction to Ernst Cassirer, *Symbol, Myth and Culture, Essays and Lectures of Ernst Cassirer,* ed. Donald Phillip Verene (New Haven and London: Yale University Press, 1979), 21 and 22.

5. In the spring of 1940 Cassirer mentioned to his wife his intention to add a fourth volume to *Philosophy of Symbolic Forms* (see Toni Cassirer, *Mein Leben mit Ernst Cassirer* [Hildesheim: Gerstenberg Verlag, 1981], 170). In his introduction to *Symbol, Myth and Culture* (page 25), Verene incontrovertibly demonstrates Cassirer's plan to write an essay on art theory.

6. Cassirer, *Individual and Cosmos,* xv.

7. For a picture of the original arrangement of the Warburg Library, see Saxl, *Die Bibliothek Warburg und ihr Ziel.* In the light of an inquiry into the theories

of the symbol and of history in Warburg and Cassirer and their differences, it seems exaggerated to affirm, as Peter Fischer-Appelt does, that "the choice of the books and the entire arrangement of this Library were such as to make one think that their founder had more or less anticipated Cassirer's conception of a theory of symbolic forms as a system of the essential functions of the spirit" (Peter Fischer-Appelt, *Zum Gedenken an Ernst Cassirer, Ansprache zur Eröffnung der wissenschaftlichen Tagung 'Symbolische Forme,' anlässlich der 100. Geburtstages von Ernst Cassirer am 20. Oktober 1974 in Hamburg* [Göttingen, 1975], 10).

8. As regards the problem of the "methodical circle" and the solution Panofsky gave to it, see chap. three.

9. Ernst Cassirer, *Das Erkenntnisproblem in der Philosophie und Wissenschaft der neueren Zeit* (Berlin: Bruno Cassirer, 1911), 1:74, 97, and 171.

10. Cassirer, *Individual and Cosmos*, 3. Concerning Burckhardt's Hegelianism, see Gombrich, *In Search of Cultural History*, 14–25, where the author attempts, without persuasive argumentation, to demonstrate that Burckhardt's image of culture derived from the scheme of an evolution of the spirit in Hegel.

11. Cassirer, *Individual and Cosmos*, 3–4.

12. Ibid., 4.

13. Cassirer, *Das Erkenntnisproblem*, 17.

14. See Guido De Ruggiero, *Storia della filosofia*, part three, "Rinascimento Riforma e Controriforma" (Bari: Laterza, 1950), 1:5, where the author expresses mistrust with regard to the formula Burckhardt used to sum up the Renaissance period. By "individualism" De Ruggiero means the polemical and negative form of opposition to rigid medieval schematization, and this was certainly not the sense this word has taken on in the modern age—the individual setting himself as universal in his self-sufficiency and independence. "In vain would one search for such a meaning in the cultural and social world of the Renaissance." Neither the Reformation, so bound to the Scriptures, nor philosophy, which depended upon Plato just as the philosophy of the preceding period had depended upon Aristotle, nor even humanism, which was anchored to the authority of the classical philosophers and artists, manifested the total essence of the individual. "Usually one takes for 'individual' that which is only original, eccentric and which in fact *is* only a barely inchoate individuality that is yet inharmonious and discordant with its environment. In this pejorative sense, one can say that the epoch we are discussing is the age of individualism, that is to say, the age of modern man's first efforts to assert his autonomy against all the forces of tradition, authority and customs." In this sense De Ruggiero gives Burckhardt's aestheticizing interpretation its full authority: the work of art is the ephemeral result in which the Renaissance sought a temporary anchor for its mania for renewal. Thus De Ruggiero observed in the Renaissance above all the slow evolution—which still took place in the sense of the closest connection—from the Scholastic mentality to the

modern age, pointing out the unsystematic character of medieval philosophy which, unlike modern systems of thought, "is the almost impersonal and anonymous custom of an age that barely felt the value of the human personality," an age which engendered the persistent, tenacious force that yet attracts the Renaissance into its sphere, because it is the negation of all striving for the new and differentiated.

15. Cassirer, *Individual and Cosmos*, 35.
16. Ibid., 38–39.
17. Ibid., 11.
18. Ibid., 15.
19. Ibid., 16.
20. Ibid., 38.
21. Ibid., 22–23.
22. Ibid., 86–87.
23. In 1910 Cassirer had noted how the importance of Ficino's thought lay not in his mystical pantheism, but in having handed down, rather than a form of Platonism related to natural science, a Platonism related to the immortality of the soul and thus to the problem of knowledge (*Das Erkenntnisproblem*, 89ff.).
24. Cassirer, *Individual and Cosmos*, 86.
25. Ibid., 86–87. See Hans Baron, "Literaturbericht, Renaissance in Italien," *Archiv für Kulturgeschichte* 21 (1931), 112ff., on Renaissance philosophy according to Cassirer. Baron criticizes Cassirer's demonstration of Cusanus's influence on Renaissance intellectuals as being insufficient. He points out that Cusanus's writings were utilized in Italy only in the circle of artists and "technical" scholars who operated outside the school tradition and thus it was not possible for Cusanus to have had any influence upon the Platonists, especially Ficino and Pico. On this same subject see also Hans Baron, "Towards a More Positive Evaluation of the Fifteenth-Century Renaissance," *Journal of the History of Ideas* 4 (1943), 21–49.
26. Cassirer, *Individual and Cosmos*, 87f.
27. Ibid., 88–89.
28. Carolus Bovillus, *De sapiente,* in Ernst Cassirer, *Individuum und Kosmos in der Philosophie der Renaissance* (Leipzig: G. Teubner, 1927), 303–412. The essay by Bovillus is not reproduced in the English edition of Cassirer's book.
29. Cassirer, *Individual and Cosmos*, 102.
30. Ibid., 102.
31. Ibid., 2. See also Cassirer, *Das Erkenntnisproblem*, 21ff., on the struggle Cusanus waged to realize a new language, and also Cassirer, "Some Remarks on the Question of the Originality of the Renaissance," *Journal of the History of Ideas* 4 (1943), 49–56.
32. In this regard, see chap. three.

33. Ernst Cassirer, *Freiheit und Form. Studien zur deutschen Geistesgeschichte* (Berlin: Bruno Cassirer, 1916; now in Darmstadt, 1975; see chap. 1, n. 63).

34. David R. Lipton, *Ernst Cassirer. The Dilemma of a Liberal Intellectual in Germany 1914–1933* (Toronto-Buffalo-London: University of Toronto Press, 1978). After a brief and rather superficial analysis of Cassirer's book on the Renaissance and on his relationship with Burckhardt, Lipton observes: "Cassirer based much of his own argument on Burckhardt's standpoint because he shared with Burckhardt the nineteenth-century liberal belief that the history of European man since the Renaissance was, for the most part, the story of the growth of individual freedom." And further on: "From an ideological standpoint, Cassirer's praise of the Renaissance amounted to a defence of a cosmopolitan liberalism" (ibid., 136). Evidently this "ideological standpoint" betrays a noteworthy shortsightedness.

35. Cassirer, *Individual and Cosmos*, 75.

36. Ibid., 75.

37. Ibid., 75–76.

38. Ibid., 75ff.

39. Ibid., 76.

40. Ibid., 80.

41. Cassirer, "Eidos und Eidolon. Das Problem des Schönen und der Kunst in Platons Dialogen," *Vorträge der Bibliothek Warburg*, vol. 2 (1922–23; Leipzig-Berlin, 1924), 25ff. See also chap. three above.

42. Cassirer, *Individual and Cosmos*, 125.

43. Ibid.

44. Ibid., 127.

45. Ibid., 127–28.

46. Ibid., 128.

47. Baron, *Renaissance in Italien*, 114.

48. In this regard see also Cassirer, *Das Erkenntnisproblem*, 88.

49. Cassirer, *Individual and Cosmos*, 67f.

50. Ibid., 99.

51. Ibid., 101.

52. Ibid., 118–19.

53. Cassirer, *Das Erkenntnisproblem*, 154ff.

54. Cassirer, *Individual and Cosmos*, 106.

55. Ibid., 110–11.

56. Ibid., 149.

57. Boll, Bezold, and Gundel, *Storia dell'astrologia*, 41ff, 55ff.

58. Cassirer, *Individual and Cosmos*, 169. Once again Hans Baron criticizes this view of astrology, but in a rather confused way. He notes a slight inconsistency in Cassirer's thesis of a transcending of astrology on the part of a new spirituality

and a new mode of investigating nature, and sees on the other hand in the essence of the Renaissance a new institution of astrology as an apparently exact science. He notes the same in vitalism, which was not transcended but on the contrary reached its height in the second half of the sixteenth century. In Baron's view the renewal of mathematics took place only with Galileo and Descartes (Baron, *Renaissance in Italien*, 115) and, contrary to what Cassirer affirms, vitalism is rather the sole and true expression of the Renaissance world view.

59. Cassirer, *Individual and Cosmos*, 142–43.

60. Cassirer, *The Philosophy of Symbolic Forms*, vol. 2, *Mythical Thought*, trans. Ralph Manheim (New Haven and London: Yale University Press, 1955), xvi. (Hereafter the three volumes of this work will be cited as *PSF I, PSF II*, and *PSF III*.) The second volume of *PSF* was published in Berlin in 1925.

61. Cassirer, *PSF I, Language*, trans. Ralph Manheim (New Haven and London: Yale University Press, 1965), 78. The first volume of *PSF* was published in Berlin in 1923.

62. Ibid., 95.

63. Cassirer, "Der Begriff der symbolischen Form im Aufbau der Geisteswissenschaften," *Wesen und Wirkung des Symbolbegriffs* (Darmstadt, 1977), 174. The first edition of this work was published in *Vorträge der Bibliothek Warburg*, 1921–22.

64. Cassirer, *PSF II*, 31.

65. For a discussion of the concept of identity in the Marburg school and Cohen's interpretation of Parmenides' being as "matter," which is opposed by the form of thinking in a "correlation" and which also inspired Cassirer's notion of "thought activity," see Sigfried Marck, "Die Lehre vom erkennenden Subjekt in der Marburger Schule," *Logos*, 4 (1913), 364–86.

For Cassirer's relations with the Marburg school, see William Henry Werkmeister, "Cassirer's Advance beyond Neo-Kantianism," *The Philosophy of Ernst Cassirer*, ed. Paul Arthur Schilpp (Evanston, Ill.: The Library of Living Philosophers, 1949), 759–98; Henri Dussort, *L'école de Marbourg* (Paris: Presses Universitaires de France, 1963); Leo Lugarini, "Criticismo e 'fondazione soggettiva,'" *Il Pensiero* (1966), 77–97 and 158–182, and by the same author, *Critica della ragione e universo della cultura. Gli orizzonti cassireriani della filosofia trascendentale* (Rome: Edizioni dell'Ateneo, 1983); Alexis Philonenko, "L'école de Marbourg: H. Cohen, P. Natorp, E. Cassirer," *La Philosophie du monde scientifique et industriel, 1860–1940* (Paris: Hachette, 1973); Andrea Poma, "Il mito nella filosofia delle forme simboliche di Ernst Cassirer. I. I precedenti della filosofia delle forme simboliche; II. La comprensione cassireriana di Kant," *Filosofia* 31 (1980), 2–3, 205ff. See also Irene Kajon, *Il concetto dell'unità della cultura e il problema della trascendenza nella filosofia di Ernst Cassirer* (Rome: Bulzoni,

1984) and, by the same author, "Un convegno a Zurigo su Ernst Cassirer," *Archivio di Filosofia* 55 (1987), 495–504.

On the problem of Cassirer's departure from the Marburg school in extending his system into a plurality of functions that all bear witness in different ways to the productivity of the spirit, see Heinz Paetzold, "Zur Sprachphilosophie Ernst Cassirers," *Philosophisches Jahrbuch* 88 (1981), 301–15.

An interesting analysis of Cassirer's relationship with Kant on the one hand and with Neo-Kantianism on the other is to be found in Edgar Wind, "Contemporary German Philosophy," *The Journal of Philosophy* 22 (1925), 18, 479ff.

66. Cassirer, *PSF I*, 268.
67. Cassirer, "Der Begriff," 174.
68. Ibid., 185f.
69. Ibid., 176.
70. Ibid., 176.
71. Cassirer, *PSF II*, 30.
72. Ibid., 30.
73. Ibid., 30–31.
74. Cassirer, *PSF II*, 29.
75. In general it must be noted that immediacy is a singular category that has a figurative meaning indicative of an event considered in itself in an extrinsic way rather than on the basis of a logically deducible position. It almost has a psychological connotation, or responds to a need to isolate the terms of a logical discourse, but appears wholly inadequate to express a mode of cognition. The difficulty in apprehending immediacy is the same one encounters in the problem of defining the origin.
76. Cassirer, *PSF II*, 29ff.
77. See the doubt expressed in this regard by Martin Heidegger in his review of the second volume of *PSF* in *Deutsche Literaturzeitung* 21 (Berlin, 1928), 1008. For his part, Erich Unger criticizes the analysis of myth proposed by Cassirer because it is effected from within the epistemological categories proper to scientific thought (*Wirklichkeit, Mythos, Erkenntniss* [Munich and Berlin: Verlag von Oldenbourg, 1930], 12–23).
78. Cassirer, "Der Begriff," 182.
79. Later on however, in the synthesis effected in *Language and Myth* (first published in 1925), Cassirer admits a common origin for language, myth, and art (ibid., 89, 97).
80. Cassirer, "Der Begriff," 183.
81. Ibid., 188.
82. Cassirer, *PSF II*, 26.
83. Let us not forget here that Warburg's conception of the symbol lacks above

all a structural change in the images, which, however, seems to be essential to the nature of Cassirer's symbolic form. As their essential content remains unchanged, what changes is the style in relation to the original expressive element. It is the choice of style that reveals the direction of a civilization, its more or less conscious will to restore a certain meaning to the symbol. The changes style undergoes in time and space constitute the history of the degree of memory that humanity conserves in relation to its patrimony of images. When total consciousness of this patrimony has been attained and the stylistic choice has matured, then the very power of the archetypal image leads to a new formulation of the ancient meaning, and creative effort liberates the essence of the artistic phenomenon from the bonds through which it has been bequeathed.

84. Cassirer, "Der Begriff," 190.

85. Friedrich Theodor Vischer, "Das Symbol," *Philosophische Aufsätze, zu Eduard Zellers fünfzigjährigem Doktor-Jubiläum* (1887; Leipzig: Zentral-Antiquariat der Deutschen Demokratischen Republik, 1962), 154.

86. Ibid., 157.

87. Cassirer, *PSF I*, 178.

88. Vischer, "Das Symbol," 165.

89. Ibid., 162.

90. Ibid., 168.

91. Cassirer, *PSF II*, 1–2.

92. Ibid., 40.

93. Georg Wilhelm Friedrich Hegel, *Aesthetics, Lectures on Fine Art*, trans. T. M. Knox (Oxford: Clarendon Press, 1975), Pt. 2, Sect. 1: "The Form of Symbolic Art," 303–424, esp. 306–10.

94. Vischer, "Das Symbol," 172. See also chap. one.

95. Ibid., 181.

96. Cassirer, "Das Symbolproblem und seine Stellung im System der Philosophie," *Zeitschrift für Aesthetik und allgemeine Kunstwissenschaft* 21 (1927), 295.

97. Cassirer, *Der Begriff*, 176.

98. Cassirer, "Die Begriffsform im mythischen Denken," *Wesen und Wirkung des Symbolbegriffs*, 7.

99. Cassirer, *Der Begriff*, 188.

100. Cassirer, "Die Begriffsform," 7f.

101. Ibid., 44.

102. Ibid., 48.

103. Ibid., 49.

104. Ibid., 54.

105. Cassirer, *Language and Myth*, 13.

106. Ibid., 19.

107. Cassirer, *PSF II*, 69.

108. Ibid., 70.

109. Concerning the accusation of mysticism the Marburg Neo-Kantians made against Bergson, see Paul Natorp, *Allgemeine Psychologie* (Tübingen: J. C. B. Mohr, 1912), 305–29, where a criticism is made of Bergson's position regarding the categories of the intellect and the lack of continuity in maintaining the original dualism, but where points in common with Natorp's own philosophy are also to be noted. See also Ernst Cassirer, "Henry Bergsons Ethik und Religionsphilosophie," *Die Morgen* 9 (1933), 20ff, where Rickert's vitalism is compared to Bergson's irrationalistic vitalism.

110. Cassirer, *PSF II*, 40.

111. Cassirer, *PSF III: The Phenomenology of Knowledge*, trans. Ralph Manheim (New Haven and London: Yale University Press, 1957), 27. This volume was first published in Berlin in 1929.

112. Cassirer, *PSF II*, 217.

113. Cassirer, *Der Begriff*, 199.

114. Ibid., 200.

115. Cassirer, *PSF I*, 106–07.

116. Cassirer, *PSF II*, 20.

117. Cassirer, *PSF I*, 83.

118. Cassirer, "Das Symbolproblem," 298.

119. Ibid., 300.

120. Ibid., 301.

121. Cassirer, *PSF III*, 27.

122. Cassirer, "Das Symbolproblem," 303.

123. Cassirer, "Mythischer, ästhetischer und theoretischer Raum," *Vierter Kongress für Aesthetik und allgemeine Kunstwissenschaft* (Hamburg, 1930), now in *Bericht vom Zeitschrift für Aesth. und allgem. Kunstwiss.* (1931), 31.

124. Ibid., 28.

125. Cassirer, *PSF I*, 86–87.

126. Ibid., 79.

127. Cassirer, *PSF III*, 101.

128. Ibid., 112.

129. Ibid., 298.

130. Ibid., 180.

131. Ibid., 180ff.

132. Ibid., 182.

133. Ibid.

134. Ibid., 188.

135. The historical-cultural background that gave rise to the idea of a philos-

ophy of symbolic forms, and the occasion for this, are to be found in Dimitry Gawronsky, "Ernst Cassirer: His Life and His Work," in Paul Arthur Schilpp (ed.), *The Philosophy of Ernst Cassirer*, 24ff.

136. Cassirer, "'Geist' und 'Leben' in der Philosophie der Gegenwart," *Die neue Rundschau* 41 (1930), 2, 259.

137. Ibid., 250.

138. Ibid., 254.

139. With regard to the return, in *PSF III*, to the positions upheld in *Substance and Function* (written in 1910), see the interesting article by Donald Phillip Verene, "Kant, Hegel and Cassirer: The Origins of the Philosophy of Symbolic Forms," *Journal of the History of Ideas* 30 (1969), 1, 40.

140. Cassirer, "'Geist' und 'Leben,'" 255.

141. Ibid., 256.

142. Verene quite clearly grasped what most interpreters of Cassirer have failed to note. Often one falls into the error of analyzing the philosophy of symbolic forms in the light of Kantian criticism solely because Cassirer came from the Marburg school and is identified with it. However an explicit reference is made to Hegel's *Phenomenology of the Spirit* in all three volumes on symbolic forms, and the very design of their ideal evolution is taken from Hegelian speculation. Verene also quite lucidly explains how Cassirer differs from Hegel in three respects: the initial schema of movement of consciousness, the division of the stages that it passes through, and the aim set for philosophy. As far as this last point is concerned, Cassirer criticizes Hegel's passage from *Phenomenology of the Spirit* to *Science of Logic* because he separates the individual categories from their phenomenal appearances: "Cassirer's system is an attempt not only to join in principle the categories of thought with their appearances; it is an attempt actually to present each through the other" ("Kant, Hegel and Cassirer," 42).

143. Hegel, *Hegel's Science of Logic*, 170ff., 502ff.

144. Cassirer, "'Geist' und 'Leben,'" 262.

145. Ibid., 264.

146. Lorenz Dittmann, *Stil, Symbol, Struktur* (Munich: Wilhelm Fink, 1967), 108: "The concept of the symbolic form is a *latent aesthetic concept*."

147. Lipton, *Ernst Cassirer, The Dilemma*, 137.

3: ERWIN PANOFSKY

1. Toni Cassirer, *Mein Leben mit Ernst Cassirer*, 150–52. For a description of the Warburg Library, see Salvatore Settis, "Warburg 'continuatus'. Descrizione di una biblioteca," *Quaderni storici* 58a, 20 (1985), 5–38.

2. Edgar Wind, *Einleitung zur Kulturwissenschaftliche Bibliographie zum Nachleben der Antike* (Leipzig: Teubner Verlag, 1934), vii.

3. Ernst Cassirer, "Eidos und Eidolon," cf. 126, n. 2.

4. Ernst Cassirer, "Goethe und Platon," *Goethe und die geschichtliche Welt* (Berlin: B. Cassirer, 1932), 110, first published in *Sokrates,* 48 (Berlin, 1922), 1.

5. Cassirer, "Eidos und Eidolon," 6.

6. Ibid., 8.

7. Paul Natorp, *Platons Ideenlehre. Eine Einführung in den Idealismus* (Leipzig: F. Meiner, 1921), 111.

8. Plato, *Theaetetus,* trans. Harold North Fowler, The Loeb Classical Library (London–New York: William Heinemann and Harvard University Press, 1921), 201d ff.

9. Cassirer, "Eidos und Eidolon," 10.

10. Ibid., 11.

11. Ibid., 13.

12. Karl Justi, *Die ästhetischen Elemente in der platonischen Philosophie. Ein historisch-philosophischer Versuch* (Marburg: N. G. Elwert'sche Universitätsbuchhandlung, 1860), 84ff.

13. Ibid., 88.

14. Cassirer, "Eidos und Eidolon," 14.

15. Ibid., 14.

16. Justi, *Die ästhetischen Elemente,* 63.

17. Ibid., 61.

18. Ibid., 167.

19. Ibid., 179.

20. Schopenhauer, *The World as Will,* 1:169.

21. In his book on Plato written in 1928 (*Platone, Eidos-Paideia-Dialogos* [Berlin: De Gruyter, 1964]), Paul Friedländer had already pointed out Justi's proximity to Schopenhauer and how Schopenhauer's interpretation of the Platonic idea influenced all the different ways of facing the problem of a so-called art theory in Plato. In Friedländer's view, art does not weigh too heavily on metaphysics, since there is no art theory in Plato. He was at once an artist and a philosopher in the sense that dialectics in the end cannot help finding a resolution in art, in contemplation, and in the intuition of reality that is impossible to define conceptually. Friedländer overturns the Hegelian perspective, even though he utilizes it in his analysis of an evolution in Platonic dialectics studied through the change effected in myth and its meaning in the dialogues. He therefore accepts Schopenhauer's point of view, setting it in relief as the original thought of a discrimination between the study of dialectics as that procedure that exhausts the understanding of reality in the conceptual connection, and the history of culture as the research into the representations of the world that have determined civilizations. There is perhaps

more coherence in Justi's view than in Friedländer's; in fact, the art historian, though he too falls into the erroneous contamination of art and philosophy with regard to Plato, still makes a precise choice in favor of the history of culture and elaborates a concept of culture as the expression of a struggle between contrasting forces in the epoch as well as in the individual, a concept that lies at the base of an entire German school of philosophy whose foremost representatives were Burckhardt and Nietzsche.

22. Justi, *Die ästhetischen Elemente,* 167.
23. Ibid., 171.
24. Ibid., 180.
25. Cassirer, "Eidos und Eidolon," 18.
26. Ibid., 24.
27. Ibid., 25.
28. Ibid., 26.
29. Ibid., 27. Concerning art and its function in the state according to Plato, see Edgar Wind, "Theios-Phobos, Untersuchungen über die platonische Kunstphilosophie," *Zeitschrift für Aesthetik und allgemeine Kunstwissenschaft* 26 (1932), 356ff., now in Wind, *The Eloquence of Symbols,* 6. On the problem of art in Plato, see, among other works, Arnold Ruge, *Die platonische Aesthetik* (1832; Osnabrück: Zeller, 1965); Eduard Zeller, *Die Philosophie der Griechen in ihrer geschichtlichen Entwirklung,* Vol. 2, Pt. 1 (Leipzig: Silver, 1922), 936ff., in particular the treatment of Plato's extraneousness to art theory and his being unable to separate the Beautiful from the Good. As regards the moralization of art among the Greeks, see Bruno Snell, "Aristophanes und die Aesthetik," in Bruno Snell, *Die Entdeckung des Geistes, Studien zur Entstehung des europäischen Denkens bei den Griechen* (Hamburg: Claassen Verlag, 1955), 161–83, especially 163–64, and also Walter Pater, *Plato und der Platonismus,* Vorlesungen (Jena-Leipzig: E. Diedrichs, 1904), 10: "Die Aesthetik Platos." See also Benedetto Croce, *Estetica come scienza dell'espressione* (Bari: Laterza, 1922), 172ff, for whom the Platonic beautiful, as it coincides with the supreme good, eludes any appraisal of an aesthetic nature; Doro Levi, *Il concetto di Kairos e la filosofia di Platone,* a report of the Reale Accademia Nazionale dei Lincei, Classe di Scienze Morali, Storiche e Filosofiche, ser. 5, vol. 33, 4/6, 1924, where the author sets out to demonstrate that in all Greek philosophy ethics and aesthetics are not clearly distinct but connected and mingled with one another; John Dewey, *Art as Experience* (New York: Minton, Bulch, 1958), 289, on the intrinsic link between knowledge and a work of art; Pierre-Maxime Schuhl, *Plato et l'art de son temps* (Paris: F. Alcan, 1933). And concerning the moralization of the state in the Platonic critique of poetry and the relationship this critique has with the Platonic myth, see Hans Georg Gadamer, *Plato und die Dichter* (Frankfurt am Main: V. Klostermann, 1934); Robin George Collingwood, "Plato's Philosophy of Art,"

Mind 35 (1925), 154–72, where the battle against art is understood as aiming at resisting the emotional fascination of the symbol in order to penetrate what it means. Collingwood does not manage to distinguish the theory of knowledge from art theory, because in his view the two converge.

In addition, see Luigi Stefanini, *Il problema estetico in Platone* (Turin: Edizioni Scientifiche Italiane, 1935), and, by the same author, *Platone* (Padua: CEDAM, 1949), 113–22, on art in Plato; Giovanni Napoleone Giordano Orsini, "L'estetica platonica e la scuola di Marburgo," *Letterature Moderne* 6 (1952), 2, where Panofsky's *Idea*, Cassirer's "Eidos und Eidolon," and the relations between Croce and the Marburg school are dealt with. See also Ranuccio Bianchi Bandinelli, "Osservazioni storico-artistiche a un passo del 'Sofista' platonico," *Studi in onore di Ugo Enrico Paoli* (Florence: Le Monnier, 1955), 81ff, according to whom Plato's condemnation of art is historically conditioned and connected to a certain artistic reality; by the same author, see "L'artista nell'antichità classica," *Archeologia classica* 9 (1957), n. 1. For in-depth and critical information on the interpretative currents concerning Platonic aesthetics, see Margherita Isnardi Parente, "La valutazione dell'estetica di Platone in alcuni momenti della critica filosofica contemporanea," *Critica e storia letteraria*, studies presented to Mario Fubini (Padua, 1970), 37–49. And last, Rupert C. Lodge, *Plato's Theory of Art* (London: Routledge & K. Paul, 1953), and Iris Murdoch, *The Fire and the Sun. Why Plato Banished the Artists* (Oxford: Clarendon Press, 1977).

30. Cassirer, "Eidos und Eidolon," 21.

31. Julius Stenzel, "Üben den Einfluss der griechischen Sprache auf die philosophische Begriffsbildung," in Julius Stenzel, *Kleine Schriften zur griechischen Philosophie* (Darmstadt: H. Gentner, 1957), 72ff.

32. Friedländer, *Platone, Eidos-Paideia-Dialogos*, 290.

33. Erwin Panofsky, *Idea. A Concept in Art Theory* (New York: Harper and Row Publishers, Icon Editions, 1968), 3–4. On the relationship between Panofsky and Cassirer, see Michael Ann Holly, *Panofsky and the Foundations of Art History* (Ithaca, New York: Cornell University Press, 1985), 114ff.

34. Panofsky, *Idea*, 3.

35. Ibid., 4.

36. Ibid., 7.

37. Ibid., 14.

38. Aristotle, *The Metaphysics*, trans. Hugh Tredennick, The Loeb Classical Library (London-New York: William Heinemann and Harvard University Press, 1947), Book 7, Chap. 7, 1032b, 339.

39. Ibid., Book 7, Chap. 7, 1034a, 2–5.

40. Panofsky, *Idea*, 17.

41. Ibid., 27.

42. Ibid., 29–30.

43. Ibid., 41–42.

44. Ibid., 193–94, n. 7.

45. St. Augustine, *Confessions,* trans. Vernone J. Bourke, Book 10, Chap. 34, *Fathers of the Church* (Washington, D.C.: The Catholic University of America Press, 1966), 309–10.

46. St. Jerome, *The Letters of St. Jerome,* trans. Charles Christopher Mierow, Vol. 1, Letter 22, in *Ancient Christian Writers* (Westminster, Md.: The Newman Press, and London: Longmans Green, 1963), 166.

47. Panofsky, *Idea,* 43.

48. Ibid., 50.

49. Ibid., 52.

50. Ibid., 54–55.

51. Ibid., 55–56.

52. Ibid., 64.

53. Ibid., 64–65.

54. Ibid., 68.

55. Ibid., 62.

56. Ibid., 79–80.

57. Ibid., 83–84.

58. Ibid., 84.

59. Ibid., 228, n. 31.

60. Ibid., 90.

61. Ibid., 93–94.

62. Ibid., 98.

63. Ibid., 104.

64. Plato, *The Republic,* trans. Paul Shorey, Book 7, 524d, in The Loeb Classical Library (London-New York: William Heinemann and Harvard University Press, 1953), 2:159.

65. Ibid., 524e–525a, 161.

66. Plato, *Phaedo,* trans. Harold North Fowler, 75a-b, in The Loeb Classical Library (London-New York: William Heinemann and Harvard University Press, 1923), 261.

67. Plato, *Theaetetus,* 186c, 165.

68. Giovan Pietro Bellori, *L'idea del Pittore, dello Schultore e dell'Architetto,* in Panofsky, *Idea,* Appendix II, 157.

69. See chap. 3, n. 32, below.

70. Concerning this problem, see Schuhl, *Platon et l'art,* 22ff.

71. Friedrich Nietzsche, "David Strauss, The Confessor and Writer," *Thoughts out of Season,* trans. Anthony M. Ludovic, 2 vols. (Edinburgh–London: T. N. Foulis, 1910), 1:20, 22.

72. Friedrich Theodor Vischer, "Das Schöne und die Kunst. Zur Einführung in die Aesthetik," *Vorträge* (Stuttgart–Berlin, 1907), 11.

73. Panofsky, *Idea*, 126.

74. Ibid., 248–49, n. 38.

75. Erwin Panofsky, "Das Problem des Stils in der bildenden Kunst" (1915), *Aufsätze zu Grundfragen der Kunstwissenschaft*, ed. H. Oberer (Berlin: E. Verheyen, 1974), 19–20.

76. Ibid., 21.

77. Ibid., 22.

78. Ibid., 25.

79. Hans Sedlmayr, Introduction to Aloïs Riegl, *Gesammelte Aufsätze* (Augsburg-Vienna: Dr. B. Filser, 1929), xiii. Sedlmayr rejected an interpretation of Riegl in a Kantian or Neo-Kantian key, of the type Panofsky or Karl Mannheim used, and proposed in its stead a reading in a Hegelian key of this art historian, both because of the nature of movement immanent to *Kunstwollen,* which is thus viewed in the light of vitalistic dynamism, and because of Riegl's conviction that even in the historical sciences, theory is the final aim of scientific labor (ibid., xxxii). Sedlmayr's introduction is interesting above all for its reference to Dilthey and to the influence Riegl exerted on Oswald Spengler. However one notes there certain inconsistencies precisely in the reference to Hegel and to history as becoming to which an aim is intrinsic. This is not exactly the theory we find in *Kunstwollen* and in naturalism. Sedlmayr himself emphasizes a conception of nature that is determined in Riegl quite differently from Hegel. For Panofsky's 1920 essay on *Kunstwollen,* see Michael Podro, "Panofsky: de la philosophie première au relativism personnel," *Pour un temps* (Paris: Pandora Edition, 1983), 61–69, a monographic volume on Panofsky.

80. Panofsky, "Der Begriff des Kunstwollen," *Aufsätze,* 29.

81. Ibid., 31–32.

82. Wilhelm Dilthey, "Der Aufbau der geschichtlichen Welt in der Geisteswissenschaften," *Gesammelte Schriften* (Stuttgart: B. G. Teubner, 1958), 7, 86ff.

83. Panofsky, "Der Begriff des Kunstwollen," 34.

84. Ibid., 36.

85. Ibid., 38.

86. Ibid., 38.

87. Ibid., 40. For Panofsky's criticism and his concept of a priori, see Podro, *Critical Historians of Art,* 178–208.

88. Erwin Panofsky, "The History of the Theory of Human Proportions as a Reflection of the History of Styles," *Meaning in the Visual Arts* (Harmondsworth: Penguin Books, 1970), 84–86.

89. Ibid., 89f.

90. Ibid., 100.
91. Ibid., 102–04.
92. Ibid., 107–09.
93. Ibid., 118.
94. Ibid., 119.
95. Ibid., 129.
96. Ibid., 129–30.
97. Erwin Panofsky, *Dürers Kunsttheorie. Vornähmlich in ihrem Verhältnis zur Kunsttheorie der Italiener* (Berlin: G. Reimer, 1915). As a dissertation this book received the Grimm-Stiftung prize of the Faculty of Philosophy at Berlin in 1913, and it was probably his reading of this remarkable work that induced Warburg to meet the young scholar.
98. Ibid., 104.
99. Ibid., 105.
100. Panofsky, "Albrecht Dürer and Classical Antiquity," *Meaning in the Visual Arts*, 279.
101. Ibid., 283.
102. Apropos of this personalization of artistic intention in Dürer, mention should be made of Warburg's thesis of Botticelli's "too pliant" artistic temperament in his 1893 paper.
103. Panofsky, "Albrecht Dürer and Classical Antiquity," 303.
104. Ibid., 305–06.
105. Ibid., 309.
106. For the problem of the concept of the ideal in classicist art theory, see chap. one.
107. Panofsky, "Albrecht Dürer and Classical Antiquity," 311–12.
108. Ibid., 312.
109. Ibid.
110. Ibid., 314.
111. Ibid., 321.
112. Ibid., 323.
113. Ibid., 329.
114. Panofsky and Saxl, "Dürers 'Melencolia I,'" 10.
115. Ibid., 15. For a remarkable study of the historiographic inquiry into this theme, see Raymond Klibansky, Erwin Panofsky, and Fritz Saxl, *Saturn and Melancholy. Studies in the History of Natural Philosophy, Religion and Art* (London: Thomas Nelson & Sons, 1964).
116. Panofsky and Saxl, "Dürers 'Melencolia I,'" 32ff.
117. Ibid., 37.
118. Ibid., 41, n. 3.
119. Ibid., 50.

120. Ibid., 57.
121. Ibid., 71f.
122. Ibid., 73.
123. Ibid., 74.
124. Ibid., 75f.
125. Erwin Panofsky, "Die Perspektive als 'symbolische Form'" (1924), *Aufsätze*, 108.
126. Ibid., 101–02.
127. Ibid., 109.
128. Ibid., 110.
129. Julius Stenzel, *Zahl und Gestalt bei Platon und Aristoteles* (Leipzig-Berlin: G. Teubner, 1924), chap. 4, "Diairesis des Räumlichen," esp. 83–89.
130. Panofsky, "Die Perspektive," 110–11.
131. Ibid., 111f.
132. Ibid., 122.
133. Ibid., 123.
134. Ibid.
135. Ibid., 126.
136. Ibid. For a critique of the concept of perspective in Panofsky's essay, see Kim Veltman, "Panofsky's Perspective a Half Century Later," *La Prospettiva Rinascimentale. Codificazioni e trasgressioni* (Florence, 1980), 1:565–84.
137. Edgar Wind, "Zur Systematik der kunstlerischen Probleme," *Zeitschrift für Aesthetik und allgemeine Kunstwissenschaft* 18 (1925), 440. The ideality of the problem consists in its need to be posed in order to explain a contradiction that however is removed in the stable result of the phenomenon. It is necessary at this stage to note that in this regard a difficulty arises that is not perceived by Panofsky and Wind: one conceives the problem as ideal, yet presupposes its reality, its concreteness of opposition and antinomical nature, at the very base of the phenomenon. This latter seems to possess an entelechy that rests upon an unresolved antinomy that is actually excluded from the concrete fact. The historian feels the need to pose the problem in order to seek an explanation for the datum, because only in this way can the foundation of that energy that is explicated in the phenomenon, its intimate structure, be made *visible*. But if the ideal problem is not only a clarification but also a foundation of the real, of becoming as well as of the already become, it can no longer be ideal and one must admit an ontological consistency to it which is impossible to realize because it is antinomical and contradictory; thus artistic intention is obliged to make a choice.
138. Ibid., 444.
139. Ibid., 448. In a review of Michael Ann Holly's book on Panofsky (see n. 33 above), Jan Bialostocki points out how Edgar Wind's influence on Panofsky is often overlooked (*Kunstchronik* 40 [1987], 23–28; esp. 23ff.).

140. Panofsky, "Über das Verhähltnis der Kunstgeschichte zur Kunsttheorie," *Aufsätze*, 50.
141. Ibid., 57.
142. Ibid., 59.
143. Ibid., 65.
144. Ibid., 67.
145. Ibid.
146. Ibid., 69.
147. Ibid., 70.
148. Panofsky, "Titian's 'Allegory of Prudence,' a Postscript," *Meaning in the Visual Arts*, 194.
149. Ibid., 205.
150. Panofsky, "Zum Problem der historischen Zeit," appendix to "Über die Reihenfolge der vier Meister von Reims," *Jahrbuch für Kunstwissenschaft* (1927), 55–82. Now in Panofsky, *Aufsätze*, 77.
151. Ibid., 78.
152. Ibid., 79.
153. Ibid., 81.
154. Georg Simmel, "Das Problem der historischen Zeit," *Philosophische Vorträge der Kantgesellschaft* (Berlin, 1916), 6.
155. Ibid., 10.
156. Ibid., 12.
157. Ibid., 15f.
158. Ibid., 21.
159. Ibid., 29f.
160. Ibid., 31.
161. Cassirer, "Die Begriffsform," here quoted in a reprint in Cassirer, *Wesen und Wirkung des Symbolbegriffs*, 4f. On this subject, see also the article by Martin Heidegger, "Der Zeitbegriff in der Geschichtswissenschaft," *Zeitschrift für Philosophie und philosophische Kritik* 161 (Leipzig, 1916), 173ff., and also Edgar Wind, "Some Points of Contact between History and Natural Science," *Philosophy and History, Essays Presented to Ernst Cassirer*, ed. by Raymond Klibansky and H. J. Paton (1936; Gloucester, Mass.: Peter Smith, 1975), 255ff.
162. Panofsky, "The First Page of Giorgio Vasari's 'Libro,'" *Meaning in the Visual Arts*, 206–65.
163. Ibid., 209.
164. Ibid., 244.
165. Ibid., 245.
166. Ibid.
167. Ibid., 260.

168. Panofsky, "Herkules am Scheidewege, und andere antike Bildstoffe in der neuren Kunst," *Studien der Bibliothek Warburg*, 18 (Leipzig-Berlin, 1930).

169. Ibid., Foreword, vii.

170. Panofsky, "Zum Problem der Beschreibung und Inhaltsdeutung von Werken der bildenden Kunst," *Aufsätze*, 90.

171. Ibid., 91. See also Panofsky, "Iconography and Iconology: An Introduction to the Study of Renaissance Art," *Meaning in the Visual Arts*, 56, 65, where explicit reference is made to Cassirer's theory of the symbol.

172. Panofsky, "Zum Problem," 92.

173. Raymond Klibansky, "The Philosophic Character of History," *Philosophy and History*, 334, says that "these dialectical subreptions of metaphysical thought do violence to the phenomena themselves."

174. Panofsky, "Zum Problem," 93.

175. Ibid., 93f.

176. Ibid., 94.

177. Ibid.

178. Ibid.

179. Ibid., 97, n. 16.

180. See also Guido Neri's criticism of excessive conceptualism in his introduction to the Italian edition of Panofsky's *Die Perspektive—La prospettiva come 'forma simbolica' e altri scritti* (Milan: Feltrinelli, 1973), 19. In addition, see Lorenz Dittmann, *Stil, Symbol, Struktur*, 118, in which the author criticizes Panofsky's connection between form and content, but does so by making incorrect (to say the least) use of philosophical concepts such as the "phenomenon" as being "external" which characterizes sensibility, and the "form of internal intuition" which conditions phenomena "only indirectly."

181. Carlo Ginzburg, "Da Aby Warburg a E. H. Gombrich," *Studi medievali*, 3d ser., 7 (1966), 1038, n. 92, now in Carlo Ginzburg, *Miti emblemi spie* (Turin: Einaudi, 1986), 29–106.

182. Panofsky, "Herkules am Scheidewege," 15.

183. Concerning the problem of the irrationality of weltanschauung and its use in the field of historiography, as well as its Diltheyian origin, see Karl Mannheim, "Beiträge zur Theorie der Weltanschauungsinterpretation," *Jahrbuch für Kunstgeschichte*, n.s., 1 (1922), 236ff.

184. From Panofsky's viewpoint one could criticize Guido Neri's proposal of a "structural genesis of the different artistic forms" as a new sort of empiricism.

185. Martin Heidegger, "Die Zeit des Weltbildes," *Holzwege* (1938; Frankfurt am Main: Vittorio Klostermann, 1977), 75–114.

186. Eugenio Garin, Introduction to Fritz Saxl, *La storia delle immagini* (Bari: Laterza, 1965), xviii, where he speaks of Panofsky: "That in this concern there

should emerge a new 'historical' and rational mode of understanding not only artistic activity, but religious life and logical thought as well, and, in the end, all human vicissitudes—this for the most part was not grasped." But see also Ginzburg, *Da Aby Warburg,* 1043: "Like Spitzer, albeit more cautiously, Panofsky postulates an interpretative method—the iconographical one—based on irrational intuition; on the other hand, faced with the most openly irrational forcing and arbitrariness (Heidegger in Panofsky's view, Stefan George's school in Spitzer's), both called for objective verification by means of the texts and documentary material."

187. Garin, Introduction, *La storia delle immagini,* xxi: "Without a doubt, in Panofsky's synthesis there was not merely a convergence of Warburg's stimuli, the data collected by Saxl and Cassirer's mediation. The references at a certain moment to Husserl or Heidegger were not casual, even though precisely during the 1931 lecture Panofsky, in controversy with Heidegger, emphasizes the need to resort to the historicization of the 'content' of the work of art as an objective corrective of the moment of the 'existential experience of life.'"

188. See also, as an example, Cassirer's long review of Heidegger's book on Kant in *Kant-Studien* 36 (1931), 1.

189. Panofsky, "Zum Problem," 95.

190. For Warburg's interpretation of Dürer, see chap. one.

191. Eugenio Montale, *Ossi di seppia, 1920–27. Sarcofaghi* (Milan: Arnoldo Mondadori Editore, 1963).

192. See Klibansky, "The Philosophic Character of History," 328ff., for the role of the creative imagination according to Kant and Goethe.

193. Panofsky, "Zum Problem," 95.

194. Ibid., 95.

195. Panofsky and Saxl, "Dürers 'Melencolia I,'" 75.

196. José Ortega y Gasset, "History as a System," *Philosophy and History,* 312.

197. Martin Heidegger, *Sein und Zeit* (Tübingen: M. Niemeyer, 1927), sect. 72.

198. Wilhelm Dilthey, "Allgemeine Sätze über den Zusammenhang der Geisteswissenschaften," *Gesammelte Schriften,* 7, 126.

199. Ibid., 130ff. On historicism in Dilthey and in contemporary consciousness, see Eugenio Garin's recent essay, "Lo storicismo nel Novecento, Materiali per una definizione," *Giornale critico della filosofia italiana,* 6th ser., 3, 62 (64), (1983), 1–57.

200. Wilhelm Dilthey, "Allgemeine Sätze," 135.

201. Wilhelm Dilthey, "Plan der Fortsetzung zum Aufbau der geschichtlichen Welt in den Geisteswissenschaften," *Gesammelte Schriften,* 7, 197.

202. Ibid., 255.

203. Johan Huizinga, "A Definition of the Concept of History" (1921), *Philosophy and History*, 1–10.

204. S. Alexander, "The Historicity of Things," *Philosophy and History*, 11–25.

205. Giovanni Gentile, "The Transcending of Time in History," *Philosophy and History*, 91–105.

206. José Ortega y Gasset, "History as a System," 314: "the mutability of everything human . . . is precisely our ontological privilege."

207. Giovanni Gentile, "Veritas filia temporis, Postilla bruniana," *Giordano Bruno e il pensiero del Rinascimento* (Florence: Vallecchi, 1920), 87–110.

208. Klibansky, "The Philosophical Character of History," 327: "This mode of scientific contemplation under the aspect of the image is history."

209. Martin Heidegger, *Die Zeit des Weltbildes*.

210. Fritz Saxl, "Veritas Filia Temporis," *Philosophy and History*, 197–222.

211. Panofsky, "Et in Arcadia Ego, On the Conception of Transcience in Poussin and Watteau," *Philosophy and History*, 223–54.

INDEX

abstraction, 10
Abū Mā'sār, 51
action, 29, 124, 135, 139
Aeneid (Virgil), 26
aesthetics, 27, 55, 115, 140, 153, 154, 157; idealist aesthetics, 144, 171, 172
Aesthetics (Hegel), 114, 193
"age of transition," xviii, 70–77, 80, 81, 82, 100
Alberti, Leon Battista, 11, 163, 164–65, 188, 203
"Albrecht Dürer and Classical Antiquity" (Panofsky), 185, 190
Alciati, Andrea, 212
Alexander, Samuel, 233–34
allegory, 114
Analytic of Principles (Kant), 129
antinomy, principle of, 174–76, 189, 203, 210, 217
Apollo, 95
Apollo Belvedere, 24, 191, 192
Apollonian/Dionysian polarity, 2, 194; in Dürer, 52–53; Nietzsche on, 54–55, 58, 60–62, 194; in Renaissance, 66–68
Apologia (Pico della Mirandola), 201
appearance, 54, 139; appearance/illusion, 55, 56
Aquinas, Thomas, 96
Arab science, 163
Argiropulo, Giovanni, 47
Aristotelian philosophy, 89, 96, 166, 167

Aristotle, 47, 67, 159, 160, 162; on melancholy, 199; on space, 203–04; on infinity, 205
art: aim and nature of, 21, 22, 125, 210; as means of knowledge, 153–54; nature and, 159; as manifestation of idea, 160–61, 168; as science, 167, 208–11. *See also* symbol formation
art history: Warburg's devotion to, 2–3; as new science, 208–11. *See also individual authors and concepts*
art theory, 31, 220; Plato on, 143–44, 151, 153; history of, 156–57
—Panofsky's views: Plato and, 157–59; art theory as science, 163–64; premises for, 160–61; Mannerism and, 168–69; solutions to problem of, 174–76; Riegl on, 179, 208–11. *See also* genius, theory of
artist: nature of, 97, 160, 161; artist as mediator, 98; Plato on, 147, 148, 149, 150, 153
artistic form, 111
artistic image, 112, 114–15. *See also* symbol formation
artistic intention (*Kunstwollen*), 189–90, 207–11; Panofsky on, 179–80, 181–82, 185–88, 194–95, 197; historical time and, 214–15
artistic phenomenon, 9, 14–15, 17, 30, 39, 42, 144, 183, 184, 185; Panofsky on, 210–11, 222–23, 229; time and, 213–18. *See also* genius, theory of

artistic problem, 207, 208–11
Asclepius, 72
astral deities. *See* pagan demonism
astral demonology, 50
astrology, 63, 64, 77, 82, 118, 200; Warburg on, 50, 51; Luther on, 65–66; Cassirer on, 92–94, 95, 98–99, 119
Astronomica (Manilius), 51
atmosphere, 20
attraction, 140
Augustine, St., 90, 161, 162, 171
Averroism, 96, 97

Baron, Hans, 97, 253n58
beauty, 12, 40, 58, 168, 172, 195, 220; tragedy and, 53, 54; F. Vischer on, 115; Justi on, 148, 149; Plato on, 152, 158; St. Augustine on, 161; Panofsky on, 163–64, 165, 188, 235; as measure of idea, 172–73; Dürer on, 201–02. *See also* classical antiquity
becoming, process of, 5–6, 42, 68, 70, 76, 80, 84; ideal and temporal, 100–01; in symbol formation, 131–37; knowledge and, 144–45; natural becoming, 146, 147, 148; antinomy and, 176; historical becoming, 203, 205. *See also* consciousness
being, 145, 155; being and thought, 103; language and, 126; nonbeing, 145, 146
Being and Time (Heidegger), 231
being-there, 73–75, 80; being-there objectivity, 111
Bellori, Giovanni Pietro, 168–69, 171, 172–73, 193
Bergson, Henri, 34, 121, 135, 185, 217, 234
Bing, Gertrud, 34
Birth of Tragedy (Nietzsche), 38, 53, 59
Boll, Franz, 99
Botticelli, Sandro, 15, 23, 25, 26, 43, 61–62, 93

Bovillus, C., 91, 92, 94
Brueghel, Pieter (elder), 43
Brunelleschi, Filippo, 206
Bruno, Giordano, 3, 234
Buoninsegna, Duccio di, 206
Burckhardt, Jacob, xii, xiii, xviii; Warburg and, 12, 22, 23, 27, 36, 57, 68; on genius, 29; on Renaissance, 31, 32, 33, 35, 81–82; on demonism, 63–64, 65; Cassirer on, 87, 88–89, 90, 91; Panofsky on, 228, 229; on Fortune, 245n115
Byzantine art, 187, 205

Cantimori, Delio, 250n2
causal schema, 200
causality, 35, 36, 56, 71, 132, 183; mythical causality, 69, 72, 118–19; demoniac causality, 98–99
cause and effect, 118
Cassirer, Bruno, 202
Cassirer, Ernst, xiv, xv, 72, 219, 229, 233; memorial address for Warburg, 1–6; interest in antiquity, 6–7, 12–14; unity in, 84–85; admiration for Warburg, 85–86; polarity in, 90–91, 92–93, 94, 96–97; development of symbol theory, 137–40; differences with Warburg, 143; criticizes Justi, 147–49, 150–55; on art and idea, 153–54; conceptual structures in, 198. *See also* idea and ideal; symbol formation *and other individual authors and concepts*
centaur, 46
chance, 150, 151
change, 102, 176, 221
chora (space), 204
chorismòs (separation), theme of, 90–91
Christian tradition, 11, 38, 39, 53, 96, 97, 192; paganism and, 46, 64–65; renewal of culture in, 162
Cicero, 90, 157, 159
Cimabue, Giovanni, 219
classical antiquity: role in Warburg's thought, 7–8, 11–14; ideal of

beauty in, 13, 38, 39, 41; Winckelmann on, 24, 25, 26; Panofsky on, 193–95. *See also* Apollonian/Dionysian polarity; Renaissance
Classicism, 157, 168, 171, 190
cognitive process, 112, 118, 127
coincidentia oppositorum, 89, 91. *See also* polarities
concept, 151, 152, 202
"Conceptual Form in Mythical Thought" (Cassirer), 117
conceptual structure, 198
"conceptual transparency," 27
Confessions (St. Augustine), 161
conflict, 90
conformity, 28
Confutation of Idealism (Kant), 217
connection, 51, 70, 87
"connection of perceptions," 182
consciousness, 101–02, 118; creativity and, 104–05; function of, 107–08; Kant on, 108; artistic consciousness, 115; discontinuity in, 120; totality of, 121; reality and, 123–24; evolution of, 124–25; becoming and, 130–31; in symbol formation, 132, 134, 135, 136
consciousness-experience relationship, 132–33
construction, theory of, 186
contemplation, 31, 97, 199, 200
content, 112, 222–23
"Copernican revolution," 109–10, 128, 176, 184, 207
correlation, principle of, 99
cosmological dynamism, 200
Cratylus (Plato), 145
creativity: creative faculty of consciousness, 104–05, 106, 108, 109, 111; creative objectivity, 111; becoming and, 133–34. *See also* symbol formation
Creuzer, Frederick, 68, 248n178
Critique of Judgement (Kant), 28
Critique of Pure Reason (Kant), 184
Croce, Benedetto, 16
Cronus, myth of, 199

culture, 111, 112, 128, 134; history of, 5, 135; process of, 131; Justi on, 150–51; concept of, 173
Cusanus, 89, 90, 91, 92, 94, 97

Dante Alighieri, 199
Darwin, Charles, 8, 9, 11
Dasein, 231
De Martino, Ernesto, 70–71, 72–75
De Ruggiero, Guido, 251n14
De Sapiente (Bovillus), 91
De vita triplici (Ficino), 200
Demiurge, 103
Democritus, 204
demonism. *See* pagan demonism
Descartes, René, 73, 83, 233
design, theory of, 166, 167
destiny, 27
development, concept of, 226–27
diaeresis, 146
dialectics, 154
Dialogues (Petrarch), 90
Dilthey, Wilhelm, 180–81, 182, 185, 231–33
Diodorus of Sicily, 186–87
Dionysian. *See* Apollonian/Dionysian polarity
divination, 62
divine prescience, 95
Dodgson, Campbell, 212
dogmatism, 220–21
Donatello, 55
Doren, Alfred, 244n111
Dürer, Albrecht, 25, 42, 89, 99, 231; genius of, 31; movement in, 52, 53; polarities in, 59, 66, 68; spirituality of, 77; idea in, 174; from Middle Ages to Renaissance, 188–92, 195, 196, 197; melancholy in, 197–202, 226
"Dürer and Italian Antiquity" (Warburg), 52

Egyptian art, 60, 186–87, 201, 212
eidos and *eidolon*, 144, 145, 146, 152. *See also* form; image

"Eidos und Eidolon" (Cassirer), 143, 154, 156
élan vital, 135
empathy, concept of, 14–16, 114, 115, 126; R. Vischer on, 17–20, 21
empirical datum, 122
"empirical thought" and mythical thought, 106–07
"empirical truth," 129
empiricism, 174
energy, 34
enlightenment, search for, 51–52, 68
Epistle VII (Plato), 155
Erlebnis (inner experience), 6, 180–82, 190, 223; cultural *Erlebnis*, 184, 195, 197; Dilthey on, 231, 232
eros, 153
Eros, theory of, 97
eternal mobility, concept of, 140
eternity, image of, 103
Etruscan art, 25
Euripides, 38
evolution, 9, 51, 79, 136, 184, 225
exaggeration, 18
exorcism, 73
experience, 107, 129, 132, 134, 209
expression, 40, 75, 128, 152, 178; sensory content and, 126, 127
Expression of Emotions in Man and Animals (Darwin), 8
Expressionism, 164, 196
expressive gesture, 178

factuality, 225, 226, 227
Faith in the Stars and Astrology (Boll), 99
fantasy, 18, 19, 20, 21, 31, 115, 147, 168, 176
feeling, 18, 170, 182
Ficino, Marsilio, 47, 48–49, 92, 95, 97, 98, 163, 164, 168; on melancholy, 199–201
Florentine art: Classicism *v* Northern realism, 39–43. *See also* Renaissance; Sassetti Chapel
flux, 102, 130

form, 19, 20–21, 145, 160, 222; form and content, 94
formalism, 222
Fortuna, goddess, 45–46
Fortuna Occasio, 45–46
Fortune, concept of, 2, 44–49, 76, 82, 94–95, 245n115
free will, 95
Friedländer, Paul, 156, 259
Friedländer, Walter, 187
future, 135

Galilei, Galileo, 13, 164
Gauricus, 65–66
genius, theory of, 27–33, 51, 165, 199
Gentile, Giovanni, 234
German Enlightenment, 28
Germany: medieval tradition, 64–65
gesture, 17
Ghirlandaio, Domenico, 37, 38, 42, 46
Giotto di Bondone, 37, 206
givenness, 180, 215, 227, 232
gnostic-pessimist tradition, 199
Goethe, W., 111, 140, 192–93
"Goethe und Plato" (Cassirer), 144
Gombrich, Ernst, xi, xii, xvii–xviii
good: beauty and, 163–64
"good European," 51–52, 58
Gothic art, 187, 219, 220–21
Gotternamen (Usener), 15–16
Greece. *See* classical antiquity

harmonistic cosmology, 188
harmony, 32, 40, 115, 152, 190
Hegel, G. W. F., xviii, 41–42, 91, 94; themes in, 112; on symbol, 114; Cassirer and, 124–25, 138; theory of overcoming, 139; concept of life, 139–40
Hegelian philosophy, xviii, 5, 14, 53, 171
Heidegger, Martin, 224, 225, 228, 229, 231, 234
Helios Pantokrator, 192
Hercules, Bust of, 24

"Hercules at the Crossroads" (Panofsky), 212, 222, 228
hero, 83
heroism *v* happiness, 3–4, 6
historian, 4–5, 221
historical consciousness, 77–80
historical interpretation, 198
historical necessity, 190–91, 197
historicism, xvii, 235
historicity, 231; of magical world, 74–75
historiography, xi–xii, xvii, 227
history, xvii, 117, 124, 184; cultural history, 84; nature and object of, 157, 215–16; Panofsky on, 183–85; history and life, 216–17; idea of, 232; of mind, 233; as science, 233–34. *See also* "age of transition"; space; time *and individual authors*
History of Ancient Art (Winckelmann), 60
"History of the Theory of Human Proportions as a Reflection of the History of Styles" (Panofsky), 185
Homer, 23, 41, 54, 58
Huizinga, Johan, 81, 82, 233, 259*n*1
humanism, 61, 62, 80, 95, 96, 97
"humanistic disciplines," 210

Icarus, 3
iconographic tradition, 222, 223
iconology, 36, 212, 228; critical iconology, 50–51
Idea. A Concept in Art Theory (Panofsky), 39–40, 97, 156, 187, 189–90, 193, 202
idea and experience, 165
idea and ideal: Plato on, 148; original meaning, 149; Cassirer on, 152–53, 155–56, 165–66; Panofsky on, 157–58, 159, 171–72, 174–77; idea into ideal, 173
—idea, 47, 169; Plato on, 145; Panofsky on, 160–61, 175–77; sensory and, 170–71; Cassirer on, 174–75

—ideal, 3, 40, 138, 175, 193; Schiller on, 40–41; Hegel on, 41–42. *See also* beauty
idea and image, 94, 159
idea and matter, 168
idea and sensation, 174
Idea of Painters, Sculptors and Architects (Zuccari), 167
"ideal mediation," 118
idealism, 21, 193, 196, 228
ideality, concept of, 59, 136
ideality/idealization: in symbol formation, 129–30
idealization, 37, 162; *v* actuality of Christian faith, 36–39; Warburg's use of term, 38–39; Florentine classicism and, 39–43; problem of in Renaissance, 42–44
ideell, 42
illusion, 54
image, xv, 7, 139; nature of, 4–5, 51–52; R. Vischer on, 19; in myth, 114; externalization of, 123; spheres of stability, 127; history of, 130; Cassirer on, 142, 143; Plato on, 172; Panofsky on, 234, 235. *See also* idea and ideal
imagination, xv, 10, 18, 20, 28, 33, 76, 134, 139, 201; primitive, 73; Bellori on, 172, 173; Panofsky on, 174
imitation, 20, 21, 22, 26, 41, 105, 167; in symbol formation, 108–09; Panofsky on, 159–60, 163; Plato on, 172; Dürer and, 191–92
immediacy, problem of, 106, 108–09, 180; in symbol formation, 123, 124, 139; defined, 255*n*75
impotency, 82
Impressionism, 164
In Search of Cultural History (Gombrich), xvii–xviii
India, 64
Indian Decans, 50–51
individual, concept of, xiv
Individual and Cosmos in Renaissance Philosophy (Cassirer), xvi–xviii, 82, 85, 87, 88, 89, 92, 94

individuality, 27, 96
individualization, 88–89
infinite, 3, 8, 60, 203, 204, 205, 221;
    affirmative infinity, 41, 42
ingenuousness, 55
initiative: as characteristic of genius,
    25, 27
inner experience. *See Erlebnis*
"inner Idea," concept of, 167
intellect, concept of, 29, 145, 172,
    175, 189
intellect-sensibility, 97, 98
intellectuals, 31
intelligence, 9, 10
interpretation, 222, 223; historical interpretation, 6; violence of, 224–30
intrinsic meaning, 223, 226
intuition, 9, 18, 29, 106, 119, 151;
    mythical, 120, 121; in symbol formation, 127–28; meaning and, 128; in art theory, 208–09
"involuntary thought," 120
irony, 77, 82, 196
Italian idealism, 67–68

Jerome, St., 162
Joseph and His Brothers (Mann), 77–79
Jupiter, 95
Justi, Karl, xiii, 25, 26, 29, 30; on
    Platonic aesthetics, 147, 148, 149,
    150, 151, 152, 154–55

Kaegi, Werner, 42, 65
Kant, Immanuel, 5, 21; on genius, 28,
    29; on being-there, 73–74; doctrine
    of transcendental apperception, 73,
    74, 75; on time and space, 103,
    107, 119, 128; sensory and, 156;
    "thing-in-itself," 174; on subject
    and will, 178–79; influence on Panofsky, 182, 184; on nature, 193;
    Heidegger on, 224, 229. *See also*
    subject-object relationship
Kant and the Problem of Metaphysics
    (Heidegger), 224
Kantorowicz, Ernst, xi

Kepler, Johannes, 13
Klibansky, Raymond, 233, 234
knowing, 231
knowledge, xvii, 82, 144–45, 146;
    Cassirer on, 84–90; being and,
    145; image and, 152; sensory and,
    169; theory of, 182–83; universality of, 198, 199; historical knowledge, 215, 233. *See also* becoming,
    process of; self-knowledge
Kunstwollen. *See* artistic intention

Lamprecht, Karl, 240*n*35
language, 93, 94, 105, 108, 140, 156;
    Cassirer on, 106, 122; artistic form
    and, 111; autonomy of, 125; formation of, 125, 126, 127
Language and Myth (Cassirer), 118–19
Laocoön (Lessing), 23, 24
Laocoön group, 24, 26, 72
Last Supper (Leonardo), 223
"legitimate construction," 206
Leibniz, G. W. von, 91, 94, 134
Leonardo da Vinci, 25, 42, 164, 188, 223
Lessing, G. E., 23, 24, 26, 28, 54, 172, 173, 222
Lévy-Bruhl, Lucien, 72
liberation, struggle for, 6
L'Idea del Pittore, dello Schultore e dell'Architetto (Bellori), 168–69
life as energy, motif of, 27
Lipton, David R., 253*n*34
logic, 65, 69–70, 117, 121, 122;
    dominance over sensory, 124–25;
    symbolic, 127; concept and, 176
logos, 144, 147, 208
Lomazzo, Giovanni Paolo, 166–67
Lorenzo the Magnificent, 11, 23, 43
love, 153, 154
Lovejoy, Arthur, xi
Luther, Martin, 6, 62, 63, 77, 99; astrology and, 65–66; against paganism, 66–67, 68, 69

Machiavelli, Niccolò, 95

macrocosm and microcosm, 91
magic, 65, 69–70; religious magic, 71; De Martino on, 73–74; Cassirer on, 92–94, 99
magnanimity, 48
manifold, 154, 155, 170
Manilius, 51
Mann, Thomas, xv, 40, 77–79
Mannerism, 157, 165, 166, 168, 190
mathematical symbols, 4, 60, 76, 103, 127, 152, 190, 201
meaning, xv, 126, 127, 128, 232
measure, concept of, 152, 163, 194. *See also* proportion, theories of
mediation, 77, 80, 144, 154, 203; mediated result, 73, 74; of *eidolon*, 152–53; creative energy as, 153. *See also* immediacy, problem of; symbol formation
Medieval tradition, 43, 64–65. *See also* Middle Ages
Meier, Hans, xi
melancholy, motif of, 59–60, 66; in Dürer, 197–202
Melanchthon, 63, 65, 159
Melencholia (Dürer), 31, 59, 226, 230
memory, xvii, 34, 79, 80, 86, 134, 135–36, 235; collective memory, 232
Metamorphosis (Ovid), 191
metaphysics, 174
Metaphysics (Aristotle), 159
methodical circle, 225
methodological unity, 85–86
Michelangelo Buonarroti, 42, 174
Middle Ages, 50, 86, 165, 205; movement in, 52–53; relationship with Renaissance, 87–91, 94, 99; art and theology in, 160, 161–65; proportion in art of, 187, 188–89. *See also* Dürer, Albrecht
modality, problem of, 132, 226, 227
moderation, 194
"momentary gods," 8
"monistic pathos," xi
monotheism, 8, 68
Montale, Eugenio, 230

movement, motif of, 9, 10–11, 25, 26, 55, 119; defined, 20, 21–22; will to movement, 27; accessories of, 45; Warburg on, 52–53; magic and, 74; proportion and, 186
movement/serenity, 52
multiplicity, 152
music, 54
mystery cult, 63
mystical theology, 161
mysticism, 49, 121, 192; number mysticism, 187
myth, 2, 4, 9, 10, 105, 108, 142, 202; classical, 38–39; Cassirer on, 94, 95–96; artistic form and, 111; symbol in, 113, 114; historicization of, 116–17; as mediation, 118; myth to science, 124; autonomy of, 125; in Plato, 147–48, 153. *See also* symbol formation
Myth and Science (Vignoli), 9
mythical theory of knowledge, 117–18
mythical thought, 122

naive/good, 51–52
naïveté, 55, 56
nationalism, 197
Natorp, Paul, 145–46
natural man, 41
natural science and cultural science, 213–14
naturalism, 168–69, 193
nature, 18–19, 47, 92, 150, 193; man and nature, 40–41, 55, 72, 165–66; in Plato, 146–47; art and, 164; genius and, 165; idea and, 169; artist and, 171
nature and spirit, 139
necessity and freedom, 94
negativity, 160
Neoplatonic-optimistic tradition, 199
Neoplatonic philosophy, 21, 42, 47, 89, 96, 98, 144, 154, 166, 167; demonism and, 63–64; Panofsky on, 159–60; Ficino on, 163, 164

Nichomachean Ethics (Aristotle), 47, 67
Nietzsche, Friedrich, 12, 24–25, 56, 234; on genius, 30; on myth, 38–39; on tragedy, 53–54, 58; polarities in, 60–62, 67–68; on hero, 83. *See also* Apollonian/Dionysian polarity
nonbeing, 145, 146
Northern art, 37–38, 39–43, 52, 195, 196; realism in, 39–43, 50, 67–68. *See also* Florentine art
Notes on the History of Art in Italy (Burckhardt), 36
nous, 96, 160
numbers, 152. *See also* mathematical symbols
nymph, 32, 191

object. *See* subject-object relationship
objectivity, 30, 227, 232; kinds of, 111; construction of, 114; attainment of, 125; of will, 151; determination of, 166
objectivization, 104, 107–08; of science, 119
oblivion, epoch of, 205
old and new, 91, 92–93
"On the Aesthetic Education of Man" (Schiller), 139
On the Naive and Sentimental in Literature (Schiller), 40–41
On the Optical Perception of Form (Vischer, R.), 15
On the Relationship between Art History and Art Theory (Panofsky), 207
One, ontology of, 170
"one-many" relation, 133–34
opinion, 146
opposites. *See* polarities
"optical attitude," 177
"optical perception," 178
Orator (Cicero), 159
order, 127–28
order and function, theory of, 103
originality, 28

Orpheus, iconography of, 52
Ortega y Gasset, José, 234
overcoming, theory of, 139
Ovid, 191

pagan demonism, 49–50, 51–52, 58–62, 98–99; nature of demoniac beings, 63–64, 69–70. *See also* Apollonian/Dionysian polarity
paganism, 6, 7–8
"pain and greatness" theme, 3–4
painting, 23
Palazzo Schifanoia frescoes, 27, 49, 50, 61
Panofsky, Erwin, xv, xvii, 31, 59, 89, 93, 143, 156, 157; concept of idea, 39–40; Cassirer on, 97, 98; departure from Cassirer, 158–59; on man and nature, 165–66; on style and representation, 177–79; on *Erlebnis*, 180–82; on ideal unity, 183–84; theory and practice in, 187–88; on Dürer, 188–92, 195, 197–202; Warburg's influence on, 190–91, 192, 211; definition of symbolic form, 202–03; art theory in, 208–11; on pragmatism and dogmatism, 220–21; on violence of interpretation, 224–30; disagrees with Warburg, 231. *See also* art theory; classical antiquity; idea and ideal; perspective; Renaissance; time
Parmenides, 12, 103
Parmenides (Plato), 155–56
participation, concept of, 72, 146
passivity, 160
past, 134, 135
pathos, 75, 82, 197
"pathos formulas," 2, 4, 11, 70, 93–94, 95
"pathos of distance," 190, 191
patience, 48
patrology, 161
perception, 102, 109, 128, 129, 232; as function of knowledge, 122–23
perfection, 220
perspective, 60, 196, 197, 202–07

Perspective as "Symbolic Form" (Panofsky), 197
pessimism, 72
Petrarch, 90, 97
Phaedon (Plato), 169
phantasm, 10
phenomenal planes: in Panofsky, 222–23
phenomenal sense and intrinsic meaning, 223–24
Phenomenology of Knowledge, The (Cassirer), 122
Phenomenology of the Spirit (Hegel), 120, 140
phenomenon, concept of, 101, 118
Philebus (Plato), 152, 155, 170
philology, 59
philosophy, 12–13, 84, 97, 114, 139, 148–49. *See also individual authors*
Philosophy and History (Klibansky, ed.), 233
Philosophy of Symbolic Forms (Cassirer), 72, 84, 113, 124–25, 193, 202, 211
physical world, 41
physis, 12–13
Pico della Mirandola, 91, 92, 95, 201
Piero della Francesca, 25
Plato, xii, 12, 13, 90, 103; on ideal, 40; myth in, 95–96; Cassirer on, 141, 143–44, 145; Platonism and, 156; art theory in, 157–59, 161; on sensory world, 169–70; admiration of for Egyptian art, 186–87; on space, 204. *See also* art theory; beauty *and individual authors and concepts*
Platonic philosophy, 60, 89, 150–51
play, 139
plenum of sensory data, 209
Plotinus, 160, 163
poet, 41
poetry, 23, 54
polarities, 61–62, 66, 70; in Renaissance, 42, 66; movement/serenity, 52–53; between Middle Ages and Renaissance, 67–68; magic and logic, 69, 71, 72, 77; theory and practice, 91–92; of beings, 170–71; Panofsky on, 206–07. *See also* Apollonian/Dionysian polarity *and other individual concepts*
Poliziano, Angelo, 11, 23, 37, 191
Pollaiuolo, Antonio del, 39, 55
Polyclitus, 186
popularization of culture, 33
"Portraiture and the Florentine Bourgeoisie" (Warburg), 36
positivism, 125
potential, concept of, 160
Poussin, Nicolas, 234, 235
pragmatism, 220–21
precision, 163
"preconscious," 120
prescience, 126, 136
presentation, act of, 134
prestructural world, 126
Primal Unity, 56, 61
primary substance, 25
primitive expression and cognitive act, 106
principium individuationis, 97
"Problem of Historical Time" (Simmel), 215
Problem of Knowledge, The (Cassirer), 83, 85, 87, 88, 89, 90
"Problem of Style in the Figurative Arts" (Panofsky), 177
Problemata (Aristotle), 67
progress, 21, 31–32, 41, 79; historical progress, 3, 76; Cassirer's faith in, 5; symbols and, 33–34; ideal and, 42; as emancipation, 51–52; expression of, 93; basis for, 135. *See also* symbol formation
Prolegomena (Kant), 193
proportion, theories of, 152, 185–88, 189–90
Protestant Reformation, 66, 69
prudence, 47, 48
psychological aesthetics, 15
psychology: folk psychology, 9
Pueblo Indians, 71

Raphael Sanzio, 42, 56, 57, 66

rationality/irrationality, 19, 29, 30, 31, 35, 230; rationality of genius, 28
realism, 38, 39–43, 196
reality, xvii, 37, 41, 138, 139, 151, 217, 236; image and, 114; sensory reality, 162, 163
reason, 3, 76, 170
reconnection, 92
rediscovery, epoch of, 205
religion, 2, 113. *See also* Christian tradition; Middle Ages
Rembrandt van Rijn, 31
Renaissance: Warburg on, 2, 191; Greek archetypes in, 7–14; empathy for antiquity in, 14–16, 22–23, 35, 56, 57; style of movement in, 20, 26; meaning of term, 32, 35, 49; self-consciousness in, 32–33, 38; polarities in, 37, 39; Renaissance philosophy, 85, 86–87, 88–93; Panofsky on, 163–65; artistic intention in, 187–89, 190. *See also other individual authors and concepts*
representation, 18, 41, 42, 127, 151, 201; in symbol formation, 128, 129; Panofsky on, 177, 178
Republic (Plato), 161, 169–70
repulsion, 140
reunification, process of, 151–52
Riegl, Aloïs, 174, 179, 183, 208, 214
Ripa, C., 212
risk, 75, 76, 77, 225, 235–36
Rohde, Erwin, 58–59
romanticism, 40, 53
Rucellai, Giovanni, 44, 45, 46, 47, 48, 95

Sassetti, Francesco, 36–37, 43–44, 95; Warburg on, 44–49, 93; character of, 76, 81–82
Sassetti Chapel, 37
Saturn, 66, 231; myth of, 198–200, 201, 212
satyr, 43

Saxl, Fritz, xi, xv, 31, 59, 77, 185, 234–35; on Cassirer, 142, 143; Panofsky and, 192; on Dürer, 197–98, 201–02; on Titian, 212
Scheler, Max, 138, 139
Schelling, Friedrich, 8
Schiller, Friedrich, 3, 40–41, 55, 139, 140
Scholasticism, 89, 161, 163, 168, 205
school, concept of, xiii–xiv
Schopenhauer, Arthur, 3, 18, 20–21, 24, 53, 151; on genius, 28, 29, 30
science, 10, 13, 60, 76, 77, 99, 156; Cassirer on, 104, 105; spiritual world and, 117, 119, 120, 121
Science of Logic (Hegel), 41–42, 140
"sciences of the spirit," 210, 218–19, 231–32
scientific symbols: as apex of symbolic process, 131, 132
sculpture, 23
secondary substance, 25, 27
Sedlmayr, Hans, 263n79
selection theory, 165
self-consciousness, 32, 33, 38, 74
self-in-humanity, 19
self-knowledge, 80, 83
self-mediation, 140
sensation, 110
sensation and idea, 145
sensibility, 110, 125–26, 128–29, 227, 228
sensism, 125
sensory consciousness, 120
sensory experience, 102–03
sensory intuition, 106
sensory unity, 214–15
sensory world, 3, 14, 76, 107; emancipation from, 122; in symbol formation, 125, 126; contamination by, 152; importance of, 152, 169; idea and, 168; in Plato, 170–71; intellect and, 172; in art, 209–10
separation, theme of, 90–91, 146, 151–52
serpent, symbol of, 71, 72, 77, 212
Signorelli, Luca, 17
Simmel, Georg, 215–17, 218

Sophistes (Plato), 155
Sophocles, 38–39, 140, 145, 169
soul, 96, 145–46, 182
space, 106, 107, 119, 132, 211; language and, 127–28; Panofsky on, 203–07; historical time and historical space, 214–15
spirit: becoming and, 136–37; nature of, 139–40; history of, 157
spiritual world, 41, 101–02
spiritualization, 6, 42, 60, 66, 76
Stufe, 117
Sturm und Drang, 28
style, 49, 111, 179, 189, 256n83
subject and will, 179
subject-object relationship, 17, 18, 19, 95, 96–97, 229; in artistic act, 21; Cassirer on, 105, 106, 108; Kant on, 109–10; F. Vischer on, 115; in symbol formation, 138; Panofsky on, 163–64, 165, 195–96; measure between, 166; ideal and, 175
subjectivism, 189
subjectivity, 30, 96, 111, 190, 222–23
substance, 160
substance and being, 103
substantiality, 131
suffering, motif of, 2
superman, theory of, 82
superstition, 2, 6, 11, 50, 61, 66, 68, 71, 76; Cassirer on, 98–99
symbol, xv, xvi, xvii, 12, 47, 93; role of, 2, 33–34; Warburg's concept of, 9, 34–35, 39; R. Vischer on, 17; De Martino on, 72–73. *See also* mathematical symbols
Symbol, Das (Vischer, F.), 15, 112
symbol formation, 3, 5, 72, 90, 94; as median phase, 14, 101–02, 103, 106, 116, 118, 122; Warburg on, 71–75; universal character of, 104–05; immediacy and, 106, 108–09; levels of Cassirer's theory, 110, 126–27; progress in, 110–11; evolution and function of, 112–14, 123–24; origin of symbolic activity, 115, 126; problem of, 116; mythical world and, 117–21, 156; apex of process, 130–31; origin of, 134–35; development of theory of, 137–40; images in, 139; emancipation of symbol, 157; structure and, 198, 203, 205
Symposium (Plato), 168
syncretism, 97, 98
synthesis/antithesis, 8

talent, 27
Tani, Angelo, 38
taste, 21, 28–29, 63
telos, 208
Tertullian, 162
Theaetetus (Plato), 95, 96, 145, 146, 155, 170
theodicy, 97
theology, 89, 160–61
theory and practice, 88, 91–92, 94, 197–98
"thing-in-itself," 21, 28, 174, 176
thought, 106–07; image and, 152
Timaeus (Plato), 96, 146, 152
time, 35, 69, 70, 92, 211; historical time, xv, xvi, 93, 230, 231–32; Cassirer on, 84, 101–02, 103, 106, 118, 119; Kant on, 107, 129; order and, 128; symbol formation and, 132, 136, 137; intuition of, 134; consciousness and, 135–36; Plato on, 146; artistic problem and, 213–18; art history and, 219–21, 230
Titian, 212
totality of spirit, 131
tradition, 34, 35, 46–47
transcendental apperception, 73, 74, 75
"transcendental truth," 129
truth, 129, 161, 163; "courage of truth," 3; truth and error, 145; beauty and, 152
types, theory of, 223–24, 225

unitary development, 128–29
unitary essence, 226

unity, sense of, xii, 17, 19, 40, 84, 85, 86, 152; concept of universal unity, 8, 9, 10, 14, 132; of inner and outer world, 166
unity of intellect, 96
unity of knowledge, 5
universal foundation, 82
Usener, Hermann, xiii, 7, 8, 15, 27, 120, 192

Valla, Lorenzo, 95
value, notion of, 185
vanishing point, 203, 206
Vasari, Giorgio, 166, 219, 220, 221
Verene, D. P., 258*n*142
vicious circle/methodical circle, 225, 228
Vico, G. B., 10, 234
Vignoli, Tito, 9, 10
Virgil, 23, 235
virtue, 47
Vischer, Friedrich Theodor, 14, 15, 17, 72, 112–15, 173
Vischer, Robert, 15, 17, 30–31
vision, 223
Von Gent, Henrich, 201
Von Melle (Hamburg burgomaster), xv

Warburg, Aby, xii, 222, 228; concept of history, xii–xiv; Burckhardt and, xviii, 33, 36, 38, 43, 65, 81, 82; "pain and greatness" in, 2–4; historiographic instinct of, 15–16; Winckelmann and, 24, 25, 57, 61–62; on life as energy, 27; on Laocoön group, 34–35; on Sassetti Chapel, 37–38; on Renaissance idealization, 42–44, 130; on fortune, 48–49; influence of Nietzsche, 53–56, 58; on Olympian gods and demonism, 62–63, 67–69; age of transition concept, 70–77, 80; meeting with Cassirer, 142–43; on iconology, 228, 229. *See also* Apollonian/Dionysian polarity; classical antiquity; Renaissance; symbol formation *and other individual authors and concepts*
Warburg Library, 2; publications of, 142, 153, 156, 197, 202
Welcker, F. G., 8
weltanschauung, 228, 231
will, 18, 20, 27–28, 30, 151, 179; objectivization of, 29; of fantasy, 31; of consciousness, 135
Winckelmann (Justi), 25
Winckelmann, Johann, 22, 24, 39, 149, 173, 193; on beauty, 38, 40, 41, 172; Warburg's opposition to, 52–53. *See also* classical antiquity
Wind, Edgar, 208, 225, 265
Wölfflin, Heinrich, 177–78, 189, 202
word, 17, 155
word origin, 7
World as Will and Representation, The (Schopenhauer), 3
World War I, 62

Zeus, 8
Zuccari, Federico, 167–68

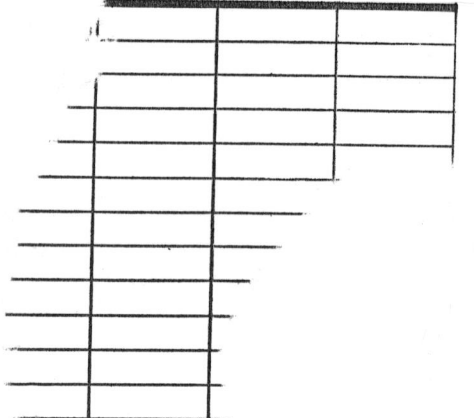